THE WISEST COUNCIL IN THE WORLD

THE
WISEST
COUNCIL
IN THE
WORLD

Restoring *the* Character Sketches
by William Pierce *of* Georgia
of the Delegates *to the*
Constitutional Convention
of 1787

JOHN R. VILE

The University of Georgia Press
Athens and London

Publication of this book was supported in part by the
Kenneth Coleman Series in Georgia History and Culture.

© 2015 by the University of Georgia Press
Athens, Georgia 30602
www.ugapress.org
Designed by Kaelin Chappell Broaddus
Set in by 10.5/13.5 Bulmer MT Std Regular
Printed and bound by Thomson-Shore, Inc.
The paper in this book meets the guidelines for
permanence and durability of the Committee on
Production Guidelines for Book Longevity of the
Council on Library Resources.

Most University of Georgia Press titles are
available from popular e-book vendors.

Printed in the United States of America
15 16 17 18 19 C 5 4 3 2 1

Library of Congress Cataloging-in-Publication Data
The wisest council in the world : restoring the character
sketches by William Pierce of Georgia of the delegates to the
Constitutional Convention of 1787 / edited by John R. Vile.
    pages cm
ISBN 978-0-8203-4772-1 (hardcover : alkaline paper)
1. Legislators—United States—Biography.
2. United States. Constitutional Convention (1787)—Biography.
3. United States. Constitution—Signers—Biography.
4. Pierce, William, 1740–1789.
5. United States—History—1783–1815—Biography.
6. United States—Politics and government—1783–1789.
7. Constitutional history—United States. I. Pierce, William,
1740–1789. II. Vile, John R.
E302.5.W796 2015
328.73'092—dc23
[B]
2014033690

British Library Cataloging-in-Publication Data available

Dedicated to my daughters,
Virginia and Rebekah;
my grandsons,
Oliver and Christopher;
and my son-in-law,
Kenny Johnston

CONTENTS

PREFACE

Of all the verbal portraits of the delegates who attended the Constitutional Convention of 1787, few are as compelling as those that William Pierce of Georgia penned. Pierce was born in York County, Virginia, studied art under Charles Willson Peale, distinguished himself in the Revolutionary War, studied briefly at William and Mary, rejoined the armed forces, moved to Georgia, and married the daughter of a Georgia planter. Pierce established himself as a merchant and represented Georgia first in the state legislature, next in Congress, and then at the Constitutional Convention.

Scholars frequently quote Pierce's sketches, which are included in Max Farrand's *Records of the Federal Convention of 1787* (1966). A recent book, the first devoted exclusively to Pierce, gathers notes that he took and letters that he wrote into a single volume (Leffler, Kaminski, and Fore 2012). No one, however, has yet analyzed the content of Pierce's sketches in extended detail. Pierce remains elusive in other ways; he is one of the few delegates to the convention for whom scholars have been unable to locate any contemporary portrait or sketch.

Working chiefly from his writings, I attempt to rediscover Pierce in this book. I was motivated in this task when I received an invitation to present a paper at a conference funded by the National Science Foundation at the University of Georgia in March 2013 commemorating the 225th anniversary of the ratification of the U.S. Constitution. Since I had previously written both a two-volume encyclopedia on the Constitutional Convention of 1787 and a subsequent narrative of the event, the choice of Pierce was initially fortuitous. Pierce was the only one of four delegates from Georgia who spoke at the Constitutional Convention about whom scholars had not written a biography. The more I researched him, however, the more appropriate the choice proved to be.

Pierce is a worthy subject both because the details of his life have only recently begun emerging in clearer focus as a result of contemporary scholarship (previous accounts were mistaken about both his date and place of birth) and because a study of his writings provides a different lens through which to reexamine scholarly work on the convention as a whole. The title of this book is taken from Pierce's collective evaluations of his fellow delegates and plays off the fact that Pierce began as a visual artist but chose ultimately to build his portraits of colleagues in speech rather than in oils or watercolors. Much as if I were rediscovering a painting, I consider this book to be a restoration of Pierce's work; scholars have cited his descriptions far more often than they have studied them. It is common to picture the framers as somehow larger than life, but Pierce's verbal portraits show that they were men with distinct personalities and abilities. Political rhetoric was a major focus of his sketches, and reading and analyzing them offers a fresh way to "hear" the delegates in their own voices.

Outline of This Book

The first chapter, which advanced students of the American founding and Georgia history might choose to skim, outlines the situation under the Articles of Confederation that led to the Constitutional Convention of 1787 and describes the particular place of the Georgia delegation at the convention. The second chapter gathers genealogical and biographical information about the life of William Pierce Jr. and his immediate family. The next four chapters deal specifically with Pierce's character sketches. Chapter 3 describes how Pierce arranged his sketches and the subjects he covered. Chapter 4 addresses Pierce's evaluations of the delegates' personal qualities and reputations. Chapter 5 looks at Pierce's assessments of the delegates' rhetorical abilities, and chapter 6 examines his descriptions of the delegates' public service, occupations, and miscellaneous matters.

Two additional chapters provide further context. Chapter 7 examines a set of somewhat overlapping character sketches that Louis-Guillaume Otto, the French minister to the United States, penned about members of Congress in 1788. Chapter 8 describes the life of Pierce's son and namesake and analyzes a Fourth of July Oration that he delivered in 1812 and a long poem that he penned in 1813, with a view toward examining how his assessments of various Founding Fathers compares with those of his father. I conclude that Otto's and Pierce's treatments demonstrate that those who wrote the Constitution may have had a relatively brief moment to craft the compromises that they did and that scholars may have underestimated how narrow this window of opportunity actually was. A coda summarizes the book's findings and my reflections. In the appendixes are Pierce's initial character sketches, those by the French minister, and a Fourth of July Oration that Pierce delivered in 1788.

REFERENCES

Farrand, Max, ed. 1966. *The Records of the Federal Convention of 1787*. 4 vols. New Haven,
    Conn.: Yale University Press.
Leffler, Richard, John P. Kaminski, and Samuel K. Fore, eds. 2012. *William Pierce on the
    Constitutional Convention and Constitution*. Dallas, Tex.: Harlan Crow Library.

ACKNOWLEDGMENTS

I have been aided by numerous individuals in the course of my research. I grate-fully acknowledge the assistance of the reading group on the Constitution at the University of Georgia, which invited me to a conference celebrating the 225th anniversary of the ratification of the U.S. Constitution; Martha Rowe of the Museum of Early Southern Decorative Arts in Winston-Salem, North Carolina; Philip Phillips, professor of English and associate dean of the Honors College at Middle Tennessee State University (MTSU); Mary Hoffschwelle, professor of history at MTSU; Kevin Donovan, professor of English at MTSU; Patricia Boulos and the staff of the Boston Athenaeum; Arthur S. Marks, professor emeritus of the University of North Carolina, Chapel Hill; the staff of the Hargrett Library at the University of Georgia; Mel E. Smith, librarian at the Connecticut State Library; Benjamin Bromley, Public Services Archives specialist at the Earl Gregg Swem Library at the College of William and Mary; individuals at the circulation desk and Kate Middleton at the Interlibrary Loan Office at MTSU; Kaylene Gebert of the Department of Speech and Theatre at MTSU; Katie Springer at the reference desk of the Indiana State Library; Dennis L. Simpson, Search Service, DAR Library, Washington, D.C.; Kate Collins, Research Services librarian at the David M. Rubenstein Rare Book and Manuscript Library at Duke University; John Hauser, who maintains a beautiful website on the Fenwick estate; Edward O'Reilly, Manuscript Department, New-York Historical Society Library; Susan Shames and George H. Yetter, John D. Rockefeller Jr. Library, Colonial Williamsburg Foundation; Linda Rowe, historian, Colonial Williamsburg Foundation; Elizabeth Bennett, librarian for history and history of science, Princeton University Library; John Kaminski at the Center for the Study of the American Constitution at the University of Wisconsin, Madison; Christa Cleeton, Special Collections assistant and social media manager, Mudd Manuscript Library, Princeton University.

I owe special thanks to Samuel K. Fore at the Harlan Crow Library in Dallas, Texas, for providing the texts of numerous original sources and for generously sharing his wide knowledge of William Pierce; to Vilay Lyxuchouky, a graduate student at MTSU, for her translations from French into English; and to Gretchen

Jenkins, a former student from MTSU who now clerks for the New York State Supreme Court, for photographing and supplying pictures of William Leigh Pierce's commonplace books at the New-York Historical Society. I am also grateful to administrative assistants Karen Demonbreum and Kathy Davis in the Honors College at MTSU; to MTSU student aides Ashlee Kaspar, Morgan Murphy, Jeremy Robertson, Tyler Whitaker, and Birgit Northcutt; and to my long-suffering wife, Linda, who has approved wide-ranging purchases of sources for this book and who has served as a useful sounding board. I am, of course, especially indebted to the teachers who have educated me and to the university that currently employs me and entrusts me with the education of Tennessee's best students. I am also grateful to Merryl A. Sloane for professionally editing this manuscript, and to Patrick Allen, the acquisitions editor; Kaelin Chappell Broaddus, the cover designer; and John Joerschke, the project editor at the University of Georgia Press.

THE WISEST COUNCIL IN THE WORLD

The Background of the U.S. Constitutional Convention and the Role of Georgia and William Pierce Jr. in the Proceedings

The Statesman and the Phylosopher have their attention turned towards us; the oppressed and wretched look to America.

—William Pierce to Major George Turner, May 19, 1787

The Constitutional Convention that met in the Philadelphia State House (today's Independence Hall) and in which William Pierce participated in the summer of 1787 was one of the most monumental events in U.S. history. It has been widely celebrated, documented, and analyzed (see Vile 2005, 2012; Beeman 2010; Johnson 2009; Edling 2008; Stewart 2008; Robertson 2005, 2012; Hendrickson 2003; Miller 1992; Anderson 1993; Peters 1987; Bernstein with Rice 1987; Collier and Collier 1986; Rossiter 1966; Bowen 1966; Van Doren 1948; Farrand 1913), and bronze statues of its signers now grace a room in the Constitution Center not far from the document's place of birth. Although recent anniversaries have not evoked the same celebrations as the centennials and bicentennials, the year 2012 marked the Constitution's 225th birthday; 2013 marked the 225th anniversary of its ratification; and 2014 marked the 225th year during which elected officials were installed in the government that it created.

Goverment under the Articles of Confederation

Americans have long been committed to the idea of liberty under law. Before the Declaration of Independence articulated natural rights principles and proclaimed independence from Great Britain in 1776, the thirteen colonies had cited principles

stated in the Magna Carta (most notably that of "no taxation without representation") and other British documents to oppose British policies. States further
heeded the Second Continental Congress's call to write new constitutions that
would replace the charters under which many of them had been previously governed.

Before the Constitution's adoption in 1789, the states were collectively governed
by the Articles of Confederation. In the parlance of contemporary political scien-
tists, the Articles of Confederation—like the later constitution of the Confederate
States of America—created a confederal form of government in which a written
document divided powers between a central government and various states, limiting the former mostly to foreign policy, much as in a treaty among sovereign nations. Only the states could act directly on the people (Vile 2011, 93–94).[1] Article II
epitomized the states' dominance: "Each state retains its sovereignty, freedom, and
independence, and every Power, Jurisdiction and right, which is not by this confederation expressly delegated to the United States, in Congress assembled" (Solberg 1958, 42). The Second Continental Congress wrote the Articles of Confederation in 1777, but their adoption required the states' unanimous consent. Maryland,
which had been concerned about western land claims of the larger states, did not
ratify until 1781.

The government under the Articles of Confederation consisted chiefly of a unicameral Congress whose members served one-year terms. The states paid their
representatives' salaries, and each state had an equal vote. The Articles of Confederation did establish an ad hoc mechanism to resolve state boundary disputes but
did not create independent executive and judicial branches. Although members
of Congress often arrived late and left early, the Articles of Confederation required
delegations from nine states to consent to key measures, and all thirteen had to
consent to adopt amendments to the Articles of Confederation. Congress did not
have the power to act directly on citizens when raising taxes or troops. Instead, it
had to requisition these items from the states, which rarely responded with alacrity.
States printed their own currencies. States seeking revenue often taxed goods coming from other states, resulting in economic stagnation. Some states, most notably
Rhode Island, printed money that created inflation, which favored debtors over
creditors. Further weaknesses of the Articles of Confederation quickly became
evident. They included a lack of congressional powers over interstate commerce,
a weak American military force (Marks 1971), an inability to enforce U.S. treaties
against state violations (Graebner 1986), and inadequate congressional power to
defend individual states.

The Call for a New Government

Faced with such difficulties, delegates from Virginia and Maryland assembled at George Washington's Mount Vernon house in Virginia in March 1785 to discuss matters involving navigation common to the two states. They in turn proposed a September 1786 meeting of all the states in Annapolis, Maryland, to discuss issues of trade and commerce throughout the new Union. But delegates from only five states attended. Leaders like James Madison and Alexander Hamilton sought to snatch victory from such a disappointing showing by proposing a wider meeting for the following May in Philadelphia "to take into consideration the situation of the United States, to devise such further provisions as shall appear to them necessary to render the constitution of the Federal Government adequate to the exigencies of the Union; and to report such an Act for that purpose to the United States in Congress assembled, as when agreed to, by them, and afterwards confirmed by the Legislatures of every State, will effectually provide for the same" (Solberg 1958, 58–59).

That winter, a Massachusetts taxpayer revolt called Shays' Rebellion closed down courthouses and seemed to confirm the crisis surrounding the existing form of government and Congress's inadequate ability to respond to events. Congress thus adopted a resolution calling a meeting "for the sole and express purpose of revising the Articles of Confederation and reporting to Congress and the several legislatures such alteration and provisions therein as shall, when agreed to in Congress and confirmed by the states render the federal constitution adequate to the exigencies of Government and the preservation of the Union" (Solberg 1958, 64).

The Constitutional Convention

Fifty-five delegates from all of the original thirteen states except Rhode Island attended the meeting. Although some prominent Americans like Thomas Jefferson and John Adams were serving in diplomatic capacities abroad or otherwise decided not to attend (Patrick Henry, who was particularly solicitous of states' rights, reportedly professed that he "smelt a rat"), the convention included such luminaries as Roger Sherman and Oliver Ellsworth of Connecticut; Nathaniel Gorham and Rufus King of Massachusetts; Alexander Hamilton of New York; John Dickinson of Delaware; William Paterson of New Jersey; Benjamin Franklin, Gouverneur Morris, and James Wilson of Pennsylvania; George Washington, James Madison, and George Mason of Virginia; Hugh Williamson of North Carolina; and Charles

Cotesworth Pinckney of South Carolina. Members elected Washington, the hero of the Revolutionary War who had resisted calls to set himself up as a monarch and had retired to private life, to preside over the proceedings. Members also adopted rules designed to see that delegates carried out deliberations and debates in an orderly fashion. Among the most important and arguably controversial of these was a rule, which delegates almost completely honored, to keep the proceedings secret. Although everyone would have a chance to see the proposed Constitution once the details were hammered out, delegates were expected to engage in the kind of freewheeling discussion that would be difficult if daily reports were published. Rules accordingly provided that members of the convention could retake votes and that votes would be recorded under the names of states rather than of individual delegates, who might thus consider themselves freer to change their minds should other delegates persuade them that they had initially been mistaken.

Although other delegates may have shared Gouverneur Morris's observation that he was attending "as a Representative of America" (Farrand 1966, 1:529), they were actually selected and paid by state legislatures, and they reflected the concerns of those states and the regions of which they were a part. As I have explained elsewhere (Vile 2013, xxi–xxvi), it is common to divide the delegates into those from the East (Northeast), the middle states, and the South, each with different climates, crops, and cultural and religious traditions. In a poorly punctuated speech delivered at the convention on or about June 19, Jared Ingersoll, a Pennsylvania delegate, observed: "the Fisheries & Manufacturers of New England, The Flour Lumber Flaxseed & Ginseng of New York New Jersey Pennsylvania & Delaware The tobacco of Maryland & Virginia the Pitch Tar, Rice & Indigo & Cotton of North Carolina South Carolina & Georgia, can never be regulated by the same Law nor the same Legislature, nor is this diversity by any means confined to Articles of Commerce, as the Eastward Slavery is not acknowledged, with us it exists in a certain qualified manner, at the Southward in its full extent" (Hutson 1987, 203).

In the months leading up to the convention, James Madison had been doing research on confederacies and writing essays on their defects; he had concluded that a new system of government was needed. Contrary to what many delegates probably anticipated, instead of simply revising the Articles of Confederation and increasing the powers of the central government, they were soon discussing a whole new plan of government that the Virginia delegation had proposed. It called for a bicameral congress with expanded powers, with the representation in both houses apportioned according to population, which would be checked and balanced by executive and judicial branches, both to be chosen by Congress. It also included some mechanisms, like a congressional negation of state laws and a

Council of Revision, which would not make it into the final document. After about two weeks, William Paterson of New Jersey countered with a proposal on behalf of less-populous states, which would have retained key features of the Articles of Confederation, including equal state representation in Congress.

Although delegates decided to proceed with the Virginia Plan as their primary template, during the course of the summer, delegates (often relying on committees to hash out details) compromised on a variety of issues. The most important compromise, known as the Great or Connecticut Compromise, split the difference between the existing Articles of Confederation and the proposed Virginia Plan by adopting a bicameral Congress that represented states according to population in the House of Representatives and equally in the Senate. This compromise was so important that, according to Article V of the Constitution, it remains the sole constitutional provision that can only be changed with the consent of the states that would lose equal representation.

From the perspective of South Carolina and Georgia, the two southernmost states, whose economies depended most on slavery, the most important compromises were those that counted slaves as three-fifths of a person for the purposes of state representation in the U.S. House of Representatives (thus increasing southern influence in that body); limited congressional control of the slave trade for twenty years; and provided for the return of fugitive slaves. Gouverneur Morris launched an attack on slavery on August 8: "The admission of slaves into the Representation when fairly explained comes to this: that the inhabitant of Georgia and S.C. who goes to the Coast of Africa, and in defiance of the most sacred laws of humanity tears away his fellow creatures from their dearest connections & dam[n]s them to the most cruel bondages, shall have more votes in a Govt. instituted for the protection of the rights of mankind, than the Citizen of Pa or N. jersey who views with a laudable horror, so nefarious a practice" (Farrand 1966, 2:222). Morris later unsuccessfully attempted to embarrass the three southernmost states by listing them as having insisted on the uninterrupted importation of slaves so that it would "be known also that this part of the Constitution was a compliance with those States" (ibid., 2:415).

Delegates also compromised on such issues as term lengths, federal-state relations, and methods of selecting the executive and members of the judiciary. A committee compiled these compromises into a document to which Pennsylvania's Gouverneur Morris added the final rhetorical flourishes. The preamble, which evoked the authority of "We the people," articulated broad purposes for the new government. Thirty-nine of the forty-two delegates (one by proxy) who remained at the convention on September 17, 1787, signed the document, which was then sent to the states for ratification. The new Constitution was divided into seven articles, which are typically designated by roman numerals.

The New Constitution

Article I outlined the authority of the new bicameral Congress and its expanded powers over commerce and fiscal matters. It was grounded on a House of Representatives, composed of individuals who were twenty-five years or older who were elected directly by the people for two-year terms from districts in the states. The number of representatives was apportioned according to population, with slaves counting as three-fifths of a person. States were to be equally represented in the Senate, whose members would be chosen by state legislatures (this was later changed to direct election when the Seventeenth Amendment was ratified in 1913). Senators had to be thirty years or older and served for six-year terms; they had special responsibilities in ratifying treaties and reviewing and confirming presidential appointments. Article I, Section 8, enumerated numerous powers that the new Congress would exercise, including taxing, spending, declaring war, and making all laws "necessary and proper" for carrying them to fruition.

In contrast to the legislative dominance under the Articles of Confederation and consistent with the Virginia Plan, the new government also contained executive and judicial branches. The Constitution specified that the president and vice president were required to be thirty-five years or older. They were to be chosen for four-year terms through the Electoral College, whose members, also chosen every four years, were apportioned according to each state's combined representation in the House and Senate. This eased the president's dependency on Congress. Article II outlined the executive branch's powers, including designating the president as commander in chief of the armed forces and granting the president most powers of appointment; the president could veto laws, but the veto was subject to being overridden by two-thirds majorities of both houses of Congress.

Article III outlined the composition and powers of the federal judiciary, which was headed by a Supreme Court, presided over by a chief justice, which would review "cases and controversies" arising under the new Constitution and its laws and treaties. The president appointed judges and justices, with the advice and consent of the Senate, to serve for life "during good behavior." Although the Constitution does not specifically empower judges with judicial review, the power they exercise to invalidate laws that they consider to be unconstitutional, a review of the convention debates reveals that many of the delegates correctly anticipated that they would do so.

Article IV outlined the powers and responsibilities of state and national governments toward one another. It included a guarantee by the national government of a "republican," or representative, government and a more controversial pledge to return fugitives (slaves) who had fled from a slave state to a free one. With an eye to the problems under the Articles of Confederation, Article I, Section 9, prohibited states from taxing goods coming in or going to other states or independently engaging in matters of foreign policy. In contrast to the unanimity required under the Articles of Confederation, Article V provided that two-thirds majorities of Congress, or of a special convention called by two-thirds of the states, could propose amendments that would go into effect if three-fourths of state legislatures or state conventions ratified them.

Article VI provided for the supremacy of federal laws over state laws and anticipated later protections for religious freedom in the First Amendment by banning religious test oaths as a condition of holding office. Article VII spelled out how the new document would be ratified. Bypassing the inflexible amending requirement under the Articles of Confederation, which required the unanimous consent of the state legislatures, the convention proposed that the new Constitution would go into effect among consenting states when special conventions in nine or more of them ratified it. This meant that the Constitution was debated, often quite extensively, in each of the states.

Ratification Debates and the Bill of Rights

Supporters of the new Constitution called themselves Federalists, perhaps in part to undercut the perception that they were proposing excessive innovations: prior to the convention, a government like that described in the Articles of Confederation was considered to be a federal government. Federalists touted the new Constitution as a cure for most of the ills in the existing government. Anti-Federalist opponents raised numerous objections to the document, expressing fears that it was impossible to establish a republican, or representative, government over such an extensive country; fears that the new national government would be too powerful; and fears that the judges, justices, and senators (and other elected officials who might be elected to multiple-year terms) created by the new system might be too aristocratic and too unaccountable to the people.

Anti-Federalist opponents to the Constitution raised particular concerns about the absence of a bill of rights, which had been included in many state constitutions specifically to limit the powers of the new government. Although they initially resisted, some prominent Federalists agreed that they would support such a bill if the Constitution were adopted. Just two years after the new Constitution went into effect in 1789, the states ratified ten amendments, largely authored and sponsored by James Madison in the first Congress. The Bill of Rights protected individual rights against the increased powers of the strengthened national government, and did much to gain support for the new Constitution. The Constitution has subsequently been amended seventeen times, most significantly at the end of the Civil War (1861–1865), when the Thirteenth through Fifteenth Amendments freed the slaves and granted freedmen new rights, and in 1920, when suffrage was extended to women. The work of the Constitutional Convention thus largely remains in effect today. In addition, Supreme Court interpretations of the due process clause of the Fourteenth Amendment have applied most of the provisions of the Bill of Rights not simply to the national government but also to the states.

Georgia's Delegates to the Constitutional Convention

As in the Congress under the Articles of Confederation, each state that sent delegates to the Constitutional Convention had a single vote. Four of the fifty-five delegates who attended the Constitutional Convention were from Georgia, which was the most recently settled and the southernmost of the thirteen former English colonies, most of which bordered the Atlantic. Georgia's delegates were Abraham Baldwin, William Few, William Houstoun, and William Pierce. Only one of them had been born in the state.

Baldwin, who had already begun work to create Franklin College (today's University of Georgia), had immigrated to Georgia from Connecticut, where he had graduated from Yale. He served as a vital link between his state of origin, a small state that was influential in the Great Compromise, and southern delegates, who typically followed the lead of Virginia (the most populous state) on issues of representation. Baldwin had attended the Annapolis Convention and represented Georgia in the Continental Congress, and he later served in both the U.S. House of Representatives and the Senate.

Few, born in Baltimore, Maryland, had also served in the Continental Congress. He went on to become one of Georgia's first two senators and a judge before moving to New York, where he served in a number of state governmental posts. Houstoun, who was born in Savannah, had attended the British Inns of Court and served both in the Georgia state legislature and in the Continental Congress. Like Few, Houstoun eventually moved to New York and lived a fairly private life after getting married. As discussed below, Pierce, who was once thought to have been born in Georgia, was actually born in Virginia. He fought in the Revolutionary War before his election to the state legislature, which chose him to represent the state in

Congress. George Walton, who headed a prominent Georgia political faction, and Nathaniel Pendleton, a lawyer who had served as the state's attorney general, were also chosen to attend the convention, but declined to do so.

Three of the Georgia delegates who attended the convention were lawyers, but Pierce was a merchant. Although Baldwin (Coulter 1987) and Few (Sargent 2004, 2006) have merited biographies, none of the Georgia delegates was particularly prominent in convention debates. Indeed, those who took notes did not record Few, who devoted most of the summer to his congressional duties, as giving a single speech at the proceedings. The historian Clinton Rossiter, whose account of the deliberations remains one of the most complete, does not list any Georgia delegates among the most important groups at the convention, which he identifies as "The Principals," "The Influentials," and "The Very Usefuls" (1966, 247–250). Instead, he places Baldwin among what he calls "The Usefuls," Few and Houstoun among "The Visibles," and Pierce among "The Dropouts and Walkouts" (251).

Baldwin was the only Georgia delegate to serve on any of the twelve committees appointed during the session. His service on four committees put him in the same league as Roger Sherman, Nathaniel Gorham, Gouverneur Morris, and James Madison (Vile 2006, 175). This was likely attributable both to his positive reputation and to the fact that he was at a meeting where delegates appointed one representative from each state present to committees. Of the four Georgia delegates, only Baldwin and Few remained at the convention to sign the document on September 17. J. David Griffin, a history professor at West Georgia College, has concluded that "Georgia's delegation was probably the least distinguished" at the convention (1977, 8). A single thesis (Saye 1934), which focuses chiefly on biographies of the participants, appears to be the only extended treatment that focuses specifically on the Georgia delegation's work at that gathering.

Georgia's Political Situation

Although it was the most recently settled and one of the least populous states (Abbot 1957; also see Griffin 1977, 5), Georgia covered a large territory and was growing rapidly. Politically, the state was divided between the tidewater region and the upcountry. Since Pierce and Houstoun were both from Savannah, they were from the former. However, they represented rival groups, known as the Walton and McIntosh factions, which might help explain Pierce's relatively negative assessment of his colleague. Few and Baldwin were from the upcountry and represented what were known as the "newcomers" (Griffin 1977, 6). As in many other states during the confederal period (Wood 1969, 162–173), Georgia's government was almost completely dominated by the legislative branch. Unlike most other states, Georgia's legislature was unicameral, a situation altered by the adoption in May 1789 of a new state constitution, which mirrored many features of the new national Constitution (Conley and Kaminski 1988, 90–91).

At the Constitutional Convention of 1787, Georgia delegates were as attuned to the prospect of anticipated growth as to existing weakness. Delegate Gunning Bedford of Delaware observed that while Georgia was "a small State at present, she is actuated by the prospect of soon being a great one" (Farrand 1966, 1:491). In his *Genuine Information*, which he first delivered as a speech to the Maryland legislature on November 29, 1787, and which was printed during the Federalist/Anti-Federalist debates, Luther Martin of Maryland offered a similar explanation of why Georgia frequently allied with the large states that had supported the Virginia Plan:

> It may be thought surprising, Sir, that Georgia, a State *now small* and comparatively *trifling* in the Union, should advocate this system of *unequal representation*, giving up her *present* equality in the federal government, and thinking herself almost to total insignificance in the scale; but, Sir, it must be considered, that Georgia has the *most extensive* territory in the Union, being *larger* than the *whole island of Great Britain*, and *thirty* times as large as *Connecticut*. This system being designed to *preserve to the States their whole territory unbroken*, and to prevent the erection of new States within the territory of any of them, Georgia looked forward *when*, her *population* being increased in some measure *proportioned* to her *territory*, she should rise in the scale, and *give law* to the *other States*, and hence we found the delegation of Georgia warmly advocating the proposition of giving the States unequal representation. (ibid., 3:187)

Facing Spanish Florida to the south and Native Americans to the west, Georgia had cause to think that a stronger Union might be necessary to its continuing security.

William Pierce: Verbal Sketch Artist

Of the Georgians who attended the convention, Abraham Baldwin was the most important, but William Pierce is the most frequently cited. His primary fame, however, derives neither from what he said at the convention, where he barely spent a month and where he gave only four speeches, nor from some notes that he took during the first week or so of his short tenure there—although these are, on occasion, a useful supplement to the more copious notes of James Madison and others.[2] Some scholars rightly associate Pierce with his report of a unique anecdote involving Washington, which emphasized the convention's focus on secrecy,[3] but Pierce is primarily known for a set of character sketches of all but two of the delegates—William Churchill Houston of New Jersey and John Francis Mercer of Maryland—both of whom were fairly inconsequential to the deliberations.[4] Pierce's sketches serve as mini-biographies not only of such notables as George Washington, Alexander Hamilton, and James Madison, but also of lesser known individuals like Virginia's John Blair, North Carolina's Alexander Martin, and Georgia's William Few.[5]

The sketches, though written during or shortly after the convention, were not published until their appearance in the Savannah *Georgian* issues of April 19, 21, 22, 23, 24, 25, 26, and 28, 1828. They were republished in the *American Historical Review* ("Notes of Major William Pierce" 1898, 87–97) and have been published numerous times since.[6] These sketches reveal an individual of considerable literary accomplishment, a sense of humor, and excellent powers of observation. He reported, with perhaps a bit of hyperbole—albeit consistent with Thomas Jefferson's assessment that the convention had been "an assembly of demigods" (Meacham 2012, 211)—that he had participated in "the wisest Council in the World" (Farrand 1966, 3:97).

John Kaminski, who has collected a book of founders' comments on other founders, observes that character sketches can be "not only useful" but also "entertaining" (2008, xxiii). Pierce's portraits certainly fit the bill. His sketches have a certain pithiness and an occasional backhandedness about them, which classical writers sometimes called "asteism." Pierce's descriptions include such snarky observations as "nature seems to have done more for his corporeal than mental powers" (fellow Georgian William Houstoun); "he appears to me rather to indulge a sportiveness of wit, than a strength of thinking" (New Jersey's William Livingston); and "a man of specious talents, with nothing of genius to improve them" (Maryland's James McHenry). Although Max Farrand observes that "Pierce's statements of age . . . are only approximately correct" (Farrand 1966, 3:325n1), most other commentators quote Pierce's sketches almost like sacred scripture, with little attention to the accuracy of his other observations. I seek to remedy this defect by presenting the first detailed analysis and discussion of Pierce's sketches. In so doing I hope to illumine both Pierce and the delegates he described.

Pierce's Attendance and Opportunity to Observe Fellow Delegates in Action

While Pierce contributed to the writing and ratification of the Constitution, he did not live long enough to contribute significantly to its implementation, and his name would largely be forgotten were it not for his vivid character sketches and a continuing thirst for knowledge about the convention delegates. The power of

Pierce's descriptions derive in part from their economy of language, but they also gain credibility from Pierce's role as an eyewitness at the convention. He highlights this role by saying at the end of his narrative that his presence at the convention "furnished me with an opportunity of giving these short Sketches of the Characters who composed it."

Because Pierce died just two years after the convention adjourned and because he did not include any information that he might have gleaned from the subsequent Federalist/Anti-Federalist debates over ratification of the Constitution, readers can be relatively sure that his observations and analysis were contemporary to the event whose members he was describing, rather than being colored by their subsequent reputations. Max Farrand notes, however, that "[i]t is impossible to assign any exact date to the writing of these sketches" (1966, 3:87n1). Moreover, on occasion, particularly when he described the service of delegates in other governmental bodies, Pierce made a point of indicating that he derived this information from the reports of others.

By contrast, in describing Jonathan Dayton, Pierce mentioned that he "served with me as a Brother Aid to General Sullivan in the Western expedition of '79." Similarly, he knew some delegates from his service in the Georgia legislature and from his work in the confederal Congress.[7] Other delegates who were representatives in Congress at the time of Pierce's service included Baldwin (Ga.), Blount (N.C.), Butler (S.C.), Few (Ga.), Gilman (N.H.), Gorham (Mass.), Johnson (Conn.), King (Mass.), Madison (Va.), and Williamson (N.C.).[8] Pierce undoubtedly met others through his membership in the Society of the Cincinnati, whose members included Baldwin (Ga.), Brearly (N.J.), Dayton (N.J.), Dickinson (Del.), Gilman (N.H.), Hamilton (N.Y.), Lansing (N.Y.), Livingston (N.J.), A. Martin (N.C.), McClurg (Va.), Mifflin (Pa.), R. Morris (Pa.), C. C. Pinckney (S.C.), Randolph (Va.), Washington (Va.), and Yates (N.Y.) (Vile 2005, 2:732).

Pierce's attendance was limited: he was seated on May 31 (Farrand 1966, 3:32) and left on June 29 or shortly thereafter. Rossiter simply says "at the end of June" (1966, 166). Burnett—who was chiefly focused on Pierce's service in Congress—says he was at the convention "to July 1" (*Letters of Members of the Continental Congress* 1963, lxxxvi). Fortunately, Rossiter made an extensive study of the delegates' attendance records. Pairing Pierce's approximate dates of attendance with those of other delegates shows that he would have had time to observe twenty-nine delegates whom Rossiter described as "full-timers" and another ten who were there for all but a few weeks (see 1966, 164–165). The full-timers were Bassett (Del.), Bedford (Del.), Blair (Va.), Brearly (N.J.), Broom (Del.), Butler (S.C.), Clymer (Pa.), Fitzsimons (Pa.), Franklin (Pa.), Gerry (Mass.), Gorham (Mass.), Ingersoll (Pa.), Jenifer (Md.), Johnson (Conn.), King (Mass.), Madison (Va.), Mason (Va.), Mifflin (Pa.), R. Morris (Pa.), C. Pinckney (S.C.), C. C. Pinckney (S.C.), Randolph (Va.), Read (Del.), Rutledge (S.C.), Sherman (Conn.), Spaight (N.C.), Washington (Va.), Williamson (N.C.), and Wilson (Pa.). The others who attended for lesser periods but whom he would have observed were Baldwin (Ga.), Davie (N.C.), Dayton (N.J.), Dickinson (Del.), Ellsworth (Conn.), Livingston (N.J.), A. Martin (N.C.), L. Martin (Md.), G. Morris (Pa.), and Strong (Mass.).

Pierce had no occasion during the convention to observe Langdon and Gilman of New Hampshire, who did not arrive until July 23. Similarly, he could not have heard Carroll of Maryland, who did not arrive until July 9 (Rossiter 1966, 165), and Mercer of Maryland, who attended only August 6–17. Significantly, Pierce's verbal portraits include all but the last of these.

Based on Rossiter's analysis, Pierce would have had limited time at the convention to observe fellow Georgian Baldwin, who did not arrive until June 11; William Blount (N.C.), whose attendance overlapped only from June 20 to the day that Pierce left; Dayton (N.J.), who did not get to the convention until June 21; Gouverneur Morris (Pa.), who missed the last three weeks of Pierce's stay; James McHenry (Md.), who attended May 28–31 and did not return until August 6; William Churchill Houston (N.J.), who was seated on May 25 and gone by June 6; and George Wythe (Va.), who, while present on the opening day of the convention, left on June 4 to give solace to his dying wife and did not return. Pierce's descriptions include all of the above except for Houston.

During the convention, Pierce lodged at the Indian Queen (Vile 2005, 1:424). This would have put him in the company of Virginia's George Mason, whom he assessed especially favorably, and Delaware's Richard Bassett, whose religious enthusiasm appears to have grated on him. When Manasseh Cutler visited the Indian Queen on July 13, 1787, he met Gorham (Mass.), Hamilton (N.Y.), Madison (Va.), A. Martin (N.C.), one of the Pinckneys (S.C.), and Rutledge (S.C.) (Farrand 1966, 58). This was also near Mary House's boarding house, where Dickinson (Del.), Madison (Va.), McClurg (Va.), Randolph (Va.), and Read (Del.) were staying.

A perusal of Pierce's notes from the first week of the convention shows that he attributed arguments to twenty delegates. The delegates that he cited and the number of times he cited them are, by my count, as follows: Delaware's Gunning Bedford (2); South Carolina's Pierce Butler (7); Delaware's John Dickinson (3); Pennsylvania's Benjamin Franklin (2); Elbridge Gerry of Massachusetts (4); New York's Alexander Hamilton (1); Rufus King of Massachusetts (5); Virginia's James Madison (9); Virginia's George Mason (3); Georgia's William Pierce (1); South Carolina's Charles Pinckney (3); South Carolina's Charles Cotesworth Pinckney

(2); Virginia's Edmund Randolph (5); South Carolina's John Rutledge (1); Connecticut's Roger Sherman (3); North Carolina's Richard Dobbs Spaight (1); Caleb Strong of Massachusetts (1); North Carolina's Hugh Williamson (1); Pennsylvania's James Wilson (9, including one on behalf of Franklin); and Virginia's George Wythe (1).

Pierce undoubtedly listened to many other speeches in the weeks he attended after he stopped taking notes. His recollections and analyses of the speakers' style formed a core component of his character sketches. As the next chapter indicates, Pierce studied in his youth under a portrait painter and worked for a brief period as an artist. Although he was no longer part of that profession, he continued to employ his faculties of observation in his word sketches, and these observations cast light both on Pierce himself and on his fellow delegates.

NOTES

1. In a unitary government, like that of Great Britain or France, there are no permanent entities like U.S. states. A federal government, like the current governments of the United States, Germany, Mexico, and Canada, is characterized by a division of powers between a central government and various constituent units and is governed by a written constitution, but *both* the national and constituent governments have the power to act directly on individual citizens as, for example, in collecting taxes.
2. Pierce's notes on the convention debates, which are not analyzed in this book, cover May 30–31, June 1–2, June 4–6, and then, like his participation later in the convention, end. Pierce's notes are included at appropriate dates in Max Farrand's *Records of the Federal Convention* (1966) and are printed in a compilation of Pierce's writings on the Constitution (Leffler, Kaminski, and Fore 2012). Farrand's records also include the official vote tallies by William Jackson, the convention's secretary. Mary Sarah Bilder (2012) has published an article arguing that Jackson's records, which have long been in the shadow of Madison's more comprehensive notes, are far better than their reputation.
3. Pierce reported that delegates were given copies of "a number of propositions brought forward as great leading principles for the New Government to be established for the United States [presumably incorporated in or accompanying the Virginia Plan]" and were told to keep them secret. He further reported that General Thomas Mifflin (Pa.) found a copy that a member had dropped and gave it to General Washington, who expressed such concern over the document, which he placed on the table, that Pierce went forward to make sure that the document was not his own (it has someone else's handwriting on it). He later discovered to his relief that he had left his copy in the pocket of his coat, which he had left in his room at the Indian Queen. Scholars have frequently cited this story to emphasize how seriously the delegates took their vow of secrecy and for Pierce's description of Washington's actions, which showed "a dignity so severe that every Person seemed alarmed."
4. Another set of character sketches from the French archives entitled "Liste des Membres et Officiers du Congres" (1788) and reported in Farrand's *Records of the Federal Convention* (1966, 3:232–238) covers many of the same delegates, but has the disadvantage (for English-speaking readers) of having been written in French. Sadly, the sketches, which are analyzed

in chapter 7 of this book and reproduced in full in appendix II, do not include a description of William Pierce, who was no longer serving in Congress.

5. Significantly, Kaminski's book (2008), which gathers comments on key founders, including some who did not attend the convention, covers only eleven of the fifty-three individuals whom Pierce recorded: John Dickinson, Oliver Ellsworth, Benjamin Franklin, Elbridge Gerry, Alexander Hamilton, James Madison, Gouverneur Morris, Robert Morris, Roger Sherman, George Washington, and James Wilson.

6. A letter that James Madison wrote to I. K. Tefft on December 30, 1830 (Farrand 1966, 3:494), indicated that a J. V. Bevan had sent Madison a copy of the articles from the *Georgian* containing Pierce's notes. Although Madison attempted to explain a discrepancy between his own notes and those of Pierce on the executive veto, he made no mention of Pierce's character sketches.

7. Houstoun was elected in 1782, and while their terms do not appear to have overlapped, Pierce may well have learned of Houstoun and other Georgia delegates from other members.

8. Delegates who had served in Congress not during Pierce's tenure were Bedford (1783–1785), Dickinson (1774–1777, 1779), Ellsworth (1778–1783), Fitzsimons (1782–1783), Gerry (1776–1781, 1783–1785), Hamilton (1782–1782, 1788), Houston (1779–1781, 1784–1785), Ingersoll (1780), Jenifer (1779–1781), Johnson (1785–1789), King (1784–1787), Lansing (1785), Livingston (1774–1776), McHenry (1783–1785), Mercer (1783–1784), Randolph (1779, 1781–1782), Rutledge 1774–1775, 1782–1783), Sherman (1774–1781, 1784), Spaight (1783–1785), Washington (1774–1775), and Wythe (1775–1776). See "List of Delegates to the Continental Congress," Ask.com Encyclopedia, http://www.ask.com/wiki/List_of_delegates-to_the_Continental-Congress.

REFERENCES

Abbot, William W. 1957. "The Structure of Politics in Georgia: 1782–1789." *William and Mary Quarterly*, 3rd ser., 14 (January):47–65.

Anderson, Thornton. 1993. *Creating the Constitution: The Convention of 1787 and the First Congress.* University Park: Pennsylvania State University Press.

Beeman, Richard. 2010. *Plain, Honest Men: The Making of the American Constitution.* New York: Random House.

Bernstein, Richard B., with Kym S. Rice. 1987. *Are We to Be a Nation? The Making of the Constitution.* Cambridge, Mass.: Harvard University Press.

Bilder, Mary Sarah. 2012. "How Bad Were the Official Records of the Federal Convention?" *George Washington Law Review* 80:101–164.

Bowen, Catherine Drinker. 1966. *Miracle at Philadelphia: The Story of the Constitutional Convention, May to September 1787.* Boston: Little, Brown.

Collier, Christopher, and James Lincoln Collier. 1986. *Decision in Philadelphia: The Constitutional Convention of 1787.* New York: Random House.

Conley, Patrick T., and John P. Kaminski, eds. 1988. *The Constitution and the States: The Role of the Original Thirteen in the Framing and Adoption of the Federal Constitution.* Madison, Wis.: Madison House.

Coulter, E. Merton. 1987. *Abraham Baldwin: Patriot, Educator, and Founding Father.* Arlington, Va.: Vandamer.

Edling, Max M. 2008. *A Revolution in Favor of Government: Origins of the U.S. Constitution and the Making of the American States*. New York: Oxford University Press.

Farrand, Max. 1913. *The Framing of the Constitution of the United States*. New Haven, Conn.: Yale University Press.

Farrand, Max, ed. 1966. *The Records of the Federal Convention of 1787*. 4 vols. New Haven, Conn.: Yale University Press.

Graebner, Norman A. 1986. "Foreign Affairs and the U.S. Constitution, 1787–1788." *Proceedings of the Massachusetts Historical Society*, 3rd ser., 98:1–20.

Griffin, J. David. 1977. *Georgia and the United States Constitution, 1787–1798*. Augusta: Georgia Commission for the National Bicentennial Celebration and Georgia Department of Education.

Hendrickson, David C. 2003. *Peace Pact: The Lost World of the American Founding*. Lawrence: University Press of Kansas.

Hutson, James H., ed. 1987. *Supplement to Max Farrand's The Records of the Federal Convention of 1787*. New Haven, Conn.: Yale University Press.

Johnson, Calvin H. 2009. *Righteous Anger at the Wicked States: The Meaning of the Founders' Constitution*. New York: Cambridge University Press.

Kaminski, John P., ed. 2008. *The Founders on the Founders: Word Portraits from the American Revolutionary Era*. Charlottesville: University of Virginia Press.

Leffler, Richard, John P. Kaminski, and Samuel K. Fore, eds. 2012. *William Pierce on the Constitutional Convention and the Constitution*. Dallas, Tex.: Harlan Crow Library.

Letters of Members of the Continental Congress. 1963. Ed. Edmund C. Burnett. Washington, D.C.: Carnegie Institution of Washington, 1936. Reprint, Gloucester, Mass.: Peter Smith.

Marks, Frederick W., III. 1971. "A Winning Issue in the Campaign for Ratification of the United States Constitution." *Political Science Quarterly* 86 (September):444–469.

Meacham, Jon. 2012. *Thomas Jefferson: The Art of Power*. New York: Random House.

Miller, William Lee. 1992. *The Business of May Next: James Madison and the Founding*. Charlottesville: University Press of Virginia.

Peters, William. 1987. *A More Perfect Union: The Making of the United States Constitution*. New York: Crown.

Robertson, David Brian. 2005. *The Constitution and America's Destiny*. New York: Cambridge University Press.

———. 2012. *The Original Compromise: What the Constitution's Framers Were Really Thinking*. New York: Oxford University Press.

Rossiter, Clinton. 1966. *1787: The Grand Convention*. New York: Norton.

Sargent, Mildrew Crow. 2004, 2006. *William Few, a Founding Father: A Biographical Perspective of Early American History*. 2 vols. New York: Vantage.

Saye, Albert B. 1934. "Georgia's Delegates to the Federal Convention of 1787: Who They Were and What They Did." M.A. thesis, University of Georgia.

Solberg, Winton, ed. 1958. *The Federal Convention and the Formation of the Union*. Indianapolis: Bobbs-Merrill.

Stewart, David D. 2008. *The Summer of 1787: The Men Who Invented the Constitution*. New York: Simon and Schuster. 2008.

Van Doren, Charles. 1948. *The Great Rehearsal: The Story of the Making and Ratifying of the Constitution of the United States*. New York: Viking.

Vile, John R. 2005. *The Constitutional Convention of 1787: A Comprehensive Encyclopedia of America's Founding*. 2 vols. Santa Barbara, Calif.: ABC-CLIO.

———. 2006. "The Critical Role of Committees at the U.S. Constitutional Convention of 1787." *American Journal of Legal History* 47:148–176.

———. 2011. *A Companion to the United States Constitution and Its Amendments.* 5th ed. Lanham, Md.: Rowman and Littlefield.

———. 2012. *The Writing and Ratification of the U.S. Constitution.* Lanham, Md.: Rowman and Littlefield.

———. 2013. *The Men Who Made the Constitution: Lives of the Delegates to the Constitutional Convention.* Lanham, Md.: Scarecrow.

Virginia Wills and Administrations 1632–1800. 1972. Comp. Clayton Torrence. Baltimore, Md.: Genealogical Publishing. Originally published by the National Society of the Colonial Dames of America, Richmond, Va., 1930.

Wood, Gordon S. 1969. *The Creation of the American Republic, 1776–1787.* Chapel Hill: University of North Carolina Press.

CHAPTER 2

Important Biographical Facts
about William Pierce Jr.

*I am conscious of having discharged my duty as a Soldier
through the course of the late revolution with honor and
propriety; and my services in Congress and the Convention
were bestowed with the best intention towards the interests of
Georgia, and towards the general welfare of the Confederation.*

—William Pierce Jr.'s Character Sketches

As with most writers, William Pierce's life informed his observations. His place of birth, his education, his experience as a soldier in the Revolution, and his service in the Georgia legislature and in Congress all shaped his perspective and gave him opportunities to observe some of the delegates even before they assembled in Philadelphia. Unfortunately, Pierce remains one of the relative unknowns among the delegates to the Constitutional Convention. In a speech delivered to the State Society of the Cincinnati of Pennsylvania to commemorate George Washington's birthday in 1987, David A. Kimball, the team leader of bicentennial constitutional research at Independence National Park, observed, "As a nation, we've never heard of William Pierce. This is probably more our loss than his." It is likely that a beautifully bound, limited-edition book with most of Pierce's key writings on the convention (Leffler, Kaminski, and Fore 2012) will renew interest in Pierce, but, like most earlier writings, it largely presents Pierce by reproducing what he said rather than by attempting to analyze his words in any meaningful way. Because no one has yet written a biography of Pierce, this chapter seeks to piece together the narrative of his life from letters of the period, from his own speeches and notes, and from a variety of other sources.

Pierce's Genealogy

Although numerous earlier sources claimed that he was born in Georgia in 1740, scholars now believe that he was the third of three sons born to Elizabeth and Matthew Pierce in York County, Virginia, in 1753 (Fore 2008). This county, the current home of Yorktown, Virginia, was originally formed as Charles River County in 1634 and renamed York in 1643 (Mason 1939, 159). One of the earliest settled parts of Virginia, it boasted schools, government buildings, and churches (Mason 1939; Riley 1942).

Partly because first names were frequently recycled from one generation to the next, and partly because there are variants of the spelling for Pierce (including Pearce and Peirce), tracing Pierce's lineage can be a frustrating endeavor. The family appears to have been well established in Virginia. A Captain William Pierce arrived in Virginia from Great Britain with his wife, Jane, in 1610, and their daughter Jane was the third wife of John Rolfe ("Historical and Genealogical Notes" 1901, 270). Captain Pierce owned large tracts of land, and his house was reported to be "the fairest in all Virginia" (ibid.).[1]

The scholar who appears to have come closest to tracing William Pierce's immediate ancestors is Linda H. Rowe, who combed through York County records while serving as a research associate at the John D. Rockefeller Jr. Library in Williamsburg, Virginia (1988). Rowe identified Matthew Pierce (whom she called Matthew1) as the father of William Pierce (whom she designated as William1 and said was born by 1733), John Pierce, and Matthew Pierce (whom she designated as Matthew2). Matthew2 was a resident of Bruton Parish, but not of Williamsburg, and married a woman named Elizabeth (Rowe was unable to ascertain her maiden name), and they had at least four children: John Pierce, Matthew Pierce, Elizabeth Pierce, and William Pierce (I cannot ascertain their birth order). Rowe designated this William, the subject of this book, as William2 Pierce. She believed he was born around 1753.

As early as 1769, this William Pierce used the designation "Jr." in signing a manuscript; although he is often designated as William Leigh Pierce, Pierce does not appear to have had a middle name, and the practice of adding it appears traceable to his son, who did have the middle name. Although it seems odd for an individual to label himself as Jr. when his father had a different first name, Rowe (1988) believes that the son did so in order to distinguish himself from his uncle with the same name (Rowe's William1, for whom his parents might have named him?). She further notes that this practice of using a Jr. designation was not uncommon in such circumstances among "York County and Williamsburg residents."

A Matthew Pierce, who was probably William's father (although possibly his grandfather) served in 1742–1743 as one of the church wardens (along with Peyton Randolph, Thomas Cobbs, Henry Tyler, Lewis Burwell, Benjamin Waller, William Parkes, John Custis, and James Wray) of Bruton Parish, who were involved in a friendly lawsuit triggered by the will of Mary Whaley, who had bequeathed money to maintain a school (Tyler 1895, 9). Similarly, William Meade (1891, 166) lists a Matthew Pierce (and a Matthew Fierce, possibly a misspelling of the same name) as a vestryman. Carl R. Lounsbury (2005, 19–21) lists Matthew Pierce, whom he identifies as a tobacco farmer, as one of thirteen men who served five times as a commissioner of the peace from York in 1731–1732. Lounsbury notes that such individuals had some legal duties, though they typically lacked formal legal training.

Rowe (1988) says that Matthew Pierce, the Matthew2 whom she identifies as William Pierce's father, served as a justice of the peace for about a decade from 1744 until his death. Both justices of the peace and vestrymen were members of the colonial elite and held considerable responsibilities (Seiler 1956). If William grew up in such a household, or under one of its stewards or guardians, he would likely have been raised in relatively affluent circumstances and would almost certainly have received a good education.

Pierce's Early Life and Study as an Artist

Matthew2 died when William was an infant. Records of York County, Virginia, list wills for an Edith Pierce (otherwise unidentified by me) in 1739 and for a Matthew Pierce in 1737, and an inventory for a Matthew Pierce in 1755 (*Virginia Wills and Administrations* 1972, 336). Drawing from the same records, Leffler, Kaminski, and Fore (2012, 9) say that William and his siblings "'made choice' of their Uncle John as their guardian" when their father died in 1760. He would likely have been responsible for William's education.[2]

On August 26, 1774, Charles Willson Peale, a leading portrait artist and American revolutionary, who later would create a famed natural history museum in Philadelphia that was open during the convention (Sellers 1980), wrote a letter from his studio in Annapolis, Maryland, to "Willm. Pearse" (the same idiosyncratic spelling is used in the rest of this letter), presumably in response to an inquiry about serving as his teacher. Peale did not indicate whether Pierce had sent him any drawings or whether he was relying on word of mouth, but he observed, "I am quite satisfy'd of your abilitys and have not the least doubt of your success in the art with the application you promise." Outlining a course of study for Pierce, Peale said that his purpose "in this first year [is] to make you well acquaint[ed] with the Rudiments of the Art; by Drawing of Anatomy, per[spective] [and] thorough knowledge of the clare obscure and studies f[rom] figures I h[ave] collected for that purpose, after this I can sett you to colouring copying and painting [from] Nature" (Peale 1983, 1:135).[3]

Pierce could not have studied with Peale for a complete year, because by the summer of 1775, Pierce had returned to Williamsburg, apparently to set up a studio (Fore 2008). A notice under "Williamsburg" in the *Virginia Gazette*, August 11, 1775, supplement 2-2, notes, "Mr. WILLIAM PIERCE, jun. is just returned to this city from Annapolis in Maryland, where he has studied PAINTING under the celebrated Mr. PEELE, And we hear intends on residing here for some time."[4] Peale wrote to Pierce in Williamsburg on September 4, 1775, "I am glad to hear that you are employed about several pictures. . . . I will not flatter you so much as to say your [*sic*] are [a] perfect Master of the Drawing, therefore apply to that part in particular" (Peale 1983, 2:509–510). Similarly, an article in the *Virginia Gazette* of November 9, 1775, observed, "Mr. William Pierce, junior, of this city, who was in the late [military] engagement at Hampton [October 26, 1775] (and whose genius is greatly admired for many valuable productions in the celebrated art of painting) we are informed, is now executing the plan of the same in a most elegant and circumstantial manner."

Like his study under Peale, Pierce's work as an artist was short-lived. I have been unable, and do not know of anyone else who has been able, to locate any paintings or drawings by Pierce. There is thus no basis to judge Pierce's talents in that area, other than Peale's comments on his mastery of "the Drawing," but he is certainly not the only artist from the period whose work does not survive (see Pleasants 1952).

Service in the Revolution and Brief Stay at William and Mary

Pierce lived in a time of tumult, and he appears to have been a young man in a hurry. Within a year after arriving in Williamsburg, he joined the patriot forces. In a likely indication of his high social status, he served for a time as a captain (probably an elected position) and then as an aide-de-camp to General John Sullivan, who fought a brutal war against the Iroquois in New York. In a letter partially printed in the *Virginia Gazette* of October 17, 1777, Pierce wrote an account from Yorktown, Pennsylvania, about the Battle of Germantown (http://secondvirginia.wordpress.com/2010/10/04/germantown).

Pierce returned to Williamsburg in 1780 and appears to have studied at the College of William and Mary, the second oldest institution of higher education in the former colonies. *A Provisional List of Alumni, Grammar School Students, Members of the Faculty, and Members of the Board of Visitors of the College of William and Mary, from 1693 to 1888* (1941) lists Pierce as having attended in 1780. He became a member of Phi Beta Kappa on June 3 (Tyler 1896).[5] Unfortunately, this is not conclusive proof that Pierce attended William and Mary since, on December 10, 1778, the society had "[r]esolved that in future admission to this Society be not confined to collegians alone" (McBryde 1915, 210).[6]

If Pierce did attend classes, he arrived at the college at a good time. Partly because of the influence of one-time governor Thomas Jefferson and of the college's eighth president, Bishop James Madison (1749–1812),[7] a cousin of the future president James Madison, the curriculum of the college had recently been revised. Robert Polk Thomson says that professors offered lectures on "natural philosophy, moral philosophy and law" (1971, 211). He also notes, "The reformed college continued to rely heavily on disputations. They were held weekly, or monthly for law students, with the entire university present. Students were supposed to prepare their debate questions in advance. Annual declamations were also retained" (ibid.).

Pierce cannot have stayed long, however, because the next year the college was suspended due to the Revolutionary War, and Pierce was serving as an aide-de-camp to General Nathanael Greene, under whom he distinguished himself in battles at Guilford Court House and Eutaw Springs. In a report to Thomas McKean, the president of the Continental Congress, on September 11, 1781, on the latter engagement, General Greene stated that he was deeply indebted to Pierce and other aides "for their activity and good conduct throughout the whole of the Action" (Greene 1991–2005, 9:333). Greene commissioned Pierce to carry word of the victory to Congress, which on October 29, 1781, awarded him a sword for his conduct in the engagement (Moran n.d.; *Journals of the Continental Congress, 1774–1789*). According to one article, the descendants of Pierce's wife still possess the sword (Deen 1991, 220).

The short length of Pierce's stay at William and Mary was not unusual. Robert Polk Thomson observes, "Few completed the course of study and acquired degrees, and the professors did not seem to encourage them to do so. Such seemed appropriate mainly for the few students who intended to go on to advanced professional studies" (1971, 202). John Marshall, for example, attended George Wythe's law lectures for only two or three months in the same year that Pierce was in Williamsburg. Marshall was elected to Phi Beta Kappa on the same day that Pierce was, and he argued on the question of "whether any form of Government is more favourable to public virtue than a Commonwealth?" ("Original Phi Beta Kappa Records" 1919, 601).

However limited Pierce's stay may have been at William and Mary, his classical education (likely from private tutors) is evident throughout his letters.[8] Hunter Dickinson Farish in her introduction to the *Journal and Letters of Philip Vickers Fithian, 1773–1774*, which was authored by a man who came from the College of New Jersey to tutor the children of Robert Carter in the northern neck of Virginia, describes the fifty years prior to the American Revolution as a "Golden Age" in which "a remarkable civilization reached its zenith in the broad coastal plain of eastern Virginia," where planters highly valued education (1990, xiii).

Pierce's education clearly followed the classical model, which was common in colonial Virginia (Hiden 1941). In a letter to St. George Tucker (1752–1827) dated July 20, 1781, Pierce noted that the army had executed a move to draw out Lord Cornwallis using "[t]he principle . . . that actuated Scipio when he led the Carthagenian hero out of Rome to the plains of Zama" (1881, 431). Similarly, Pierce began a letter to General Greene from Kiawah Island, South Carolina (where Pierce was recovering from malaria), on September 14, 1782, by observing, "This place is not an Elysium [the abode of the dead in classical mythology], nor is it equal to the Garden of Hesrude [a mythical garden where golden apples were said to grow], happily calculated for philosophic solitude and contemplation" (Greene 1991–2005, 11:659). The letter continued with a variety of classical allusions to Greek gods and goddesses and what appears to be an allusion to Shakespeare (ibid., 660). Other correspondence contained references to events from ancient history. Citing letters that Pierce wrote to Tucker on April 14 and June 17, 1787, David A. Kimball (1987, n.p.) speculates, "Among other things, Pierce may have written the first review of an American play."

But Pierce's creative and artistic side may have sometimes prevailed over more practical skills. On May 6, 1784, Nathaniel Pendleton penned a letter from Charleston to Otho Holland Williams, in which, in a foreshadowing of Pierce's later failures in business, he observed that Pierce "has been successful in his first commercial essays; but I fear he wants stability, for such an employment. You know he was a warm advocate for great and astonishing flights of Genius. A Soberer, and more plodding turn of mind would be better suited to ~~for~~ Commercial Concerns" (provided by Sam Fore from Nathaniel Pendleton Family Papers, Yale University).

At times Pierce was caught up in the enthusiasm of the patriot cause for which he had been fighting. Writing on December 15, 1782, to St. George Tucker, a fellow veteran of the Revolution and a lawyer who studied under and eventually replaced George Wythe as a professor of law at William and Mary (Stephens 2003), Pierce

observed: "The Carolinians, so long oppressed, are now likely to enjoy the blessings of peace and tranquility. One universal joy seems to reign through the whole
country. The fetters of tyranny are taken off, and the goddess of liberty seems to be
the companion of every one. I feel myself exceedingly interested in the happiness
of these people" (1881, 445). Looking back on the Revolution in his Fourth of July
Oration in 1788, however, Pierce stressed "the spirit of moderation and wisdom
which marked every stage of the opposition" (4). He continued in a similar vein
later in the speech: "No circumstance of whim or passion moved us,—no fanatic
zeal enraged us,—no cause of a popular demagogue inflamed us,—no dethroned
monarch to replace,—no sympathetic fury caught from the injury of a favorite citizen urged us to oppose our parent country;—no,—all was the result of reason, and
a train of injuries unprovoked, which prompted us to arms" (3). Like others of his
day, Pierce interpreted the Revolution as the vindication of preexisting liberties.
Continuing in his Fourth of July oration, he thus observed, "The rights of human
nature, and the benefits of civil liberty, we contended for; the cause of all mankind
we engaged in" (ibid.). Somewhat later, he opined (in words that appear to echo
George Washington's Circular to the States of June 8, 1783):[9]

> Fortunate for mankind the American Revolution happened at a period when
> the principles of society, and the nature of government, were better understood
> than at any former existence of the world. Men were taught how to define the
> rights of nature,—how to search into, to distinguish, and to comprehend, the
> principles of physical, moral, religious, and civil liberty. The spirit of free inves-
> tigation had gone forth and stirred the genius of the civilized world; and men no
> longer fettered by false habits suffered philosophy, guided by truth, to pursue its
> way through the dark regions of ignorance and superstition, without the dread
> of persecution. (5–6)

With a clear emphasis on the need for civil liberties against repressive forces of
both church and state, Pierce further claimed that the Revolution "has since gone
into the Chambers of the Inquisition, and shaken the pillars on which that awful and bloody tribunal rested;—nay it has ventured farther,—it has dared to approach the palaces of despots, and pointed out the boundaries of regal prerogative
to Kings" (6).

Pierce was also aware that the new government was encountering numerous
problems. On June 19, 1783, for example, he wrote a letter to General Greene from
Philadelphia in which he reported that troops were on the verge of using force to
get the pay that Congress owed them (Greene 1991–2005, 13:40). Congress perceived the threat to be serious enough that it moved from Philadelphia to Princeton
(see Gallagher 1995).

Pierce's Life after the Revolution

Congress gave Pierce land as a reward for his military service. In writing an introduction for Pierce as he was leaving military service, General Greene observed on March 18, 1783, that "[a]s a Soldier he is much esteemed as a Gentleman highly respected. His genius and education do him honor, and his honor and principles are unquestionable." Greene further said that he took pleasure in giving "this general testimony of my respect and esteem for him having had full opportunity to know his merit and worth" (Greene 1991–2005, 12:536).

Pierce may also have had something of a reputation as a ladies' man during the Revolution. In a letter dated October 25, 1781, Major John Clark Jr. of Philadelphia indicated that while Pierce was a "sensible & worthy man," he could scarcely "get a word with" him because Pierce's time was "engrossed & Monopolised by the *Great* and last by the *Fair*" (Greene 1991–2005, 9:487). Inquiring how Pierce was employing himself after the British evacuation of Charleston, John Marshall observed in a letter of February 12, 1783, "You are in a Country where your *gallantry* may be as serviceable in peace as in war. I know your skill in maneuvering under the banners of Venus [the goddess of love] & I doubt not but several hearts can testify [to] your success" (Marshall 1974, 1:95).[10]

Pierce subsequently headed a trading company (initially in partnership with Anthony W. White and Richard Call, and then renamed Pierce and Co.) that opened stores in Savannah and Augusta. On December 11, 1783, he married Charlotte Fenwick (b. 1766), the daughter of Edward (1720–1775) and Mary Drayton Fenwick, wealthy and prolific South Carolina planters.[11]

A friend wrote a letter to Pierce describing his wife-to-be: "Last evening for the first time in my life I saw Miss Charlotte Fenwick. She sang 'Return Enraptured Hours' most divinely. She is rather pretty than handsome. She is live, facitious and I think abomimably clever. The whole town says you are engaged to her—it is taken for granted—and now you are ranked on the list of a Northern Gentleman marrying a Southern Lady" (http://www.fenwickhall.com/fenwickshistory.html). It seems a bit odd to describe a man from Virginia as a "Northern Gentleman," but it is possible that the writer was intending to be ironic or that he so identified Pierce because of some of his military service farther north.

Pierce and his wife had four sons. Only William Leigh Pierce, who was born after the death of his father,[12] survived into adulthood. On July 25, 1792, Pierce's widow, Charlotte, married Ebenezer Jackson (1763–1837), a veteran of the Revolutionary War who had moved to Savannah in April 1787, where, under the name E. Jackson and Company, he had created a packet line between that city and New

York (Starr 2012, 58).[13] Jackson owned a plantation at Whitmarsh Island on the Savannah River, which he named Newton, and another south of the river, on which he raised cotton. In 1801 he purchased a home named Walnut Grove on thirty acres outside Middletown, Connecticut, which he kept until 1826 (Starr 2012, 58).[14] Charlotte Fenwick Pierce and Ebenezer Jackson fathered a daughter, Harriet Jackson, who married Commodore Tattnall, a first cousin, in 1821 (http://www.fenwickhall.com/fenwickshistory.html). Charlotte and Ebenezer's son, Ebenezer Jackson Jr. (1796–1874), was born in Savannah; graduated from St. Mary's College; studied law at the Litchfield Law School; started his practice in Philadelphia; moved to Middletown, Connecticut; was elected to the Connecticut house of representatives, where he twice served; and was elected to Congress and served in 1834–1835 (http://bioguide.congress.gov/biosearch/biosearch.asp).

Charlotte died in Savannah on April 4, 1819, and Ebenezer in Middletown on October 31, 1837. Both outlived William Leigh Pierce, who died of typhus in 1814 (Starr 2012, 45–59), the third generation of Pierce males to die relatively early in life. He appears to have inherited both his father's and his stepfather's patriotism and his birth father's facility in writing; like his birth father, he gave a Fourth of July oration (1812).[15]

Pierce's Public Life

William Pierce Jr. and Charlotte had houses both in the city of Savannah and at a nearby plantation named Belmont, which was a confiscated loyalist property he had purchased from the state. Although in a letter dated December 8, 1785, Pierce turned down a request from the governor to adjudicate the charter lines of the state (letter on file at the David M. Rubenstein Rare Book and Manuscript Library, Duke University), Pierce was elected in 1786 to the Georgia Assembly, which in turn chose him to represent the state in the confederal Congress in 1787. In a letter that Pierce wrote to Thomas Washington (a land speculator who was later hanged for counterfeiting) from New York on January 14, 1787, Pierce indicated that his wife had accompanied him on a twenty-nine-day sea journey to the city, during which, after being caught in a storm on the way, they were able to see "Massachusetts, Rhode Island, Connecticut, & New York" (*Letters of Members of the Continental Congress* 1963, 24:71).

Pierce's colleagues elected him to be president of the Georgia chapter of the Society of the Cincinnati, and the *Gazette of the State of Georgia* for January 4, 1787, observed that the Georgia society had elected Pierce to be a delegate to the next general meeting, held in Philadelphia in May 1787.[16] The organization had encountered suspicions because of its "hereditary features and the honorary membership" (Davies 1948, 7). Pierce combatted the criticisms in his Fourth of July Oration to fellow Cincinnati members in 1788: "There is no pleasure so sublime as that which arises from the reflection of having faithfully served our country. It was to keep awake this reflection, and to cement the friendship we had formed amidst difficulties and dangers, that the Society of the Cincinnati was instituted. No base motive (as has been ungenerously suggested) gave birth to our association,—but the purest principles of friendly esteem, and the most sacred regard for our invaluable rights, urged us to unite" (13). He further said: "The emblazoned honors and distinctions of a military order that should mark a separation between our fellow citizens and ourselves we reject. We only desire to be known as a private society of friends who have shared together one common danger; and that posterity may be informed who aided that Revolution which gave freedom to North America" (14).

Pierce's Thoughts Leading Up to the Constitutional Convention

In what appears to be a fairly obvious reference to the taxpayer revolt known as Shays' Rebellion, Pierce and William Few sent a letter to George Mathews on January 29, 1787. They indicated that Congress was not yet in session and that "the Government of Massachusetts is greatly disturbed by a serious faction which now prevails in the State," and enclosed articles that described the situation (*Letters of Members of the Continental Congress* 1963, 24:78).[17] On April 14, 1787, Pierce, who was still in New York, sent a letter to St. George Tucker describing the sentiments surrounding the forthcoming convention: "the season being near at hand for the meeting of the Convention little else is talked of in this quarter but the changes that will likely take place in our federal Government. It is certain that the confederation is very compleat, and deficient in point of energy, but I fear we shall meet with great difficulties in amending it. The different States will not make such a surrender of their sovereignty as may be found necessary to give the federal head compleat weight in the Union. Nothing will produce such a surrender but a sense of the greatest danger" (ibid., 24:221).

A month later, on May 19, 1787, William Pierce wrote a letter to Major George Turner, a South Carolinian who was a member of the Society of the Cincinnati. Referring to the upcoming Constitutional Convention, Pierce favored "powers equal to a prompt and certain execution, but tempered with a proper respect for the liberties of the People. I am for securing their happiness, not by the will of a few, but by the direction of the Law" (Hutson 1987, 9). In the same letter, he said that it was necessary to pay respect "to the temper of the People," and he indicated that he thought this temper was incompatible with the establishment of a monarchy (ibid.). He opposed the exercise of "dictatorial power" and thought that "unless *we* can settle down into some permanent System very shortly, our condition will be as fickle and inconsistent, as that of the Romans; and our political schemes be nothing more than chimeras and disorders" (10). Clearly, Pierce recognized that the convention would be important. He concluded the letter, in his own idiosyncratic spelling, most of which I have modernized for this book, by observing, "The Statesman and the Phylosopher have their attention turned towards us: the oppressed and wretched look to America" (ibid.).

Pierce's Participation at the Constitutional Convention

Writing to Thomas Jefferson on June 6, 1787, James Madison listed the delegates in attendance at the convention, among whom in the Georgia delegation he included "Major Pierce, formerly of Williamsburg, and aid[e] to General Greene" (Madison 1865, 1:331). Pierce's notes of the first day indicated that he believed it was necessary to know "how the Senate should be appointed" before deciding on how the first legislative branch (today's House of Representatives) would be selected. His notes continued with his view that the delegates would need to balance the powers of the state and national governments: "it appeared clear to me that unless we established a Government that should carry at least some of its principles into the mass of the people, we might as well depend upon the present confederation. If the influence of the States is not lost in some part of the new Government we never shall have any thing like a national institution. But in my opinion it will be right to shew the sovereignty of the State in one branch of the Legislature, and that should be in the Senate" (Farrand 1966, 1:59). Pierce elaborated on these thoughts on June 6 when, in a possible portent of future compromise, he said that he "was for an election by the people as to the 1st. branch & by the States as to the 2d. branch; by which means the Citizens of the States wd. be represented both *individually & collectively*" (1:137).

On June 12, Pierce showed his support for greater national power by successfully proposing that members of the House of Representatives should be paid out of the national treasury rather than by the individual states (Farrand 1966, 1:216). That same day, which was still early in the convention's proceedings, Pierce supported setting the term of senators at three years. At the time, the convention was considering a seven-year term. Pierce pointed out that such a term had caused "great mischief" in Great Britain, where it had been "reprobated by most of their patriotic Statesmen" (1:218).

On June 27, Pierce wrote from Philadelphia to St. George Tucker to regret that he could tell him nothing about the proceedings because of their secret nature. Assuring his friend that he should not conclude that the convention was about to adopt a monarchy, he related a story that he got from Jean-Jacques Burlamaqui (1694–1748), a Swiss political and legal thinker. It involved a discussion among seven chiefs about what kind of government would be best for Persia on the death of Cambyses. Pierce reported: "One was of opinion that Persia ought to be a Republic; another was of opinion that it ought to be a strong aristocracy, and a third (who I think was Darius) was convinced that no other Government would suit it but a Monarchy" (*Letters of Members of the Continental Congress* 1963, 24:345).

Pierce reiterated the need to balance state and national interests on June 29 in following up a speech by Madison. Pierce observed that members of Congress had represented the interests of their states. Pointing out that the federal government under the Articles of Confederation was "no more than a compact between states," he said: "We are now met to remedy its defects, and our difficulties are great, but not, I hope, insurmountable. State distinctions must be sacrificed so far as the general government shall render it necessary—without, however, destroying them altogether. Although I am here [as] a representative from a small state, I consider myself as a citizen of the United States, whose general interest I will always support" (Farrand 1966, 1:474). As a member of a state that needed congressional help in repelling Indian attacks, Pierce may have been seen the wisdom of taking a more nationalistic view compared to delegates from states where such a dependency was less obvious.

Pierce's Life after the Constitutional Convention

As indicated in chapter 1, Clinton Rossiter (1966, 252) classified Pierce—along with Houston, Wythe, Mercer, Yates, and Lansing—as among "The Dropouts and Walkouts" at the convention. Pierce earned this designation because, while he arrived relatively early in the proceedings (May 31), he left the convention soon after June 29 (see Saye 1934, 61). Although he professed in a letter to William Short on July 25, 1787, to have thought that by then "all the first principles of the new Government were established" (Hutson 1987, 182), he departed prior to the adoption of the Great Compromise concerning state and popular representation in Congress, the invention of the Electoral College for selecting the president, and a number of other important constitutional innovations. Moreover, although Pierce told Short that "[t]he business of the Convention is now going on with some degree of harmony" (ibid.), on June 28, 1787, Benjamin Franklin provided a clue to the real discord that the delegates faced at about the time of Pierce's departure when he asked in vain for the delegates to consider opening each session with prayer (Farrand 1966, 1:451). The delegates did not adopt the Great Compromise until July 16. After noting that Pierce had returned on July 14 to the Congress from the convention, William Blount observed, presumably based on information that Pierce had shared with him, "that it is the general Opinion of the Members of that Body that it will not rise before the Middle of October" (*Letters of Members of the Continental Congress* 1963, 3:610). Although Blount reported that Pierce had preserved his pledge of secrecy, he further observed, "he says in general Terms very little is done and nothing definitive" (ibid.).

Pierce, whose financial situation was precarious and seems to have resulted in some personal antagonisms,[18] left the convention intending to engage in a duel with John Auldjo, a partner in the English mercantile house of Strachan McKenzie and Co., who was visiting New York but had apparently insulted Pierce in Philadelphia.[19] Ironically, fellow delegate Alexander Hamilton, who had also left the convention early and who later died in such an encounter with Aaron Burr, mediated to avoid this as Auldjo's designated second.[20] Although the duel was averted, instead of returning to the convention in Philadelphia, Pierce returned to Congress, which was meeting in New York, and pleaded for national help for Georgia against Indian threats.[21] Although his comments in June on balancing state and national interests suggested that he would have supported the Great Compromise on representation, he did not participate actively enough in debates during his tenure in Philadelphia for me to ascertain whether his continuing presence at the convention would have made much of a difference.

Explaining to St. George Tucker in a letter of September 28, 1787, the first part of which was published in the *Massachusetts Centinel* of May 21, 1788, and all of which was printed in the *Gazette of the State of Georgia* on May 21, 1788 (Leffler, Kaminski, and Fore 2012, 82), why he had not stayed at the convention and signed the document, Pierce referred to "a piece of business so necessary that it became unavoidable"—presumably his anticipated duel. He indicated, however, that he supported the document: "I approve of its principles, and would have signed it with all my heart, had I been present. To say, however, that I consider it as perfect, would be to make an acknowledgement immediately opposed to my judgment. Perhaps it is the only one that will suit our present situation. The wisdom of the Convention was equal to something greater; but a variety of local circumstances, the inequality of states, and the dissonant interests of the different parts of the Union, made it impossible to give it any other shape or form" ("Notes of Major William Pierce" 1898, 314). Although he supported the new Constitution, much like Benjamin Franklin, Pierce did so not because he thought it was the best possible but because he thought it was as good as any that could emerge from a convention with such diverse viewpoints.[22]

Pierce elaborated on his views by using nautical analogies, which, as the well-worn term "ship of state" suggests, are fairly common in political discourse:

> The condition of America demands a change; we must sooner or later be convulsed if we do not have some other government than the one under which we at present live. The old Federal Constitution is like a ship bearing under the weight of a tempest; it is trembling, and just on the point of sinking. If we have not another bark to take us up we shall all go down together. There are periods in the existence of a political society that require prompt and decisive measures; I mean that point of time between a people's running into anarchy and an anxious state of the public mind to be rescued from its approaching mischiefs by the intervention of some good and efficient government. (ibid.)

Expressing his view that the new Constitution "is the ark that is to save us," he opined that "as individuals in society . . . give up a part of their national rights to secure the rest, so the different states should render a portion of their interests to secure the good of the whole" (ibid). Pierce further argued that "when there are restraints on power, to prevent its invading the positive rights of a people, there is no necessity for any such thing as a Bill of Rights" (ibid., 315). Citing the authority of William Blackstone's *Commentaries on the Laws of England* (1771–1772), Pierce specifically responded to those who thought that the Constitution should have included jury trials in federal civil cases (something the Seventh Amendment later required), which drew a response from "A Planter" in the *Gazette of the State of Georgia* on April 3, 1788 (Jensen et al. 1978, 3:298–300). Pierce confessed to some concerns as to whether the executive department, which had been greatly enlarged after he left the convention, was "too highly mounted to preserve exactly the equilibrium" ("Notes of Major William Pierce" 1898, 316), but he also said that he was "at a loss to know whether any government can have sufficient energy to effect its own ends without the aid of a military power" (ibid., 317).

Pierce helped to persuade Congress to send the Constitution to the states for ratification. He brought this congressional dispatch with him when he and his wife sailed on the *Friendship* from New York to Georgia between October 3 and October 10 (Saye 1934, 222), helped to print the Constitution there, and worked for its ratification. There was, however, little opposition to ratification in Georgia, in part because many state leaders believed that it would enhance its security against Indian tribes. The debate at the Georgia ratifying convention in August was short, and the vote for approval was unanimous (26–0; Maier 2010, 123–124). Delegates signed the document on January 2, 1788 (Saye 1988, 89). Because a sufficient number of other state legislatures had ratified the Bill of Rights prior to Georgia's consideration of the amendments, it did not ratify them until 1939, when it did so as part of the sesquicentennial of their adoption (Conley and Kaminski 1988, 90).

Pierce's Fourth of July Oration

A three-man committee of the Georgia Society of the Cincinnati selected Pierce to deliver an oration at Christ Church in Savannah on July 4, 1788 (see Kaminski and Saladino 1995, 249–254), which was in part a plea for ratification of the new Constitution. Coming from a merchant who was about to go bankrupt, the speech was particularly noteworthy for linking the ills of the Articles of Confederation to the allure of "false schemes of commerce," to the temptations of "luxuries which we had for many years before been deprived of," and to "habits of expence and idle speculation, that have so entangled and disordered the economy of our affairs as to make us neglectful of every public concern" (qtd. in Kaminski and Saladino 1995, 251; for the widespread fear of such corruption, see Wood 1969, 423). Pierce concluded his speech by recommending that citizens "cherish a spirit of industry," "abandon all idle extravagance," and "introduce economy" (Kaminski and Saladino 1995, 253).

In his speech, Pierce observed, "When changes in a government take place, it is always to be expected that objections, discontents and parties, will arise." Citing Anti-Federalist objections that all that was needed was a bit more power in the national government and that the new government would result in a diminution of liberty, Pierce rhetorically asked: "Has not experience sufficiently convinced us that the present government of the United States is inadequate to every national purpose?" The government under the Articles of Confederation, Pierce said, was like the "hanging" (he meant "leaning") tower of Pisa—"kept up and supported only by props, that must one day or other fall." He compared the weakness of the Articles of Confederation to the strength of state governments: "In all the state governments the three great branches that maintain each other give each separate [state] of the Union an efficient power to execute its own laws. But, in the Federal Constitution, there is nothing but legislative and recommendatory powers, without even the shadow of authority to support or enforce its decrees." To Pierce, the situation was dire: "We are about, my Countrymen, to experience a change, the effects of which cannot yet be told. One false step now may ruin us forever;—should we look back at our former situation and repent, we are undone:—the object lies before us. We must go on, and not halt between disunion and war."

Pierce mailed a copy of his speech to George Washington on August 2, 1788, with a letter expressing "the highest sentiments of respect and esteem." Washington responded: "Sir, I am happy to find that the same patriotic sentiments have been displayed, through the Union, by the Citizens of America and particularly by those who were formerly members of the Army, on the [twelfth] Anniversary of Independence" (Washington 1997, 1:417–418). Washington's copy of the speech, inscribed by Pierce to him, is now in Washington's collection of writings at the Boston Athenaeum.

Bankruptcy, Death, and Legacy

Pierce's life took a decidedly downward turn after the convention. His youngest son, Nathanael Greene Pierce, died on May 8, 1789 (*Georgia Gazette*, May 21, 1789); a "violent whirlwind" destroyed a "machine house" on Pierce's Belmont plantation on May 12 (ibid.); and another son, his initial namesake, died on August 15 (*Georgia Gazette*, August 20, 1789). Both Pierce's business and his health failed. He attempted to secure a post as collector of the port of Savannah, which involved solicitations of Washington, Madison, John Jay, and Dickinson, but Major John Habersham was selected after the Senate rejected Washington's nomination of Major Benjamin Fisbourne. Pierce then ran for governor, but lost to Edward Telfair.

Pierce died on December 10, 1789, at his plantation near Savannah. His remains were accompanied by a group of Freemasons, members of the Society of the Cincinnati, and members of the Union Society from the house of James Seagrove at Yamacraw to an unspecified place of interment (*Georgia Gazette*, December 17, 1789).[23] A friend reported that, despite his adversities, his last words, which might be interpreted to exhibit either philosophic acceptance or Christian faith, were "Farewell! Farewell all! Now dies the happy man" (Jones 1891, 158, from death notice in *Georgia Gazette*, December 24, 1789).

Pierce's youngest son, who was named in his honor, followed his father in giving a Fourth of July Oration in Savannah in 1812. He published a long poem the following year but died before his father's character sketches were first published in a Georgia paper in 1828. This publication still preceded dissemination of Madison's notes of the event, which were not published until 1840. At a time when memories of some of the framers must have been fading from popular consciousness, it seems appropriate that citizens were reintroduced to the cast of characters before reading the notes of the debates and compromises in which they had participated.

NOTES

1. This source goes on to list a William Pierce, believed to be his son, who served as a "major and justice of Westmoreland county" ("Historical and Genealogical Notes" 1901, 271). It lists a number of other John and William Pierces, albeit none that appears to be the son of a Matthew Pierce. I therefore do not know for sure that the two families were the same, but I think that even having the last name of such a distinguished family might have counted for something in a society that was much more aristocratic than contemporary America. For further information on possible heirs of Captain Pierce, see *Adventurers of Purse and Person* 2005, 799n19.

2. For those who might be interested in further genealogical research, records from James City County indicate that Alice Browne (daughter of William, whose will was dated October 22, 1773) married John Pierce, and they had children named Anne, Alice, and John Pierce Jr. ("Historical and Genealogical Notes" 1896, 204). They also say that John Browne, identified as a "commissary general during the Revolution" (whose will was dated October 16, 1793), had a daughter Susannah, who married John Pierce Jr., and they had a son named William Pierce.

   There was a William Pierce, or Pearce (the two spellings sometimes were used interchangeably) (ca. 1754–1813), who lived in Georgia and is believed to be the son of Joshua Pierce (ca. 1735–1810) and Hannah Green. In 2009, Laura M. Cooper compiled information on the Munson, Underwood, Horn, Fairfield, and allied families, which includes a section on Joshua Pearce. See http://www.brazoriaroots.com/p2700.htm.

   For conflicting genealogical information that lists a William Pierce Sr. as being the first son of Stephen Pearce, see Stafford n.d.

3. Peale mentioned Pearse/Pierce again in a letter of January or February 25, 1775, in connection with a pamphlet that John Pinkney had conveyed through Pierce to him. Peale 1983, 1:138.

   Peale sent another letter to Pierce dated June 17, 1787, in which he reported his pleasure in hearing (contrary to fact) "that in point of fortune you rank among the wealthy" and expressed hope that Pierce would repay part of his debt to him, possibly in conjunction with a special exhibition for the Society of the Cincinnati on May 16, 1787. See ibid., 1:480.

4. This information was kindly supplied to me by e-mail on November 6, 2012, by Martha Rowe, a research associate at the Museum of Early Southern Decorative Arts in Winston-Salem, North Carolina. The notice is also found in Brock 1893, 35.

5. Noting that it was "issued as an Appeal for Additional Information," the book listed William Pierce under alumni with his year of attendance and a † symbol beside his name indicating that "[f]urther information about attendance is especially desired" (32). Other Pierces who were listed—who may or may not have been related—were John Pierce (1857–1858), John P. Pierce (1836–1840, 1841–1843), William F. L. Pierce (1817–1818, 1821–1822), and William R. Pierce (1836–1840).

   Oscar M. Voorhees, "The Fifty Founders of Phi Beta Kappa," *William and Mary Quarterly* (1936), denoted twenty-seven of these individuals with an asterisk, indicating that he desired further information about "the names of parents, place and date of birth, of marriage,

and of death, as well as occupation and services render[ed] to society; and also the names
of children especially of those who attained prominence" (420). He listed Pierce among the
fifty founders and did not indicate that he required further information.

Given the typical age of college students, Pierce's attendance at William and Mary seems
to confirm the likelihood that he was born in 1753, which would have made him twenty-seven
at the time, rather than in 1740, which would have made him forty.

6. McBryde 1915 included Pierce among the "noncollegians" in Williamsburg. However, he
also included in that category John Marshall, who is known to have attended lectures by the
college's George Wythe.

7. Madison is probably best known for the eulogy that he delivered on the death of George
Washington at the Bruton Parish Church in 1800. See Madison 1999.

8. Tyler (1898, 171) observed, "For the times and circumstances there was never any lack in colonial times of the higher education in Virginia. The sources of education were, first, private
tutors; second, English and Scotch schools and universities; third, the College of William
and Mary, and fourth, the College of New Jersey in Princeton, and the schools of Pennsylvania." He further observed that "some one wealthy planter generally assumed the main
expense of employing a tutor, but as the children of the neighboring plantations were also
invited, the tutor was generally at the head of a school" (172).

9. Pointing to "the happy conjuncture of times and circumstances, under which our Republic
assumed its rank among the nations," Washington observed, "[t]he Foundation of our Empire was not laid in the gloomy age of Ignorance and Superstition, but at an Epocha when
the rights of mankind were better understood and more clearly defined, than at any former
period" (Kurland and Lerner 1987, 1:219).

10. Although there is no particular reason to believe that Pierce was specifically referring to
amorous adventures, he wrote a letter on August 17, 1783, to General Nathanael Greene
(b. 1742) in which he implored Greene, "The follies of youth forgive, and my virtues remember." He further said, "I . . . look up to you as a Son would to a Father with veneration,
love, and respect" (Greene 1991–2005, 13:103). This seems to confirm that Pierce was born
closer to 1753 (than to the 1740 date that earlier historians cited) since it seems highly unlikely that Pierce would have written this to someone younger than himself. The willingness
to look up to Greene as a father would also be more likely for someone who had lost his
birth father relatively early in life.

11. Edward and Mary Fenwick had fifteen children; Charlotte was the eleventh. Edward Fenwick inherited 13,000 acres, which he increased by another 11,000 acres. His seven plantations were worked by about five hundred slaves. See *Biographical Directory of the South
Carolina House of Representatives* 1974, 2:242–243. Also see Fenwick Hall's plantation history at http://www.fenwickhall.com/fenwickshistory.html and Smith 1913.

12. Deen 1991, 219, says that he was born on November 30, 1790, but this seems improbable
given the date of his father's death. Sam Fore reported to me in an e-mail dated January 10,
2013, that a note "made by an unknown—obviously twentieth-century—hand, indicates later
that William Leigh's tombstone reads that he was born on June 30, 1790 and died on Dec. 17,
1814." He added that the individual did not indicate where the tombstone was located.

13. The Library of Congress purchased Jackson's papers in 1996. Nan Thompson Ernst, Manuscript Division, prepared *Ebenezer Jackson: A Register of His Papers in the Library of Congress* in 2007.

14. Papers in the Library of Congress contain correspondence between Jackson and his wife

concerning the management of "the Fenwick and Tattnall plantations near Savannah." See Ernst 2007. Additionally, the New-York Historical Society has two handwritten notebooks (358 pages) by William Leigh Pierce, which are described as follows: "Commonplace book, [1810], and volume of chronological notes recording current political and historical events, 1811–1813, kept by William Leigh Pierce of New York State. Commonplace book, entitled 'Notes and Extracts on Various Subjects, or 'Extracts and Sentimental touches from various authors in prose and verse,' contains literary extracts, many of them from the works of Shakespeare, along with homilies, maxims, sentimental definitions, etc. Volume entitled 'Spirit of Public prints and History of Principal Political Events from the month of March 1811 to [March 25, 1813],' contains chronological entries based on newspaper accounts recording current political and historical events of the day." A historical note adds: "Poet and son of William Leigh and Charlotte (Fenwick) Pierce; died in Canadaigua [*sic*], New York, Dec. 17, 1814, aged 24 of typhus fever."

15. Pierce also published *An Account of the Great Earthquakes, in the Western States, Particularly on the Mississippi River, December 16–23, 1811*, and an extended poem (1813). His previous eyewitness accounts of the earthquakes had been widely reported in contemporary newspapers. For an account originally published in the *New York Evening Post*, see "New Madrid 1811–12 First Steamboat, quakes, comet," http://www.showme.net/~fkeller/quake/lib/roosevelt.htm.

16. Pierce does not appear, however, to have attended. That meeting lasted May 7–19, 1787 (Schuyler 1886, 10), and Pierce, who did not arrive at the convention until May 31, wrote a letter to George Turner, a South Carolinian who was secretary of the general meeting, from New York on May 19, 1787 (Hutson 1987, 9).

17. Pierce was also familiar with other troubles. In his letter from South Carolina to St. George Tucker of July 20, 1781, Pierce described "[s]uch scenes of desolation, bloodshed and deliberate murder I never was a witness to before!" He continued: "Wherever you turn the weeping widow the fatherless child pour out their melancholy tales to wound the feelings of humanity. The two opposite principles of whiggism and toryism have set the people of this country to cutting each others's [*sic*] throats, and scarce a day passes but some poor deluded tory is put to death at his door. For the want of civil government the bands of society are totally disunited, and the people, by copying the manners of the British, have become perfectly savage" (1881, 434).

18. The year before, he had begged Nathanael Greene for payment on some items "that I may be enabled to stop the repeated Duns at my Door, & in all probability several Writs against me should I not be able to make some part paymt" (see Greene 1991–2005, 13:657).

19. In a letter to Nathaniel Mitchell, a member of the Continental Congress whom Pierce had designated as his second, dated July 19, 1787, Pierce observed that when in Philadelphia, Auldjo "was not only indelicate in his language as it applied to me, but insulting in his reflections on my State and the People in it" (Hamilton 1962, 4:227). In the same letter, Pierce said that Auldjo had complained about a settlement that Pierce had offered and "made a loud complaint of the irregularity of things, and called forth the attention of every Person in Savannah to my private affairs, as if they, or any other set of People had any business with them. In consequence of this report, my Enemies triumphed, and my Friends grew cold" (ibid., 225).

20. In a letter that George Washington wrote from Philadelphia to Hamilton in New York on July 10, 1787, Washington said, "I am sorry you went away. I wish you were back. The crisis is equally important and alarming, and no opposition under such circumstances should discourage exertions till the signature is fixed" (Hamilton 1962, 4:225). In a letter to Pierce

posted from New York sometime during July 20–26, Hamilton wrote that he thought he had resolved the differences between Auldjo and Pierce (ibid., 4:228). Nathaniel Pendleton, who had been selected by Georgia as a delegate to the Constitutional Convention but did not attend, was Hamilton's designated second in his fatal duel (Deen 1991, 221).

21. Burnett reported that Pierce was elected on October 9, 1786, for service from the first Monday in November 1786 to the first Monday in November 1787. Records indicate that he attended January 17–May 24, July 6–August 2, and August 27–October 2, 1787. The same records list Pierce as having attended the Constitutional Convention from May 31 to July 1. See *Letters of Members of the Continental Congress* 1963, lxxxvi.

22. In his classic closing speech to the delegates at the convention, Franklin observed:

> I doubt too whether any other Convention we can obtain may be able to make a better Constitution. For when you assemble a number of men to have the advantage of their joint wisdom, you inevitably assemble with those men, all their prejudices, their passions, their errors of opinion, their local interests, and their selfish views. From such an Assembly can a perfect production be expected? It therefore astonishes me, Sir, to find this system approaching so near to perfection as it does; and I think will astonish our enemies. . . . Thus, I consent, Sir, to this Constitution because I expect no better, and because I am not sure that it is not the best. The opinions I have had of its errors, I sacrifice to the public good. (Farrand 1966, 2:642–643)

23. The Union Society of Savannah, which was incorporated in 1786 as a successor to the St. George's Society, although composed of members of five religious denominations was largely devoted to raising money to support an orphanage (named Bethesda) for boys, which the evangelist George Whitefield had established (*Minutes of the Union Society* 1860, 125). "Wm. Pierce" is listed as being one of the society's two "Stewards" on April 24, 1786. The society adopted a resolution on September 14, 1786, praising Pierce, who is described as one of several "Esquires," for helping the society become incorporated (196). In a list of members (15), "William Pierce" is said to have joined in 1774, but it seems unlikely that it was the same person. Could this be the individual with a 1740 birthday with whom early biographers confused him? For further information on Bethesda, see Cashin 2001.

REFERENCES

Adventurers of Purse and Person Virginia 1607–1724/5. 2005. Vol. 2: *Families G–P*. Ed. John Frederick Dornam. Baltimore, Md.: Genealogical Publishing.

Biographical Directory of the South Carolina House of Representatives. 1974. Ed. Walter B. Edgar. Columbia: University of South Carolina Press.

Brock, R. A. 1893. "Virginia's Past in Portraiture." *William and Mary Quarterly* 2, no. 1 (July):30–35.

Cashin, Edward J. 2001. *Beloved Bethesda: A History of George Whitefield's Home for Boys, 1740–2000*. Macon, Ga.: Mercer University Press.

Conley, Patrick T., and John P. Kaminski, eds. 1988. *The Constitution and the States: The Role of the Original Thirteen in the Framing and Adoption of the Federal Constitution*. Madison, Wis.: Madison House.

Davies, Wallace Evan. 1948. "The Society of the Cincinnati in New England, 1783–1800." *William and Mary Quarterly*, 3rd ser., 5 (January):3–25.

Deen, Braswell D., Jr. 1991. "William Leigh Pierce: The Notetaker Who Signed with His

Heart but Not with His Pen." *Georgia Journal of Southern Legal History* 1 (Spring–Summer):219–221.

Ernst, Nan Thompson. 2007. *Ebenezer Jackson: A Register of His Papers in the Library of Congress*. Washington, D.C.: Manuscript Division, Library of Congress.

Farrand, Max, ed. 1966. *The Records of the Federal Convention of 1787*. 4 vols. New Haven, Conn.: Yale University Press.

Fithian, Philip Vickers. 1990. *Journal and Letters of Philip Vickers Fithian 1773–1774: A Plantation Tutor of the Old Dominion*. Ed. Hunter Dickinson Farish. Charlottesville: University Press of Virginia. http://www.gutenberg.org/files/40044/40044-h/40044-htm.

Fore, Sam. 2008. "William Pierce (1753–1789)." *New Georgia Encyclopedia*. http://www.georgia encyclopedia.org/nge/Article.jsp?id=h-3698.

Gallagher, Mary A. Y. 1995. "Reinterpreting the 'Very Trifling Mutiny' at Philadelphia in June 1783." *Pennsylvania Magazine of History and Biography* 119 (January–April):3–35.

Greene, Nathanael. 1991–2005. *The Papers of General Nathanael Greene*. Vols. 6–14. Ed. Dennis M. Conrad (Roger N. Parks for last volume). Chapel Hill: University of North Carolina Press for the Rhode Island Historical Society.

Hamilton, Alexander. 1962. *The Papers of Alexander Hamilton*. Ed. Harold C. Syrett. Vol. 4: *January 1787–May 1788*. New York: Columbia University Press.

Hiden, P. W. 1941. "Education and the Classics in the Life of Colonial Virginia." *Virginia Magazine of History and Biography* 49, no. 1 (January):20–28.

"Historical and Genealogical Notes." 1896. *William and Mary Quarterly* 4, no. 3 (January):200–206.

———. 1901. *William and Mary Quarterly* 9 (April):268–272.

Hutson, James H., ed. 1987. *Supplement to Max Farrand's The Records of the Federal Convention of 1787*. New Haven, Conn.: Yale University Press.

Jensen, Merrill, et al., eds. 1978. *The Documentary History of the Ratification of the Constitution*. Vol. 3. Madison: State Historical Society of Wisconsin.

Jones, Charles C., Jr. 1891. *Biographical Sketches of the Delegates from Georgia to the Continental Congress*. Boston: Houghton, Mifflin.

Journals of the Continental Congress, 1774–1789. http://lcweb2.loc.gov.

Kaminski, John P., and Gaspare J. Saladino, eds. 1995. *Commentaries on the Constitution, Public and Private*, vol. 6: *10 May to 13 September 1788*. Madison: State Historical Society of Wisconsin.

Kimball, David A. 1987. "The Role of the Cincinnati in Forming the Constitution and Its Later Adoption by the States." Paper presented to the State Society of the Cincinnati of Pennsylvania on Washington's Birthday. In possession of author.

Kurland, Philip B., and Ralph Lerner. 1987. *The Founders' Constitution*. 5 vols. Chicago: University of Chicago Press.

Letters of Members of the Continental Congress. 1963. Ed. Edmund C. Burnett. Washington, D.C.: Carnegie Institution of Washington, 1936. Reprint, Gloucester, Mass.: Peter Smith.

Lounsbury, Carl R. 2005. *The Courthouses of Early Virginia: An Architectural History*. Charlottesville: University of Virginia Press.

Madison, James. 1865. *Letters and Other Writings of James Madison, Fourth President of the United States*. 4 vols. Philadelphia: Lippincott.

Madison, James [Bishop]. 1999. *A Nation Mourns: Bishop James Madison's Memorial Eulogy on the Death of George Washington*. Ed. David Holmes. Mount Vernon, Va.: Mount Vernon Ladies' Association.

Maier, Pauline. 2010. *Ratification: The People Debate the Constitution, 1787–1788*. New York: Simon and Schuster.

Marshall, John. 1974. *The Papers of John Marshall*. Vol. 1. Ed. Herbert A. Johnson. Chapel Hill: University of North Carolina Press in association with the Institute of Early American History and Culture, Williamsburg, Va.

Mason, George Carrington. 1939. "The Colonial Churches of York County, Virginia." *William and Mary Quarterly*, 2nd ser., 19, no. 2 (April):159–180.

McBryde, John M., Jr. 1915. "Phi Beta Kappa Society: Past and Present." *Sewanee Review* 23, no. 2 (April):209–229.

Meade, William. 1891. *Old Churches, Ministers, and Families of Virginia*. Philadelphia: Lippincott. http://genealogytrails.com/vir/jamescity/oldchurchesandfamilies2.html.

Minutes of the Union Society: Being an Abstract of Existing Records, from 1750 to 1858: Comprising, Also, Chronological Lists of Its Officers, Members and Beneficiaries, with the Anniversary Address of Hon. T. U. P. Charlton, Col. Howell Cobb, Hon. Robert M. Charlton, Rev. Willard Preston and Col. Robert H. Griffin, Also, a Historical Sketch of Bethesda. 1860. Savannah, Ga.: John M. Cooper.

Moran, Donald N. n.d. *Revolutionary War Presentation Swords*. http://www.revolutionarywar archives.org/presentationswords.html.

"The Original Phi Beta Kappa Records." 1919. *Phi Beta Kappa Key* (May):546–554, 599–625.

Peale, Charles Willson. 1983. *The Selected Papers of Charles Willson Peale and His Family*. 2 vols. Ed. Lillian B. Miller. New Haven, Conn.: Yale University Press for the National Portrait Gallery, Smithsonian Institution.

Pierce, William [Major]. 1788. *An Oration Delivered at Christ Church, Savannah, on the 4th July, 1788, in Commemoration of the Anniversary of American Independence*. Savannah, Ga.: James Johnston.

———. 1881. "Southern Campaign of General Greene 1781–2." *Magazine of American History* 7 (December):431–445.

Pierce, William Leigh. 1812. *Oration on American Independence Delivered in the Presbyterian Church, Savannah, Georgia, on the Fourth of July, 1812, by Appointment of the Savannah Volunteer Guards*. Savannah, Ga.: John J. Evans.

———. 1813. *The Year: A Poem, in Three Cantoes*. New York: David Longworth.

Pleasants, J. Hall. 1952. "William Dering: A Mid-Eighteenth Century Williamsburg Portrait Painter." *Virginia Magazine of History and Biography* 60 (January):56–63.

A Provisional List of Alumni, Grammar School Students, Members of the Faculty, and Members of the Board of Visitors of the College of William and Mary in Virginia, from 1693 to 1888. 1941. Richmond, Va.: Division of Purchase and Printing.

Riley, Edward M. 1942. "The Colonial Courthouses of York County, Virginia." *William and Mary Quarterly*, 2nd ser., 22, no. 4 (October):399–414.

Rossiter, Clinton. 1966. *1787: The Grand Convention*. New York: Norton.

Rowe, Linda H. 1988. Letter to Mr. Leonard Rapport, December 6. On file at the John D. Rockefeller Jr. Library, Colonial Williamsburg Foundation, Williamsburg, Va.

Saye, Albert B. 1934. "Georgia's Delegates to the Federal Convention of 1787: Who They Were and What They Did." M.A. thesis, University of Georgia.

———. 1988. "Georgia: Security through Union." In *The Constitution and the States: The Role of the Original Thirteen in the Framing and Adoption of the Federal Constitution*, edited by Patrick T. Conley and John P. Kaminski, 77–92. Madison, Wis.: Madison House.

Schuyler, John. 1886. *Institution of the Society of the Cincinnati, Formed by the Officers of the*

American Army of the Revolution, 1783, with Extracts, from the Proceedings of Its General Meetings and from the Transactions of the New York State Society. New York: Dennis Taylor.

Seiler, William H. 1956. "The Anglican Parish Vestry in Colonial Virginia." *Journal of Southern History* 22, no. 3 (August):310–337.

Sellers, Charles Coleman. 1980. *Mr. Peale's Museum: Charles Willson Peale and the First Popular Museum of Natural Science and Art.* New York: Norton.

Smith, E. E. Huger. 1913. "An Account of the Tattnall and Fenwick Families in South Carolina." *South Carolina Historical and Genealogical Magazine* 14, no. 1 (January):3–19.

Stafford, George Mason Graham. n.d. "Three Pioneer Rapides Families: A Genealogy." Baton Rouge, La.: Claitor's Publishing Division. http://www.jimsweb.org/pearce/prchist.htm.

Starr, Frank Farnsworth. 2012. *The Edward Jackson Family of Newton, Massachusetts, in the Lines of Commodore Charles Hunter Jackson, United States Navy, Middletown, Connecticut.* 1895. Reprint, Charleston, S.C.: Nabu Press.

Stephens, Otis H. 2003. "Tucker, St. George." In *Great American Judges: An Encyclopedia.* 2 vols. Ed. John R. Vile, 760–767. Santa Barbara, Calif.: ABC-CLIO.

Thomson, Robert Polk. 1971. "The Reform of the College of William and Mary, 1763–1780." *Proceedings of the American Philosophical Society* 115, no. 3 (June):187–213.

Tyler, Lyon G. 1895. "Grammar and Mattey Practice and Model School." *William and Mary Quarterly* 4, no. 1 (July):3–14.

———. 1896. "Brief Personal Sketches." *William and Mary Quarterly* 4 (April):245–254.

———. 1898. "Education in Colonial Virginia: Part IV: The Higher Education." *William and Mary Quarterly* 6, no. 3 (January):171–187.

Virginia Wills and Administrations 1632–1800. 1972. Comp. Clayton Torrence. Baltimore, Md.: Genealogical Publishing. Originally published by the National Society of the Colonial Dames of America, Richmond, Va., 1930.

Voorhees, Oscar M. 1936. "The Fifty Founders of Phi Beta Kappa." *William and Mary Quarterly*, 2nd ser., 16, no. 3 (July):420–421.

Washington, George. 1997. *The Papers of George Washington*, vol. 6: *January–September 1788.* Ed. Dorothy Twohig. Charlottesville: University Press of Virginia.

Wood, Gordon S. 1969. *The Creation of the American Republic, 1776-1788.* Chapel Hill: University of North Carolina Press.

CHAPTER 3

The Arrangement and General Objects of Attention of Pierce's Character Sketches

One good deed dying tongueless, slaughters
a thousand waiting upon that.

—Shakespeare, *The Winter's Tale* (as cited by Pierce)

Pierce titled his collection of portraits "Characters in the Convention of the States Held at Philadelphia, May 1787." He thus provided a label for the delegates ("Characters") and a name, place, and time for the meeting.

Pierce's Descriptions of His Sketches

Samuel Johnson (1709–1784), the great British lexicographer upon whose dictionary the delegates to the convention relied (Lynch 2002, 18), described character as a "representation of any man as to his personal qualities" (definition 4, old style *f*'s changed to *s*'s in this and other citations from this dictionary) and as "the person with his assemblage of qualities" (1967, 1:definition 6). Looking specifically at the American context, Andrew S. Trees observes that the term "character" had a different meaning in eighteenth-century America than it does today: "It possessed a largely public meaning that was virtually synonymous with reputation, rather than an intrinsic quality. It was almost a tangible possession, something one fashioned, held, and protected, so that one would speak of 'acquiring' a character" (2004, 2). Although Trees thinks that this meaning shifted in the nineteenth century, when conceptions of character relied more strongly on "private life" (ibid.), he believes that, with independence from Great Britain, Americans were seeking to define their own national character (ibid., 1) and that leaders perceived that their own character in office could well influence those of others. Like Trees, the historian Gordon S.

Wood associates character with public personas (2006, 24–25). Applying such an analogy, the convention served as a stage and the delegates as actors who sought to play their parts as what Wood calls "natural aristocrats" (25).[1]

Pierce identified his sketches with a particular time (its start in May 1787) and place (the city of Philadelphia, which is one of the few times that he mentioned a city in his sketches). Consciously or not, he therefore highlighted the difference between this event and the written document it produced, and Britain's unwritten constitution, which grew largely from customs and usages rather than from a single meeting.

Pierce may have intended for his reference to a "Convention of the States" to be purely descriptive. It served, however, to remind readers that the delegates met under the government of the Articles of Confederation, where such states were sovereign. It might also have reminded readers that delegates voted at the convention by states rather than as individuals.

Pierce's Reliques

Pierce penned his sketches, like his notes of the convention, in a notebook generally referred to as *Pierce's Reliques* ("Notes of Major William Pierce" 1898, 313). Leffler, Kaminski, and Fore (2012, 23) have suggested that the title was wordplay "on the popular eighteenth-century printed collection *Percy's Reliques*," in which Bishop Thomas Percy compiled ballads and popular songs (first published in England in 1765; subsequently published in Philadelphia, Savannah, and New York, 1786–1810). Pierce's son may have provided the title of the sketches. Samuel Johnson (1967, vol. 2) defined "relick" as "1. That which remains; that which is left after the loss of decay of the rest." A second definition said, "It is often taken for the body deserted by the soul," and a third referred to it as "[t]hat which is kept in memory of another, with a kind of religious veneration." William Leigh Pierce may have especially venerated the collection as a tie to the father he had never seen. One might further liken the notebook, and the sketches it contained, to ancient religious relics. The book, like the verbal portraits it contained, would serve, like the bones or other relics of ancient saints, as testimony to their deeds, only the saints would be secular saints, responsible for founding a nation rather than a church.

Charles E. Jackson, a descendant of Pierce from Middletown, Connecticut, presented Pierce's notebook to the Connecticut State Library on September 25, 1914. Jackson labeled the notebook as having belonged to "Major Wm Leigh Pierce of Virginia [which confirms modern sources as to Pierce's place of birth] aide de camp of Gen Green, at the battle of Eutaw Springs, Member of the Convention in

1787." Although relatives reclaimed the notebook in 1927, the library has a copy, which it copied and provided to me; the original now resides in the Harlan Crow Library in Dallas, Texas, which has reprinted some of the materials (Leffler, Kaminski, and Fore 2012).[2] The notebook contains a number of items (some not previously reported) that further illumine Pierce's life. Unfortunately, it contains no drawings or doodles by which one might judge Pierce's skills as an artist, even in places (like Pierce's essay on botany, discussed below) where they might have been appropriate.

At the beginning is a bookplate over the scrolled name William L. Pierce (probably Pierce's son William Leigh Pierce).[3] It pictures the Pierce crest, or coat of arms, of which several variants are known. It features three blackbirds (with a black band between them) in a shield beneath a larger bird—probably a crane—with its wings stretched as though it were about to fly. There are garlands of flowers around the shield, and laurel-like grasses follow its curvature just below it. The family motto, IN FUTURA SPECTOR—"I am faced with the future"—is printed in a scroll below the shield.

In ascertaining the purpose of Pierce's work, one need look no further than the quotation from Shakespeare's *Winter's Tale* that begins the "Miscellanies": "One good deed dying tongueless, slaughters a thousand waiting upon that." The word "that," which seems to beg for explanation, appears to refer to the unspoken praise of a noteworthy deed.[4] In the sentence that followed, Shakespeare wrote, "Our prayses are our Wages." Praise seems to have been Shakespeare's equivalent to the framers' emphasis on fame. This suggests that the reason Pierce compiled his sketches of the delegates who had labored in Philadelphia was to serve as an inspiration to others contemplating similar exertions on behalf of their country, but it does not explain (although Pierce's truncated life may) why he did not publish the sketches in his lifetime.

Pierce followed the quotation from Shakespeare with one from Jacques Necker (1737–1804), the French minister of finance, on eloquence, which is discussed below, and—in a particularly fitting touch for a delegate from Georgia—comments on the size of a peach and a strawberry! Pierce recorded the first observation from a dinner with Sir John Temple (1731–1798), the British consul general to the United States from 1785 until 1798, in New York on September 10, 1787. At that dinner, Pierce reported seeing a "yellow clingstone peach [precision again appropriate for a Georgian] which measured eleven and one quarter inches in circumference." Another observation (likely a later addition by his son since it is dated July 1810) recorded a notice from a London paper of a Devonshire strawberry with a circumference of seven inches.

Pierce followed these descriptions of fruits with two more observations from Necker; an anecdote about Franklin's age (discussed below); an anecdote from the Revolutionary War in South Carolina; a report from September 28, 1787, of the discovery of a silver mine in Virginia; and an order between the patriots and the stadtholder of Holland regarding a fight to the finish (copied from the New York *Packet* of September 28, 1787). The notebook continued with more exotic reports from the records of New Haven, Connecticut, of a seaman who, upon his return, was fined for kissing his wife in public on the Sabbath ("an open violation of the Laws of God, and a great scandal to religion") and of another citizen of the state who was banished and fined for "luxury" after manufacturing round plates rather than square ones. Pierce followed this with epitaphs for Voltaire, Sophocles, and the king of Prussia, the latter of which reads "Hic cinis ubique fama."[5]

The rest of the notebook consisted of the anecdote about Washington's concern for preserving the privacy of communications among delegates at the convention; another note about conditions in Holland, received on October 9, 1787; a record of Pierce's travel aboard the *Friendship* and bringing the proceedings of the federal convention to Georgia; his notes from the convention; and his character sketches. The final pages of the journal consisted of a fairly technical essay, "On Botany," that Pierce appears to have authored and a copy of a letter to his wife from 1786, in which he described his arrival at the state capital in Augusta to take his seat in the state legislature.

Arrangement and Date of the Sketches

Historically, authors have organized narratives of the delegates' lives either alphabetically by the delegate's last name or geographically by state. Some sources have rearranged Pierce's descriptions in alphabetical order, a procedure that I largely follow,[6] but his own procedure mimicked the votes at the convention and the signatures that delegates later added to the bottom of the Constitution by listing the delegations from north to south.[7] He thus recorded delegates within states that he arranged in the following order: New Hampshire, Massachusetts, Connecticut, New York, New Jersey, Pennsylvania, Delaware, Maryland, Virginia, North Carolina, South Carolina, and Georgia.[8] He began the description of most delegates with the word "From" followed by the name of the state, as in "From New Hampshire." Not only did the descriptions therefore follow the convention's precedents, but this arrangement also allowed Pierce to begin by discussing the delegates from New Hampshire, who did not arrive at the convention until after he left and about whom he presumably knew the least, and to end with those from Georgia, including himself, with whom he was the most familiar.

Pierce referred to May 1787, the month and year in which the convention began, rather than to September 17, when the delegates signed the document. Although Pierce had left for New York by the end of June or the beginning of July, and the convention did not disperse until September 17, Pierce did not specify when he wrote his narratives. Pierce was not seated until May 31 (Farrand 1966, 1:35), and it seems highly improbable that he would have written the sketches on his first day (prior to hearing speeches on which he commented). Furthermore, Pierce's notebook contained few strikeouts or emendations, suggesting that he might have compiled his sketches from previously gathered notes. Although it is not dated, the entry immediately before Pierce's character sketches covers events that happened between his boarding the ship in New York on October 3, 1787, and arriving on October 10 in Savannah. This suggests that he might have composed or copied the sketches on the journey. The essay on botany that follows is also undated, and the letter to Pierce's wife is of little help in dating the entries because it was copied from February 19, 1786.

Pierce's General Objects of Attention

Like a portrait artist, even the most comprehensive biographer has to decide which elements of an individual's life to accentuate. Authors of thumbnail sketches must necessarily be even more selective. Pierce almost always provided an estimate of delegates' ages and their speaking abilities and styles, but the other information he supplied was not always uniform. His sketches varied considerably in length. He devoted a mere 21 words to John Langdon of New Hampshire, for example, but 207 words to Roger Sherman of Connecticut. He also provided extended treatments of John Dickinson (Del.), Benjamin Franklin (Pa.), Alexander Hamilton (N.Y.), William Samuel Johnson (Conn.), Rufus King (Mass.), James Madison (Va.), Gouverneur Morris (Pa.), and George Washington (Va.).

By his groupings of delegates from north to south, Pierce called immediate attention to the state (and, indirectly, the region) that each delegate represented. Pierce included other observations about the following, though not all categories for all delegates: age; physical characteristics and health; education and knowledge; personal qualities and patriotism; reputation; principles; status (indications that an individual was a "gentleman" or "esquire"); wealth and family connections; political abilities; speaking and writing abilities; military or political service;

occupation(s); and miscellaneous factors, such as marital status, religious affiliation, immigrant status, and the like.

NAMES

Pierce's mistakes in citing names are inconsequential for modern scholars since all of the delegates' names are well established, but a number of mistakes, usually corrected in reprints, likely show either that he was not always as precise as he might have been, that spellings were not as standardized as they are today, or that some combination of these factors was at work. He thus incorrectly referred to William Richardson Davie as "Davey"; used "W." for Ellsworth's "Oliver"; incorrectly identified the first name of both Caleb Strong and Alexander Martin as "Jno."; and left out the first names of Robert Yates and John Lansing, neither of whom he observed at the convention. Consistent with his idiosyncratic spelling, which he shared with other delegates, he also spelled Carroll without the final *l*, Madison with two *d*'s, and Paterson with two *t*'s, and referred to McClurg as McLurg.

AGES

The ages of the delegates to the convention varied from a low of twenty-seven (Dayton of N.J.) to a high of eighty-one (Franklin of Pa.), with an average age of forty-four (Lloyd n.d.). If, as is now believed, Pierce was born in 1753, then at thirty-four he was among the youngest delegates who attended the convention; had earlier biographers been correct in reporting his birth in 1740, he would, of course, have been forty-seven. Pierce provided an approximate age for each delegate, which he usually qualified with an "about," as in "about 37 years of age." His guesses (for such his observations largely appear to be) were not always that close to the mark. As demonstrated below, Pierce sometimes classified delegates as "young" gentlemen.

Table 1 compares the delegates' age on their birthdays in 1787—which may variously have been before, during, or after the convention—against the approximate ages that Pierce assigned to them:

ANALYSIS

Table 1 confirms the note accompanying the *American Historical Review*'s printing of Pierce's character sketches: "Pierce's statements of age, throughout the paper, are only approximately correct" ("Notes of Major William Pierce" 1898, 325). The table further demonstrates in a more systematic fashion that Pierce usually *underestimated* the ages of his fellow delegates, sometimes fairly considerably. The only delegates to whose ages he added more than two years were Abraham Bald-

TABLE 1 *Comparison of Delegates' Ages and Pierce's Estimates*

State	Delegate	Pierce's Guess (in years)	Delegate's Actual Age at Birthday in 1787 (in years)	Divergence (in years)
Ga.	Abraham Baldwin	38	32	+6
Del.	Richard Bassett	36	42	–6
Del.	Gunning Bedford	32	30	–2
Va.	John Blair Jr.	50	55	–5
N.C.	William Blount	36	38	–2
N.J.	David Brearly	40	42	–2
Del.	Jacob Broom	35	35	0
S.C.	Pierce Butler	40	43	–3
Md.	Daniel Carroll	no est.	57	NA
Pa.	George Clymer	40	48	–8
N.C.	William Richardson Davie	30	31	–1
N.J.	Jonathan Dayton	30	27	+3
Del.	John Dickinson	55	55	0
Conn.	Oliver Ellsworth	37	42	–5
Ga.	William Few	35	39	–4
Pa.	Thomas Fitzsimons	40	46	–6
Pa.	Benjamin Franklin	82	81	+1
Mass.	Elbridge Gerry	37	43	–6
N.H.	Nicholas Gilman	30	32	–2
Mass.	Nathaniel Gorham	46	49	–3
N.Y.	Alexander Hamilton	33	32	+1
N.J.	William Churchill Houston	no est.	31	NA
Ga.	William Houstoun	30	41	–11
Pa.	Jared Ingersoll	36	42	–6
Md.	Daniel of St. Thomas Jenifer	55	64	–9
Conn.	William Samuel Johnson	60	60	0
Mass.	Rufus King	33	32	+1
N.H.	John Langdon	40	46	–6
N.Y.	John Lansing	32	33	–1
N.J.	William Livingston	60	64	–4
Va.	James Madison Jr.	37	36	+1
N.C.	Alexander Martin	40	47	–7
Md.	Luther Martin	34	43	–9
Va.	George Mason	60	62	–2
Va.	James McClurg	38	41	–3
Md.	James McHenry	32	34	–2
Md.	John Francis Mercer	no est.	29	NA

TABLE 1 (*continued*)

State	Delegate	Pierce's Guess (in years)	Delegate's Actual Age at Birthday in 1787 (in years)	Divergence (in years)
Pa.	Thomas Mifflin	40	43	−3
Pa.	Gouverneur Morris	38	35	+3
Pa.	Robert Morris	50	53	−3
N.J.	William Paterson	34	42	−8
Ga.	William Pierce Jr.	no est.	34	NA
S.C.	Charles Pinckney	24	30	−6
S.C.	Charles Cotesworth Pinckney	40	41	−1
Va.	Edmund Randolph	32	34	−2
Del.	George Read	50	54	−4
S.C.	John Rutledge	48	48	0
Conn.	Roger Sherman	60	66	−6
N.C.	Richard Dobbs Spaight	31	29	+2
Mass.	Caleb Strong	35	42	−7
Va.	George Washington	52	55	−3
N.C.	Hugh Williamson	48	52	−4
Pa.	James Wilson	45	45	0
Va.	George Wythe	55	61	−6
N.Y.	Robert Yates	45	49	−4
AVERAGE		41.49	44.43	

Note: The averages include only the fifty-one delegates for whom Pierce provided estimates.

win (a fellow Georgian), for whom he added six, and Jonathan Dayton (N.J.), for whom he added three. By contrast, he underestimated by eleven years for William Houstoun (Ga.), while subtracting nine years from the ages of Jenifer (Md.) and Luther Martin (Md.), eight from Clymer (Pa.) and Paterson (N.J.), seven from Alexander Martin (N.C.) and Strong (Mass.), and six from Bassett (Del.), Fitzsimons (Pa.), Gerry (Mass.), Ingersoll (Pa.), Langdon (N.H.), Charles Pinckney (S.C.), Sherman (Conn.), and Wythe (Va.).

It is, of course, not uncommon to seek to gain favor and to flatter individuals by either guessing in their presence that they are younger or telling them that they look younger than they are, but Pierce did not appear to have had such a motive since he did not publish his descriptions during his or most of the other delegates' lifetimes. Indeed, to the extent that readers might associate wisdom with increased age, underestimating the ages might have detracted from Pierce's overall conclusion about the wisdom of the body. Charles Pinckney, who, at thirty, was three years older than Jonathan Dayton, apparently did nothing to correct the impression that he was the youngest member in attendance (Matthews 2004, 39–40), and Pierce fell for this deceit. Although he overstated Franklin's age by a year, Pierce did correctly record him as being the oldest member. In notes that he left at the library of the University of Georgia, Albert Saye observed (1934, 40n1), "In assigning ages to the delegates, it seems that he guessed from their appearance." It is possible that Pierce's general proclivity to underestimate the ages of the delegates, who would have almost all come from the upper class and who would have done much of their intellectually challenging and less-demanding physical work indoors, arose from the fact that they would have looked younger than people of comparable ages who spent their lives doing manual labor outdoors.

In the book that contains Pierce's handwritten character sketches, Pierce described how he met Franklin at his house one morning—a further confirmation of the role that informal contacts might have played during the convention—and asked his age. After recording that Franklin told him that he was eighty-two years old (he was actually eighty-one, so either Franklin misspoke or Pierce misremembered), Pierce further observed that Franklin said that "he had lived long enough to intrude himself on posterity."[9] Although Gouverneur Morris had not yet penned the preamble to the Constitution, which would include a similar reference to future generations, the story seems to confirm that the concern pervaded the deliberations.

PHYSICAL CHARACTERISTICS AND HEALTH

A notice of Pierce's death said that he had been "born with a delicate constitution," but that he had later enjoyed "a firm, uninterrupted state of health." It also reported that his health had been "undermined and destroyed" by "the fatigues of the war" and "diversities of climes and elements" and that "[h]e supported a lingering [unspecified] disease, and beheld the slow approaches of Death with philosophical calmness and serenity" (Jones 1891, 157–158). Given Pierce's artistic study under Charles Willson Peale and Pierce's death shortly after the convention, it is perhaps surprising that he did not devote more attention than he did to the delegates' physical characteristics and health. Because Pierce did not uniformly comment on these characteristics, the observations that he did make in this area likely reflected extremes of physical condition or, perhaps, indicated Pierce's greater familiarity with specific delegates.

Pierce's limited observations regarding the physical characteristics of delegates were as follows:

GUNNING BEDFORD (Del.): "very corpulent"

ALEXANDER HAMILTON (N.Y.): "of small stature, and lean"

WILLIAM HOUSTOUN (Ga.): "Nature seems to have done more for his corporeal than mental powers. His person is striking"

RUFUS KING (Mass.): "about five feet ten Inches high, well formed, an handsome face, with a strong expressive Eye, and a sweet high toned voice"; "His action is natural, swimming, and graceful"

WILLIAM LIVINGSTON (N.J.): "remarkably healthy"

GEORGE MASON (Va.): "a fine strong constitution"

THOMAS MIFFLIN (Pa.): "a very handsome man"

GOUVERNEUR MORRIS (Pa.): "he has been unfortunate in losing one of his Legs, and getting all the flesh taken off his right arm by a scald, when a youth"

WILLIAM PATERSON (N.J.): "of a very low stature"

GEORGE READ (Del.): "of a low stature, and a weak constitution"

ROGER SHERMAN (Conn.): "He is awkward, unmeaning, and unaccountably strange in his manner"

ROBERT YATES (N.Y.): "enjoys a great share of health"

Analysis of Pierce's Observations

In what could be intentional irony or mere coincidence, Pierce identified Mason, who would have been associated with the Virginia Plan, which called for a significantly stronger government in which states would be represented in both houses according to population, as having "a fine strong constitution" and Read, who favored continuing the existing system of equal state representation under the Articles of Confederation, as having a "weak" one. Although I am inclined to believe this is a mere coincidence, one reason to think that Pierce may have contrived the contrast is that Mason was far more widely known for constantly complaining of gout and other ailments, which may have included depression, than for his good health (see Broadwater 2006, 9–10, 74–75), and Read, who was a younger man, survived him by six years.

Whereas modern commentators are most likely to characterize James Madison by his small stature (variously said to be five feet four inches or five feet six) and weight (generally estimated at ninety to a hundred pounds)—Washington Irving would later call him "but a withered little apple-John" (Meacham 2012, 122)—Pierce did not comment on his physical appearance. Instead, Pierce singled out Alexander Hamilton, William Paterson, and George Read for being of "low stature" and Gunning Bedford and, possibly, William Houstoun for their excessive weight (Pierce's reference to Houstoun's "corporeal . . . powers" is arguably ambiguous and might simply be a positive reference to his overall physical state rather than to corpulence). Pierce reported both of Gouverneur Morris's fairly obvious physical deformities—a scalded right arm and a missing left leg (although Pierce neither noted which leg it was nor the fact, which artists usually capture, that Morris wore a prosthetic in its place). Pierce did not mention what ladies of his day apparently rarely missed: how handsome Morris otherwise was.[10] Morris, who was "of similar height and build" to George Washington, once posed for the sculptor Jean-Antoine Houdon in France as a stand-in for the general (Foster 2012).

Rufus King (Mass.) was about Pierce's age, and Pierce seemed almost infatuated with him. Pierce observed that King was about five feet ten inches tall (the only delegate whom he noted for tall height), and he commented on his "handsome face, with a strong expressive Eye [another comment that he did not apply to any other delegate], and a sweet high toned voice," as well as on his "natural, swimming, and graceful" manners while speaking. Pierce even used a French term, *tout ensemble*, to rank him "among the Luminaries of the present Age." Pierce also referred to Thomas Mifflin as "a very handsome man." Pierce might not have commented on the physical attributes of delegates like Benjamin Franklin (with his receding hairline in the front and long hair in the back) or George Washington (known both for his height and his strength) because he thought the public already knew how they looked through pictures and prints.

EDUCATION, KNOWLEDGE, AND ABILITIES

Citizens and scholars often assess participants in governmental bodies by their intellectual capacities and formal educational attainments. The delegates to the convention were highly educated by comparison to members of the population as a whole (see Vile 2005, 1:239–242). Thirty had attended college at a time when attendance was not that common. The College of New Jersey (today's Princeton University) supplied nine graduates. Its president, John Witherspoon, had immigrated from Scotland, championed commonsense philosophy, and signed the Declaration of Independence (Morrison 2004). London's Middle Temple educated seven delegates, William and Mary five, Yale five, Harvard three, and King's College (today's Columbia) three. Pierce often mixed observations about the formal educations (I have supplied the higher educational institutions that delegates attended), knowledge, and abilities of his colleagues.

ABRAHAM BALDWIN (Ga.) [Yale]: "a Gentleman of superior abilities"; "Having laid the foundation of a compleat classical education at Harvard College, he pursues every other study with ease. He is well acquainted with Books and Characters and has an accommodating turn of mind, which enables him to gain the confidence of Men, and to understand them"

GUNNING BEDFORD (Del.) [College of New Jersey]: "educated for the Bar"

JOHN BLAIR (Va.) [William and Mary, Middle Temple]: "acknowledged to have a very extensive knowledge of the Laws"

WILLIAM BLOUNT (N.C.): "nor does he possess any of those talents that make Men shine"

GEORGE CLYMER (Pa.): "a Lawyer of some abilities"

WILLIAM RICHARDSON DAVIE (N.C.) [College of New Jersey]: "He is said to have a good classical education, and is a Gentleman of considerable literary talents"

JONATHAN DAYTON (N.J.) [College of New Jersey]: "a young Gentleman of talents"; "He possesses a good education"

JOHN DICKINSON (Del.) [Middle Temple]: "he is a Scholar, and said to be a Man of very extensive information"

OLIVER ELLSWORTH (Conn.): "a Gentleman of a clear, deep, and copious understanding"

WILLIAM FEW (Ga.): "Mr. Few possesses a strong natural Genius, and from application has acquired some knowledge of legal matters"

BENJAMIN FRANKLIN (Pa.): "is well known to be the greatest phylosopher of the present age;—all the operations of nature he seems to understand,—the very heavens obey him, and the Clouds yield up their Lightning to be imprisoned in his rod"; "possesses an activity of mind equal to a youth of 25 years of age"

NATHANIEL GORHAM (Mass.): "He is a man of very good sense, but not much improved in his education"

ALEXANDER HAMILTON (N.Y.) [King's College]: "reputed to be a finished Scholar"

WILLIAM HOUSTOUN (Ga.) [English Inns of Court]: "was educated in England. As to his legal or political knowledge he has very little to boast of"; has a "mind very little improved with useful or elegant knowledge"

JARED INGERSOLL (Pa.) [Yale, Middle Temple]: "possesses a clear legal understanding. He is well versed in the Classics, and is a Man of very extensive reading"

WILLIAM SAMUEL JOHNSON (Conn.) [Yale]: "Dr. Johnson is a character much celebrated for his legal knowledge; he is said to be one of the first classics in America, and certainly possesses a very strong and enlightened understanding"

RUFUS KING (Mass.) [Harvard]: "He was educated in Massachusetts, and is said to have good classical as well as legal knowledge"

JOHN LANGDON (N.H.): "possesses a liberal mind, and a good plain understanding"

JOHN LANSING (N.Y.): "his legal knowledge I am told is not extensive, nor his education a good one. He is however a Man of good sense"

WILLIAM LIVINGSTON (N.J.) [Yale]: "Governor Livingston is confessedly a Man of the first rate talents, but he appears to me rather to indulge a sportiveness of wit, than a strength of thinking. He is however equal to anything, from the extensiveness of his education and genius"

JAMES MADISON (Va.) [College of New Jersey]: "He blends together the profound politician, with the Scholar"; "The affairs of the United States, he perhaps, has the most correct knowledge of, of any Man in the Union"

LUTHER MARTIN (Md.) [College of New Jersey]: "Mr. Martin was educated for the Bar"; "possesses a good deal of information"

GEORGE MASON (Va.): "a Gentleman of remarkable strong powers, and possesses a clear and copious understanding"

JAMES MCCLURG (Va.) [William and Mary, University of Edinburgh]: "a learned physician"; "he has a foundation of learning, on which, if he pleases, he may erect a character of high renown"

JAMES MCHENRY (Md.) [Newark Academy, read law] "was bred a physician"; "He is a Man of specious talents, with nothing of genius to improve them"

THOMAS MIFFLIN (Pa.): "is well known for the activity of his mind, and the brilliancy of his parts"

GOUVERNEUR MORRIS (Pa.) [King's College]: "one of those Genius's in whom every species of talents combine to render him conspicuous and flourishing in public debate"; "He has gone through a very extensive course of reading, and is acquainted with all the sciences"; "No Man has more wit"; "He was bred to the Law"

ROBERT MORRIS (Pa.): "He has an understanding equal to any public object, and possesses an energy of mind that few Men can boast of. Although he is not learned, yet he is as great as those who are"

WILLIAM PATERSON (N.J.) [College of New Jersey]: "one of those kind of Men whose powers break in upon you, and create wonder and astonishment"; "looks that bespeak talents of no great extent,—but he is a Classic [I do not know whether this was a reference to his education or not], a Lawyer, and an Orator"

CHARLES PINCKNEY (S.C.) [honorary degree from College of New Jersey]: "the most promising talents"; "in possession of a very great variety of knowledge. Government, Law, History and Phylosophy are his favorite studies, but he is intimately acquainted with every species of polite learning"

CHARLES COTESWORTH PINCKNEY (S.C.) [Christ Church at Oxford, Middle Temple]: "He has received the advantage of a liberal education, and possesses a very extensive degree of legal knowledge"

EDMUND RANDOLPH (Va.) [William and Mary]: "all the accomplishments of the Scholar, and the States-man"

GEORGE READ (Del.) [read law]: "his legal abilities are said to be very great"

JOHN RUTLEDGE (S.C.) [Middle Temple]: "He was bred to the Law"; "He is undoubtedly a man of abilities"

ROGER SHERMAN (Conn.): "in his train of thinking there is something regular, deep and comprehensive"

RICHARD SPAIGHT (N.C.) [Glasgow University]: "Without possessing a Genius to render him brilliant, he is able to discharge any public trust that his Country may repose in him"

CALEB STRONG (Mass.) [Harvard]: "he has received a liberal education, and has good connections to recommend him"

HUGH WILLIAMSON (N.C.) [College of Philadelphia, University of Edinburgh, University of Utrecht]: "a Gentleman of education and talents"

JAMES WILSON (Pa.) [University of St. Andrews]: "ranks among the foremost in legal and political knowledge. He has joined to a fine genius all that can set him off and show him to advantage. He is well acquainted with Man, and understands all the passions that influence him. Government seems to have been his peculiar [probably meaning "particular"] Study, all the political institutions of the World he knows in detail, and can trace the causes and effects of every revolution from the earliest stages of the Greecian commonwealth down to the present time"

GEORGE WYTHE (Va.): "the famous Professor of Law at the University of William and Mary. He is confessedly one of the most learned legal Characters of the present age. From his close attention to the study of general learning he has acquired a compleat knowledge of the dead languages and all the sciences"; "No Man it is said understands the history of Government better than Mr. Wythe,—nor [is there] any one who understands the fluctuating condition to which all societies are liable better than he does"

ROBERT YATES (N.Y.): "He is a Man of great legal abilities"

ANALYSIS OF PIERCE'S OBSERVATIONS

Pierce's descriptions of the educational attainments of the delegates were incomplete. He did not mention the College of New Jersey, which supplied the largest number of degrees, and only mentioned William and Mary once, and then as a place where Wythe taught rather than where he and other delegates attended. Pierce's designation of the institution as a university, while contrary to its current appellation as a college, was not unusual for the time, as demonstrated by an advertisement in the *Virginia Gazette* for August 17, 1782.[11] Pierce's reference to Abraham Baldwin's education at Harvard was mistaken (he actually attended Yale). Although Pierce did not intend humor, his mistake anticipated President John F. Kennedy's commencement address at Yale, which awarded him an honorary degree, on July 11, 1962. On that occasion, he remarked, "It might be said now that I have the best of both worlds, a Harvard education and a Yale degree." Pierce indicated that King had been educated in Massachusetts without mentioning that he had attended Harvard. William Houstoun, a fellow Georgian, is the only individual whom Pierce cited as having studied abroad.

Pierce identified as naturally gifted a number of delegates who had not attended college. He generally focused on individual characteristics rather than formal degrees. This likely indicated that in a century when many gentlemen (perhaps including Pierce himself) were largely tutored at home or read law under attorneys rather than attending law schools, Pierce considered education to be less a matter of college or university attendance and degrees and more a matter of mastering classical texts and cultivating scholarly virtues (for an insightful article on the education of the day, see Hamilton 1994).

Pierce's description of Franklin was among his most unusual. His allusions to Franklin's control over nature not only resembled classical references to the gods, but it was also similar to St. Luke's account of Jesus calming the Sea of Galilee during a storm. In that account, Luke recorded Jesus's disciples as reacting to his display of power with the words "What manner of man is this! For he commandeth even the winds and the water, and they obey him" (Luke 8:25, KJV). Given this parallel, it is unclear whether Pierce was enthusiastically highlighting, or gently mocking, Franklin and his reputation for scientific prowess. It is further unclear whether Pierce's reference to Franklin's "rod" was designed to evoke Moses's (the great lawgiver) staff.[12]

It bears noting that this was not the only time that Franklin served, if I may pun, as a lightning rod of sorts. Pierce's observations about Franklin thus provide an interesting comparison to a comment that John Adams made in a letter to Benjamin Rush. A year after the first presidential election, deeply concerned about his own fame, Adams observed, "The history of our revolution will be one continued lie from one end to the other. The essence of the whole will be that Dr. Franklin's electrical rod smote the earth and out sprang George Washington. That Franklin electrified him with his rod—and henceforward these two conducted all the policy, negotiations, legislatures, and war" (qtd. in Whitney 2011, n.p.).

People often distinguish between those who merely possess abilities and knowledge and those who are adept at using them in a wise or understanding way. Pierce variously identified the delegates with abilities or talents, knowledge or information, understanding or good sense. His observations thus linked Baldwin with both "abilities" and an understanding of men; Blair with "knowledge of the laws";

Clymer with "some abilities"; Davie with "considerable literary talents"; Dickinson with "extensive information"; Few with "some knowledge of legal matters"; Gorham with "very good sense"; Lansing with "good sense"; A. Martin with "sense"; King with "legal knowledge"; Johnson with "legal knowledge"; Livingston with "genius"; Madison with "correct knowledge"; Martin with "a good deal of information"; McClurg with "learning"; G. Morris with "talents" and with acquaintance "with all the sciences"; C. Pinckney with "a very great variety of knowledge"; C. C. Pinckney with both "a liberal education" and "legal knowledge"; Randolph with being a "Scholar"; Read with his "legal abilities"; Rutledge with "abilities"; Spaight with "genius"; Strong with a "liberal education"; Williamson with "talents"; Wilson with "genius"; Wythe with "compleat knowledge" of ancient languages and sciences; and Yates with "great legal abilities."

Pierce used other positive descriptors too. He identified Ellsworth with "copious understanding"; believed that Franklin "understand[s]" scientific matters; thought that Ingersoll had "legal understanding"; attributed Johnson with "enlightened understanding"; associated Langdon with "plain understanding"; credited Mason with "copious understanding"; associated Robert Morris with "understanding"; tied Sherman to a deep "training of thinking"; identified Wilson with an understanding of man; and credited Wythe with an understanding of government.

Pierce provided negative assessments of the talents and wisdom of only a few delegates. For example, although he praised him for his integrity, Pierce did not think that Blount had sufficient "talents." Pierce observed that Houstoun had little "useful or elegant knowledge." He questioned whether McHenry had sufficient "talents" or "genius."

The high number of positive descriptions over negative ones is consistent with Pierce's design to show that the convention was one of the "wisest" councils in world history. Pierce continued with this purpose by calling attention to other virtues of the delegates, including how they patriotically applied their wisdom in the interests of their country.

NOTES

1. The commonplace books kept by Pierce's son contain a quotation from Junius, possibly a pseudonym of Sir Philip Francis, on the subject of "Character": "every common dauber writes rascal and villain under his pictures, because the pictures themselves have neither character nor resemblance. But the works of a master require no index. His features and coloring are taken from nature" (in the picture provided by the New-York Historical Society Library, the page number is obscured by a finger). In words not quoted, Junius went on to

say, "The impression they make is immediate and uniform; nor is it possible to mistake his characters."

2. Leffler, Kaminski, and Fore 2012, 23, report that the book was sold at the Parke-Bernet Galleries in 1938 to Lucius Wilmerding Sr. (d. 1949) from whom it passed to Ursus Rare Books, which sold it to the Harlan Crow Library in 2003.

3. Leffler, Kaminski, and Fore 2012, 17–22, have included pictures of the original book cover as well as some of the pages. A bookplate of the same design is found in the commonplace books compiled by Pierce's son.

4. William Shakespeare, *The Winter's Tale*, edited by Robert K. Turner et al. (New York: Modern Language Association of America, 2005), 54.

5. Pierce appears to have been fascinated with epitaphs. He published "An Epitaph—Intended for the Monument of Major General Greene" in the *American Museum* (1789) under the byline "William Pierce, esq. of Savannah" that reads as follows:

> Like other things, this marble must decay,
> The cipher'd characters shall fade away,
> And naught but ruin mark this sacred spot,
> Where Greene's interr'd—perhaps the place forgot;
> But time, unmeasured, shall preserve his name,
> Through distant ages shall roll on his fame,
> And in the heart of every good man, raise
> A lasting monument of matchless praise.

6. I have chosen this method out of no disrespect to William Pierce but in the belief that most modern readers will find it easier to locate information about delegates listed alphabetically than by having to remember which states they represented. Although it is somewhat repetitive, I include the state affiliation of each of the delegates as Pierce mentions them in the narrative.

7. At first inspection, the placement of the names is confusing because delegates began by signing in a column on the right side of the document, which proceeded from New Hampshire to Pennsylvania, but they ran out of space and had to continue in a column to the left. As president of the convention, George Washington heads the signatures on the right, and the signature of William Jackson (the official secretary) is at the bottom on the left. See Vile 2005, 2:721.

8. Pierce did not arrange the names of the delegates within states alphabetically. In some cases (for example, Delaware, Pennsylvania, and Virginia), it seems that Pierce treated the leading man first, but if there is a pattern to his presentation (or to the order in which those who remained at the convention signed the Constitution), I have been unable to find it. Pierce's order of presentation within states was as follows: New Hampshire—Langdon, Gilman; Massachusetts—King, Gorham, Gerry, Strong; Connecticut—Johnson, Sherman, Ellsworth; New York—Hamilton, Yates, Lansing; New Jersey—Livingston, Brearly, Paterson, Dayton; Pennsylvania—Franklin, Mifflin, R. Morris, Clymer, Fitzsimons, Ingersoll, Wilson, G. Morris; Delaware—Dickinson, Bedford, Read, Bassett, Broom; Maryland—Martin, McHenry, Jenifer, Carroll; Virginia—Washington, Wythe, Mason, Madison, Blair, Randolph, McClurg;

North Carolina—Blount, Spaight, Williamson, Davie, Martin; South Carolina—Rutledge, C. C. Pinckney, C. Pinckney, Butler; and Georgia—Few, Baldwin, Houstoun, Pierce.

9. This quotation is similar to James Madison's comment in his own old age: "Having outlived so many of my contemporaries, I ought not to forget that I may be thought to have outlived myself" (McCoy 1989, xi).

10. When John Jay learned that Morris had lost a leg, he wrote a letter to Robert Morris expressing disappointment that Gouverneur Morris had not "lost *something* else" (Brookhiser 2003, 61).

11. This notice was kindly provided by Benjamin Bromley, a Public Services Archives specialist at the Earl Gregg Swem Library of the College of William and Mary, in an e-mail of November 14, 2012.

12. On a much different note, could the reference to Franklin's "rod," in a pre-Freudian era, be a veiled reference to Franklin's reputation as a ladies' man?

REFERENCES

Broadwater, Jeff. 2006. *George Mason: Forgotten Founder*. Chapel Hill: University of North Carolina Press.

Brookhiser, Richard. 2003. *Gentleman Revolutionary: Gouverneur Morris, the Rake Who Wrote the Constitution*. New York: Free Press.

Foster, Thomas A. 2012. "Recovering Washington's Body-Double: Disability and Manliness in the Life and Legacy of a Founding Father." *Disability Studies Quarterly* 32, no. 1. http://dsq-sds.org/article/view/3028/3064.

Hamilton, Philip. 1994. "Education in the St. George Tucker Household: Change and Continuity in Jeffersonian Virginia." *Virginia Magazine of History and Biography* 201:167–192.

Jones, Charles C., Jr. 1891. *Biographical Sketches of the Delegates from Georgia to the Continental Congress*. Boston: Houghton, Mifflin.

Leffler, Richard, John P. Kaminski, and Samuel K. Fore, eds. 2012. *William Pierce on the Constitutional Convention and the Constitution*. Dallas, Tex.: Harlan Crow Library.

Lloyd, Gordon. n.d. "The Age of the Delegates in 1787." http://teachingamericanhistory.org/convention/delegates/age.

Lynch, Jack. 2002. "Introduction to This Edition." In *Samuel Johnson's Dictionary: Selections from the 1755 Work That Defined the English Language*, edited by Jack Lynch, 1–21. New York: Walker.

Matthews, Marty D. 2004. *Forgotten Founder: The Life and Times of Charles Pinckney*. Columbia: University of South Carolina Press.

McCoy, Drew R. 1989. *The Last of the Fathers: James Madison and the Republican Legacy*. New York: Cambridge University Press.

Meacham, Jon. 2012. *Thomas Jefferson: The Art of Power*. New York: Random House.

Morrison, Jeffry H. 2004. "John Witherspoon's Revolutionary Religion." In *The Founders on God and Government*, edited by Daniel L. Dreisbach, Mark D. Hall, and Jeffry H. Morrison, 117–146. Lanham, Md.: Rowman and Littlefield.

"Notes of Major William Pierce on the Federal Convention of 1787." 1898. *American Historical Review* 3, no. 2 (January):310–334.

Pierce, William. 1789. "An Epitaph—Intended for the Monument of Major General Greene." *American Museum* 6:86.

Saye, Albert, comp. Extracts from the Writings of William Pierce. William Pierce Collection. Hargrett Rare Book and Manuscript Library. University of Georgia.

Trees, Andrew S. 2004. *The Founding Fathers and the Politics of Character*. Princeton, N.J.: Princeton University Press.

Vile, John R. 2005. *The Constitutional Convention of 1787: A Comprehensive Encyclopedia of America's Founding*. 2 vols. Santa Barbara, Calif.: ABC-CLIO.

Whitney, Gleaves. 2011. "American Founding—John Adams 3: The Thorn of Fame." History Gadfly. http://gleaveswhitney.blogspot.com/2011/07/american-founding-john-adams-3.html.

Wood, Gordon S. 1969. *The Creation of the American Republic, 1776–1787*. Chapel Hill: University of North Carolina Press.

———. 2006. *Revolutionary Characters: What Made the Founders Different*. New York: Penguin.

CHAPTER 4

Pierce's Analysis of the Delegates' Personal Qualities and Reputations

*Power dies away; great Offices disappear; praise itself is transitory;
forgetfulness, lassitude, inconstancy, and levity all conspire to
disperse it; and nothing will remain with the Minister but faint
and melancholy images of the great Offices he filled, if in a happy
or at least peaceful private station he cannot recall to his mind
some honorable actions which may exalt him in his own Eyes.*

—Jacques Necker, *Treatise on the Administration of the
Finances of France* (as quoted in *Pierce's Reliques*)

Because they relied on more than a record of the delegates' college degrees and professional attainments, Pierce's assessments of their abilities involved considerable judgment on his part. In describing the "Characters" at the Constitutional Convention, Pierce also discussed their personalities and virtues. Such judgments were frequently tied to Pierce's perceptions of the delegates' statuses and reputations as well as their political abilities.

Personal Qualities and Patriotism

It is as common for citizens to assess the moral capabilities of their leaders and their commitment to the common good as it is to judge their abilities and educational attainments. In his sketches, Pierce frequently listed character traits and virtues, some of which he directly associated with patriotism or love of country. Although most of his characterizations were positive, as with other aspects of his descriptions, some of these had a backhanded quality to them.

In the handwritten notebook *Pierce's Reliques*, Pierce quoted Jacques Necker's *Treatise on the Administration of the Finances of France* (first published in English in 1786) on politics and the public good: "We should attach ourselves to one general principle of administration, and be as it were totally absorbed in it, rather than be so selfish, or rather than have always two open accounts, one with our vanity, and the other with the public welfare." Pierce followed with another quotation from the same source, indicating the importance of honor, which is the epigraph of this chapter.

In his character sketches, Pierce associated delegates with the following varied personal qualities:

RICHARD BASSETT (Del.): "He is a Man of plain sense, and has modesty enough to hold his tongue"

GUNNING BEDFORD (Del.): "he is warm and impetuous in his temper, and precipitate in his judgment"

JOHN BLAIR (Va.): "his good sense, and most excellent principles, compensate for other deficiencies"

WILLIAM BLOUNT (N.C.): "is a character strongly marked for integrity and honor"; "plain, honest, and sincere"

DAVID BREARLY (N.J.): "a man of good, rather than of brilliant parts"; "as a Man he has every virtue to recommend him"

JACOB BROOM (Del.): "a plain good Man, with some abilities, but nothing to render him conspicuous"

PIERCE BUTLER (S.C.): "much respected for the many excellent virtues which he possesses"

DANIEL CARROLL (Md.): "He possesses plain good sense"

GEORGE CLYMER (Pa.): "a respectable Man"

JONATHAN DAYTON (N.J.): "There is an impetuosity in his temper that is injurious to him; but there is an honest rectitude about him that makes him a valuable Member of Society"

OLIVER ELLSWORTH (Conn.): "attentive to his duty"; "much respected for his integrity"

WILLIAM FEW (Ga.): "served . . . with fidelity to his State, and honor to himself"

BENJAMIN FRANKLIN (Pa.): "a most extraordinary Man"

ELBRIDGE GERRY (Mass.): "Mr. Gerry's character is marked for integrity and perseverance"; "cherishes as his first virtue, a love for his Country"; "very much of a Gentleman in his principles and manners"

NICHOLAS GILMAN (N.H.): "is modest, genteel, and sensible. There is nothing brilliant or striking in his character, but there is something respectable and worthy in the Man"

NATHANIEL GORHAM (Mass.): "He is a Man of very good sense"; "rather lusty, and has an agreeable and pleasing manner"

ALEXANDER HAMILTON (N.Y.): "His manners are tinctured with stiffness, and sometimes with a degree of vanity that is highly disagreeable"

WILLIAM HOUSTOUN (Ga.): "of an amiable and sweet temper, and of good and honorable principles"

JARED INGERSOLL (Pa.): "There is a modesty in his character that keeps him back"

DANIEL OF ST. THOMAS JENIFER (Md.): "he is always in good humour, and never fails to make his company pleased with him"

WILLIAM SAMUEL JOHNSON (Conn.): "engages the Hearts of Men by the sweetness of his temper"

RUFUS KING (Mass.): "His action is natural, swimming, and graceful, but there is a rudeness of manner sometimes accompanying it"

JOHN LANGDON (N.H.): "possesses a liberal mind, and a good plain understanding"

JOHN LANSING (N.Y.): "a Man of good sense, plain in his manners, and sincere in his friendships"

JAMES MADISON (Va.): "a Gentleman of great modesty,—with a remarkable sweet temper. He is easy and unreserved among his acquaintance[s], and has a most agreeable style of conversation"

ALEXANDER MARTIN (N.C.): "He is a Man of sense"

GEORGE MASON (Va.): "steady and firm in his principles"

JAMES MCCLURG (Va.): "of a fair and unblemished character"

JAMES MCHENRY (Md.): "a Man of specious talents, with nothing of genius to improve them"

GOUVERNEUR MORRIS (Pa.): "But with all these powers he is fickle and inconstant,—never pursuing one train of thinking,—nor ever regular"

ROBERT MORRIS (Pa.): "a worthy Patriot"[1]

WILLIAM PATERSON (N.J.): "He is a Man of great modesty"; "of a disposition so favorable to his advancement"

WILLIAM PIERCE (Ga.): "my services in Congress and the Convention were bestowed with the best intention towards the interest of Georgia, and towards the general welfare of the Confederacy"; "I possess ambition"

EDMUND RANDOLPH (Va.): "a fine person and striking manners"

GEORGE READ (Del.): "He is a very good Man, and bears an amiable character with those who know him"

ROGER SHERMAN (Conn.): "Mr. Sherman exhibits the oddest shaped character I ever remember to have met with. He is awkward, un-meaning, and unaccountably strange in his manner"; "yet he deserves infinite praise"; "no Man has a better Heart or a clearer Head"; as a member of Congress, he "discharged the duties of his Office with honor and credit to himself, and advantage to the State he represented"

RICHARD DOBBS SPAIGHT (N.C.): "a worthy Man"; "able to discharge any public trust that his Country may repose in him"

GEORGE WASHINGTON (Va.): "Having conducted these States to independence and peace, he now appears to assist in framing a Government to make the People happy. Like Gustavus Vasa [probably Gustav I of Sweden, 1496–1560, generally credited for having freed the Swedes from the Danes], he may be said to be the deliverer of his Country;—like Peter the Great [of Russia, 1672–1725] he appears as the politician and the States-man; and like Cincinnatus [of Rome, 519–430 B.C.] he returned to his farm perfectly contented with being only a plain Citizen, after enjoying the highest honor of the Confederacy,—and now only seeks for the approbation of his Country-men by being virtuous and useful"[2]

HUGH WILLIAMSON (N.C.): "There is a great degree of good humour and pleasantry in his character; and in his manners there is a strong trait of the Gentleman"

JAMES WILSON (Pa.): "Mr. Wilson ranks among the foremost in legal and political knowledge. He has joined to a fine genius all that can set him off and show him to advantage"

GEORGE WYTHE (Va.): "He is remarked [probably meaning either remarkable, or famous] for his exemplary life"

Analysis of Pierce's Observations

William Blount's later impeachment by the U.S. Senate for his role in conspiring to stir up an Indian war against Spain (Melton 1998) calls into question Pierce's assessment of Blount as having "a character strongly marked for integrity and honor." Whitney (1974, 55) appears to have come closer to the truth when he identified Blount as someone who "was more interested in what his country could do for him than in what he could do for his country." Pierce's description of Hamilton as having "a degree of vanity" was probably understated (see, for example, Hamilton's dispute with Washington as documented in Chernow 2004, 152–153). Pierce's analysis of Madison is consistent with recent scholarship, while his assessment of Wythe's virtues was consistent with other reports from his era. Thomas Jefferson, one of Wythe's many distinguished students, said, "His virtue was of the purest tint; his integrity inflexible, and his justice exact" (qtd. in "George Wythe" n.d.).

Virtue has both a private and a public dimension. The latter stresses public commitment and service and is often particularly associated with republicanism. The four classical virtues are temperance, fortitude, prudence, and justice. St. Paul described "love, joy, peace, longsuffering, gentleness, goodness, faith" as "fruits of the Spirit" (Galatians 5:22–23), and delegates who were Masons (see Vile 2005, 1:463–464)—a movement that is known to have influenced Phi Beta Kappa, of which Pierce was a member (Current 1990, 10)—would further have been familiar with the virtues of friendship, morality, and brotherly love.

George Washington is, of course, known for having transcribed *Rules of Civility and Decent Behaviour in Company and Conversation* (1971) when he was sixteen. Surveying the libraries in the plantation culture of eastern Virginia in the years leading up to the American Revolution, Hunter Dickinson Farish observes in her introduction to the *Journal and Letters of Philip Vickers Fithian 1773–1774* (1990) that "English 'courtesy' and 'conduct' books were on every gentleman's shelves" (xvii). She elaborates: "Richard Allestree's *A Gentleman's Calling* and Henry Peacham's *The Compleat Gentleman*, and other works which portrayed fortitude, prudence, temperance, justice, liberality, and courtesy as cardinal virtues appear again and again in the inventories of the period, along with the writings of Castiglione and other Italians of an earlier day from whom English authors had derived ideas of courtly conduct" (xvii–xviii).

Pierce used versions of the word "virtue" in a number of his descriptions.[3] He noted that Butler was respected for his "many excellent virtues," Brearly "has every virtue to recommend him," Gerry had patriotism as his "first virtue," and Washington was "virtuous and useful." Specifically, Pierce referred to the following sometimes overlapping virtues: modesty (Bassett, Gilman, Ingersoll, Madison, Paterson);[4] integrity (Blount, Gerry); honor (Blount); honest rectitude (Dayton); attention to duty (Ellsworth); fidelity (Few); perseverance (Gerry); patriotism and love of country (Gerry, R. Morris); sincerity (Blount, Lansing); and steadiness and firmness (Wythe). Pierce listed far more virtues than vices, but he did link Hamilton to vanity and Gouverneur Morris to fickleness and inconstancy.

At a time when the distinction between the heart (the seat of emotions) and the head (the seat of intellect) was a common literary motif (see, for example, Jefferson 1786), Pierce described Sherman by saying "no Man has a better Heart or a clearer Head." He said that Johnson "engages the Hearts of Men by the sweetness of his temper" and (as detailed in the following chapter on oratory) that Hamilton's eloquence also appealed to both. Although Pierce also associated Sherman with a "strange New England cant," he was the only delegate for whose head and heart Pierce directly vouched since his references to Johnson and Hamilton had to do not with the characteristics of their own heads and hearts but with Pierce's assessments of their ability to engage the heads and hearts of others. John Adams confirmed Pierce's judgment of Sherman in a letter of November 1822, in which Adams associated Sherman with "the clearest head and steadiest heart" (qtd. in Hall 2012, 2).

Pierce recorded a number of observations that seemed to assess the characters of some delegates from an inward rather than an outward perspective. He observed that Gerry "possesses a great degree of confidence"; that Sherman despised "the lowness of his condition" as a shoemaker; that G. Morris "disliked" the profession of law; that Jenifer "seems to be conscious that he is no politician"; and that Madison possessed "a spirit of industry and application . . . in a most eminent degree." Pierce vouched for himself by citing his good intentions toward both his state and the confederacy.

Reputations

Pierce's observations were undoubtedly shaped by the opinions of others, but on occasion (especially when discussing oratorical skills), he demonstrated confidence in his own judgments by contrasting his perspective with what he had previously heard. At times he blended the two judgments by referring to individuals as "respectable" or as having "rank" in their states. Observations about the popularity and respectability of delegates would not only have been consistent with eighteenth-century ideas of character but would also have bolstered the delegates' authority to draft a document on behalf of "We the People."

Pierce included the following observations that related chiefly to the reputations of the delegates:

RICHARD BASSETT (Del.): "serves his Country because it is the will of the people that he should do so"; "is in high estimation among the Methodists"

JOHN BLAIR (Va.): "is one of the most respectable Men in Virginia, both on account of his Family as well as fortune"

DAVID BREARLY (N.J.): "is very much in the esteem of the people"

PIERCE BUTLER (S.C.): "a character much respected"; "takes rank among the first in South Carolina"

DANIEL CARROLL (Md.): "a Man of large fortune, and influence in his State"; "is in the full confidence of his Countrymen"

GEORGE CLYMER (Pa.): "much esteemed"

WILLIAM RICHARDSON DAVIE (N.C.): "his opinion was always respected"

JONATHAN DAYTON (N.J.): "secures to him the esteem of all good Men"

JOHN DICKINSON (Del.): "Mr. Dickinson has been famed through all America, for his Farmers Letters"; "I had often heard that he was a great Orator"; "will ever be considered one of the most important characters in the United States"

OLIVER ELLSWORTH (Conn.): "venerated for his abilities"

BENJAMIN FRANKLIN (Pa.): "is well known to be the greatest phylosopher of the present age"

NATHANIEL GORHAM (Mass.): "high in reputation, and much in the esteem of his Country-men"

ALEXANDER HAMILTON (N.Y.): "deservedly celebrated for his talents"

WILLIAM SAMUEL JOHNSON (Conn.): "he laid the foundation of a reputation which will probably last much longer than his own life"; "a character much celebrated for his legal knowledge"

RUFUS KING (Mass.): "He has served for three years in the Congress of the United States with great and deserved applause, and is at this time high in the confidence and approbation of his Country-men"; "But take him *tout en semble*, he may with propriety be ranked among the Luminaries of the present Age"

JAMES MADISON (Va.): "every Person seems to acknowledge his greatness"; "always thought one of the ablest Members that ever sat in that Council [Congress]"

JAMES MCCLURG (Va.): "a Gentleman of great respectability"

JAMES MCHENRY (Md.): "He is however, a very respectable young Gentleman, and deserves the honor which his Country has bestowed on him"

WILLIAM PATERSON (N.J.): "every one seemed ready to exalt him with their praises"

WILLIAM PIERCE (Ga.): "the flattering opinion which some of my Friends had of me"

CHARLES COTESWORTH PINCKNEY (S.C.): "served with great reputation through the War"

JOHN RUTLEDGE (S.C.): "one of those characters who was highly mounted at the commencement of the late revolution;—his reputation in the first Congress gave him a distinguished rank among the American Worthies"

ROGER SHERMAN (Conn.): "yet he deserves infinite praise"

CALEB STRONG (Mass.): "a Lawyer of some eminence"; "greatly in the esteem of his Colleagues"

GEORGE WASHINGTON (Va.): "well known as the Commander in chief of the late American Army"; "The General was conducted to the Chair as President of the Convention by the unanimous voice of its Members"

GEORGE WYTHE (Va.): "the famous Professor of Law at the University of William and Mary"; "universally esteemed for his good principles"

Analysis

Pierce identified six delegates as occupying special places on the national and world stage. He described Rufus King (Mass.) as "among the Luminaries of the present Age"; called Benjamin Franklin (Pa.) "the greatest phylosopher of the present age"; said that John Dickinson (Del.) "has been famed through all America, for his Farmers Letters"; reported that John Rutledge's (S.C.) reputation in the first Congress "gave him a distinguished rank among the American Worthies";

compared George Washington (Va.) to statesmen throughout the world; and referenced Wythe (Va.) as "one of the most learned legal Characters of the present age." Consciously or otherwise, Pierce thus included one or more representatives from the northeastern states, the middle states, and the southern states. Few contemporaries would have challenged Pierce's assessments of Franklin and Washington, although Dickinson, King, Rutledge, and Wythe would probably not have received the same contemporary accolades.

References to Principles

It is common to discuss public servants with respect to their principles. Pierce mentioned the delegates' principles in five sketches:

JOHN BLAIR (Va.): "his good sense, and most excellent principles, compensate for other deficiencies"

WILLIAM HOUSTOUN (Ga.): "of good and honorable principles"

GEORGE MASON (Va.): "steady and firm in his principles"

EDMUND RANDOLPH (Va.): "He came forward with the postulate, or first principles, on which the Convention acted"

GEORGE WYTHE (Va.): "universally esteemed for his good principles"

As these references indicate, the term principle can be either a postulate, or "first principle," or a matter of conscience to which one adheres. Samuel Johnson defined a "principle" as an "[e]lement; constituent part; primordial substance" (definition 1), as a "[g]round of action; motive" (definition 5), and as a "[t]enet on which morality is founded" (definition 6) (1967, vol. 2). Pierce appears to have used the term in the first sense to refer to Randolph and the plan that he introduced and in the second sense to refer to Blair, Houstoun, Mason, and Wythe. What is most fascinating is that Pierce employed the term in one fashion or the other for four of the six Virginia delegates and, with the exception of Houstoun, *only* to those delegates. Almost as though he were following John Adams's somewhat jealous quip—"In Virginia all Geese are Swans" (Ellis 2001, 79)—Pierce seemed to hold these delegates in higher esteem than he did those from the state he was representing, or any other state.

In examining why he so associated the Virginia delegation with principles, one might hypothesize either that he simply used the word once and unconsciously repeated it a number of times in portraits in close proximity to one another (as previously indicated, he grouped his biographies under the individual states).[5] Alternatively, he may have used the term because he associated the convention with the principles of the initial Virginia Plan, which that state's delegates had introduced. Perhaps Pierce still identified with his place of birth or had developed a special esteem for Virginians when he spent time in Williamsburg. Whatever the case, the term seems to place the Virginia delegates on a higher plane with respect to their good intentions.[6]

Use of the Word "Gentleman"

One of the fascinating aspects of Pierce's descriptions was his frequent use of the word "gentleman" or a variant.

ABRAHAM BALDWIN (Ga.): "a Gentleman of superior abilities"

RICHARD BASSETT (Del.): "He is a Gentlemanly Man"

PIERCE BUTLER (S.C.): "He is a Gentleman of fortune, and takes rank among the first in South Carolina"

DANIEL CARROLL (Md.): "This Gentleman"

JONATHAN DAYTON (N.J.): "a young Gentleman of talents"

OLIVER ELLSWORTH (Conn.): "a Gentleman of a clear, deep, and copious understanding"

ELBRIDGE GERRY (Mass.): "very much of a Gentleman in his principles and manners"

WILLIAM HOUSTOUN (Ga.): "He is a Gentleman of Family"

DANIEL OF ST. THOMAS JENIFER (Md.): "a Gentleman of fortune in Maryland"

WILLIAM SAMUEL JOHNSON (Conn.): "possesses the manners of a Gentleman"

RUFUS KING (Mass.): "This Gentleman"

JAMES MADISON (Va.): "a Gentleman of great modesty"

LUTHER MARTIN (Md.): a "Gentleman" who "possesses a good deal of information"

GEORGE MASON (Va.): "a Gentleman of remarkable strong powers"

JAMES MCCLURG (Va.): "a Gentleman of great respectability"

JAMES MCHENRY (Md.): "a very respectable young Gentleman"

GOUVERNEUR MORRIS (Pa.): "This Gentleman"

WILLIAM PATERSON (N.J.): "This Gentleman"

CHARLES PINCKNEY (S.C.): "a young Gentleman of the most promising talents"

CHARLES COTESWORTH PINCKNEY (S.C.): "a Gentleman of Family and fortune in his own State"

EDMUND RANDOLPH (Va.): "a young Gentleman"

JOHN RUTLEDGE (S.C.): "This Gentleman is much famed in his own State as an Orator"; "a Gentleman of distinction and fortune"

CALEB STRONG (Mass.): "This Gentn."

HUGH WILLIAMSON (N.C.): "a Gentleman of education and talents"

Analysis

Samuel Johnson listed as the first definition of "gentleman" "[a] man of birth; a man of extraction, though not noble." A fifth definition reported that the term "is used of any man however high" (1967, vol. 1). Focusing more specifically on America, Susan Rather has observed: "By the eighteenth century, and especially in colonial British America, where few were titled, the term had wider application [than being born to wealth]. Birth and patronage still counted for a great deal; so did wealth, though it alone did not a gentleman make, especially if gained by trade. Gentlemen were never defined by what they did, by the usefulness of their trades, but by their 'quality' and condition as men of learning, manners, taste, and character" (1997, 269).

Gordon Wood believes that in the eighteenth century, the term gentleman "assumed a moral meaning that was more important than its social significance" (2006, 14). He associates positive character with "being reasonable, tolerant, honest, virtuous, and 'candid'" (15). The term was sometimes used to designate a man educated in the liberal arts. Wood quotes John Adams as saying, "By gentlemen are not meant the rich or the poor, the high-born or the low-born, the industrious or the idle: but all those who have received a liberal education, an ordinary degree of erudition in liberal arts and sciences" (ibid.). Wood believes that gentlemen "were all those at the top of the social hierarchy who were wealthy enough not to have to work, or at least not to have to work with their hands, and who thus seemed able to act in a disinterested manner in promoting a public good" (16).

Like the term "esquire" (described below), Pierce appears to have used the term "gentleman" not so much to distinguish delegates from one another as to distinguish or elevate them above the general populace. He designated at least two delegates (Dayton and Randolph) as "young" gentlemen. Perhaps because he bestowed so many other accolades upon him, or perhaps because he thought that he ranked even higher, Pierce did not specifically use the term "gentleman" to refer to Washington.

Wealth and Family Connections

The historian Charles Beard is among those scholars who highlight the economic status and motivations of the framers in *An Economic Interpretation of the Consti-*

tution, which he first published in 1913 (1949; also see McGuire 2003; for critiques, see McDonald 1958; Brown 1956). At the time of the convention, delegates like Robert Morris (a merchant and financier who later went bankrupt) and George Washington (an entrepreneurial planter) were among the wealthiest in North America, and many of the southerners came from large plantations, although this did not always mean that they had cash on hand. Pierce singled out a number of delegates for their wealth and family connections, and sometimes linked references to gentlemen with statements about wealth and property:

JOHN BLAIR (Va.): "Mr. Blair is one of the most respectable Men in Virginia, both on account of his Family as well as fortune"

PIERCE BUTLER (S.C.): "a Gentleman of fortune, and takes rank among the first in South Carolina"

DANIEL CARROLL (Md.): "Mr. Carrol is a Man of large fortune"

ELBRIDGE GERRY (Mass.): "is a Man of property"

WILLIAM HOUSTOUN (Ga.): "He is a Gentleman of Family"

DANIEL OF ST. THOMAS JENIFER (Md.): "Mr. Jenifer is a Gentleman of fortune in Maryland"

JOHN LANGDON (N.H.): "Mr. Langdon is a Man of considerable fortune"

ROBERT MORRIS (Pa.): "Robert Morris is a merchant of great eminence and wealth; an able Financier"

CHARLES COTESWORTH PINCKNEY (S.C.): "A Gentleman of Family and fortune in his own State"

JOHN RUTLEDGE (S.C.): "a Gentleman of distinction and fortune"

RICHARD DOBBS SPAIGHT (N.C.): "Mr. Spaight is a worthy Man, of some abilities, and fortune"

Pierce identified far more southerners for their wealth, which was largely based on the slave economy but which Pierce did not mention, than he did others.

Political Abilities

It is common to assess the political skills of those who hold public office, or even of those who engage in occupations like the law, which so frequently involve interactions with governmental bodies. As the following excerpts show, Pierce appears to have used the terms "politician" and "statesman" as synonyms (unlike in the present day, when they are sometimes used as antonyms) in assessing the political savvy of his fellow delegates. He thus followed Samuel Johnson's first definition of a "politician" as "[o]ne versed in the arts of government; one skilled in politicks" rather than the second definition of "[a] man of artifice; one of deep contrivance"

(1967, vol. 2).[7] On occasion, Pierce specifically tied the politician role to speaking, showing the necessity of combining Pierce's assessment of the delegates' political abilities with his assessment of their rhetoric.

PIERCE BUTLER (S.C.): "But as a politician or an Orator, he has no pretentions to either"

BENJAMIN FRANKLIN (Pa.): "But what claim he has to the politician, posterity must determine"; "nor does he seem to let politics engage his attention"

DANIEL OF ST. THOMAS JENIFER (Md.): "He sits silent in the Senate, and seems to be conscious that he is no politician"

RUFUS KING (Mass.): "great parliamentary talents"

WILLIAM LIVINGSTON (N.J.): "seems little acquainted with the guiles of policy"

ALEXANDER MARTIN (N.C.): "undoubtedly is a good politician"

GEORGE MASON (Va.): "undoubtedly one of the best politicians in America"

JAMES MCCLURG (Va.): "having never appeared before in public life his character as a politician is not sufficiently known"

JAMES MCHENRY (Md.): "As a politician there is nothing remarkable in him"

EDMUND RANDOLPH (Va.): "the States-man"

ROGER SHERMAN (Conn.): "He is an able politician, and extremely artful in accomplishing any particular object;—it is remarked that he seldom fails"; "He has been several years a Member of Congress, and discharged the duties of his Office with honor and credit to himself, and advantage to the State he represented"

GEORGE WASHINGTON (Va.): "Having conducted these States to independence and peace, he now appears to assist in framing a Government to make the People happy. Like Gustavus Vasa, he may be said to be the deliverer of his Country;—like Peter the Great he appears as the politician and the States-man; and like Cincinnatus he returned to his farm perfectly contented with being only a plain Citizen, after enjoying the highest honor of the Confederacy,—and now only seeks for the approbation of his Country-men by being virtuous and useful"

GEORGE WYTHE (Va.): "yet from his too favorable opinion of Men, he is no great politician"

ROBERT YATES (N.Y.): "Some of his Enemies say he is an anti-federal Man, but I discovered no such disposition in him"

Analysis

It is unclear why Pierce failed to provide his own assessment of Franklin's political skills, although Franklin's age may have made the display of such skills less obvious at the convention than in other political theaters in which he participated. Pierce's assessment of George Mason as "undoubtedly one of the best politicians in America" seems overly generous, but Pierce was likely basing his assessment on the first month of the convention, when the Virginia Plan was dominating the discussion and before Mason began raising objections to and ultimately chose not to sign the Constitution. As late as July 5, Mason proclaimed that "he would bury his bones in this city rather than expose his Country to the Consequences of a dissolution of the Convention without any thing being done" (Farrand 1966, 1:533). By contrast, Pierce's assessment of Roger Sherman seems on the mark. Scholarship has indicated that Sherman was one of the savviest and most successful of the delegates in getting what he wanted (Robertson, May 2005). Perhaps because of George Washington's international reputation, Pierce found himself attempting to explain him with references to foreign leaders and to the classical Cincinnatus. Pierce's observation that Wythe's skills as a politician were undercut by his "too favorable opinion of Men" shows that Pierce possessed a realistic view of human nature, not unlike the view so prominently reflected in *The Federalist Papers*.[8]

Although Washington certainly stood out above the rest of the delegates, the overall picture that emerges from Pierce's sketches is of a body that was more patriotic, more virtuous, more principled, and more politically skilled than the members of the general population whom they were representing. The delegates' medium for representing the interests of their constituents was speech, and, as the following chapter shows, Pierce's descriptions of the delegates' speaking styles and abilities constituted a major part of his character sketches.

NOTES

1. Pierce had dealings with Robert Morris during the Revolution; Morris had reimbursed his superior (General Greene) "for secret [spy] services" for which Greene had paid out of his own pocket. See Greene 1991–2005, 9:636.
2. In his Fourth of July Oration of 1788, Pierce referred to Washington as "immortal" (see Kaminski and Saladino 1995, 255; and appendix III in this book).
3. I am in this section omitting Pierce's references to "good sense" and variants because I think they more accurately fall under the section concerning education and abilities.
4. Some of these references appear to be less to a virtue than to a character trait (a lack of confidence).
5. In back-to-back portraits of Franklin, Mifflin, and R. Morris (all from Pennsylvania), Pierce described each according to their activity of mind, an expression he does not utilize elsewhere in his sketches. Similarly, in another back-to-back pair of descriptions involving Massachusetts delegates, Pierce observed both that Gerry's speech "possesses a good deal of confidence" and that Strong was "without confidence."
6. By contrast, Madison reported that on June 15 John Dickinson of Delaware told him that the rising opposition to Madison's insistence on representation solely on the basis of population in Congress showed "the consequences of pushing things too far." Dickinson further explained to Madison: "Some of the members from the small States wish for two branches

in the General Legislature, and are friends to a good National Government; but we would sooner submit to a foreign power, than submit to be deprived of an equality of suffrage, in both branches of the legislature, and thereby be thrown under the domination of the larger States" (note marked with * in Farrand 1966, 1:242).

7. In attempting to prove that eighteenth-century Americans associated politics with corruption, Trees 2004, 1, ignores Johnson's first definition and focuses only on the second.

8. In Federalist No. 51, James Madison observed: "If men were angels, no government would be necessary. If angels were to govern men, neither external nor internal controls on government would be necessary. In framing a government which is to be administered by men over men, the great difficulty lies in this: you must first enable the government to control the governed; and in the next place oblige it to control itself."

REFERENCES

Beard, Charles A. 1949. *An Economic Interpretation of the Constitution of the United States*. 1913. Reprint, New York: Macmillan.

Brown, Robert E. 1956. *Charles Beard and the Constitution: A Critical Analysis of "An Economic Interpretation of the Constitution."* Princeton, N.J.: Princeton University Press.

Chernow, Ron. 2004. *Alexander Hamilton*. New York: Penguin.

Current, Richard Nelson. 1990. *Phi Beta Kappa in American Life: The First Two Hundred Years*. New York: Oxford University Press.

Ellis, Joseph. 2001. *Founding Brothers: The Revolutionary Generation*. New York: Knopf.

Farrand, Max, ed. 1966. *The Records of the Federal Convention of 1787*. 4 vols. New Haven, Conn.: Yale University Press.

Fithian, Philip Vickers. 1990. *Journal and Letters of Philip Vickers Fithian 1773–1774: A Plantation Tutor of the Old Dominion*. Ed. Hunter Dickinson Farish. Charlottesville: University Press of Virginia. http://www.gutenberg.org/files/40044/40044-h/40044-htm.

"George Wythe." n.d. *Colonial Williamsburg*. http://www.history.org/almanack/people/bios/biowythe.cfm.

Greene, Nathanael. 1991–2005. *The Papers of General Nathanael Greene*. Ed. Dennis M. Conrad. Chapel Hill: University of North Carolina Press for the Rhode Island Historical Society.

Hall, Mark David. 2012. *Roger Sherman and the Creation of the American Republic*. New York: Oxford University Press.

Hamilton, Alexander, James Madison, and John Jay. 1961. *The Federalist Papers*. New York: New American Library.

Jefferson, Thomas. 1786. "Head and Heart Letter" to Maria Cosway. http://www.pbs.org/jefferson/archives/documents/ih195811.htm.

Johnson, Samuel. 1967. *A Dictionary of the English Language*. 1755. 2 vols. Reprint, New York: AMS.

Kaminsky, John P., and Gaspare J. Saladino, eds. 1995. *Commentaries on the Constitution, Public and Private*, vol. 6: *10 May to 13 September 1788*. Madison: State Historical Society of Wisconsin.

McDonald, Forrest. 1958. *We the People: The Economic Origins of the Constitution*. Chicago: University of Chicago Press.

McGuire, Robert A. 2003. *To Form a More Perfect Union: A New Economic Interpretation of the United States Constitution*. New York: Oxford University Press.

Melton, Buckner F., Jr. 1998. *The First Impeachment: The Constitution's Framers and the Case of Senator Blount.* Macon, Ga.: Mercer University Press.

Rather, Susan. 1997. "Carpenter, Tailor, Shoemaker, Artist: Copley and Portrait Painting around 1770." *Art Bulletin* 79 (June):269–290.

Robertson, David Brian. 2005. "Madison's Opponents and Constitutional Design." *American Political Science Review* 99 (May):225–243.

Trees, Andrew S. 2004. *The Founding Fathers and the Politics of Character.* Princeton, N.J.: Princeton University Press.

Vile, John R. 2005. *The Constitutional Convention of 1787: A Comprehensive Encyclopedia of America's Founding.* 2 vols. Santa Barbara, Calif.: ABC-CLIO.

Washington, George. 1971. *Rules of Civility and Decent Behaviour in Company and Conversation: A Book of Etiquette.* Williamsburg, Va.: Beaver Press.

Whitney, David C. 1974. *Founders of Freedom in America: Lives of the Men Who Signed the Constitution of the United States and So Helped to Established the United States of America.* Chicago: Ferguson.

Wood, Gordon S. 2006. *Revolutionary Characters: What Made the Founders Different.* New York: Penguin.

ABRAHAM BALDWIN

RICHARD BASSETT

GUNNING BEDFORD

JOHN BLAIR

WILLIAM BLOUNT

PIERCE BUTLER

DANIEL CARROLL

GEORGE CLYMER

WILLIAM RICHARDSON DAVIE

JOHNATHAN DAYTON

JOHN DICKINSON

OLIVER ELLSWORTH

WILLIAM FEW

BENJAMIN FRANKLIN

ELBRIDGE GERRY

NICHOLAS GILMAN

NATHANIEL GORHAM

ALEXANDER HAMILTON

JARED INGERSOLL

DANIEL OF ST. THOMAS JENIFER

WILLIAM SAMUEL JOHNSON

RUFUS KING

JOHN LANGDON

JOHN LANSING

WILLIAM LIVINGSTON

JAMES MADISON JR.

ALEXANDER MARTIN

LUTHER MARTIN

GEORGE MASON

JAMES McCLURG

JAMES McHENRY

JOHN FRANCIS MERCER

THOMAS MIFFLIN

GOUVERNEUR MORRIS

ROBERT MORRIS

WILLIAM PATERSON

CHARLES COTESWORTH PICKNEY

CHARLES PINCKNEY

EDMUND RANDOLPH

GEORGE READ

JOHN RUTLEDGE

ROGER SHERMAN

CALEB STRONG

GEORGE WASHINGTON

HUGH WILLIAMSON   JAMES WILSON

GEORGE WYTHE

CHAPTER 5

Pierce's Analysis of the Delegates'
Rhetorical Abilities

*The power of eloquence is not a vain power: we often obey it
and frequently are captivated by it when we think we yield to
our own reflections.—Words and phrases are the interpreters
of our sentiments, and the representatives of our thoughts.*

—Jacques Necker, *Treatise on the Administration of the
Finances of France* (as quoted in *Pierce's Reliques*)

The study of rhetoric was an established part of college curricula in the eighteenth
century in both America and Britain (Richard 1994, 20; Mahoney 1958). Pierce
would likely have learned most of what he gleaned about the delegates, especially
those from other states, by listening to the speeches they gave at the convention
or in Congress or by reading what they had published. A book about eighteenth-
century rhetoric in Connecticut, a state that had been particularly influenced by
clerical rhetoric (see, however, Mahaffey 1957), captures the political importance of
speech by referring to the state's leaders as "a speaking aristocracy" (Grasso 1999).
Jurgen Heideking has also explored the importance of rhetoric to the founders,
with special emphasis on the states' ratifying conventions of the U.S. Constitution (2012, 273–285). I have written an article examining Pierce's assessment of the
rhetoric of his fellow delegates (Vile 2014).

Pierce's Rhetorical Background

As noted in chapter 2, the reformed curriculum at William and Mary, where Pierce
appears to have spent several months, employed disputations. Pierce may also
have developed his interest and proficiency in speaking as a member of Phi Beta
Kappa. Although the organization is today chiefly known as an honor society that

recognizes individuals in the liberal arts for their good grades, at the time of its founding in 1776, it was chiefly "a forensic club" (Current 1990, 8). The historian Richard Nelson Current explains that a typical meeting consisted of two participating students presenting papers, arguing from opposing sides, and three judges deciding between them (ibid.). Such experience would likely have given Pierce confidence not only in delivering his own speeches but in judging those of others. I cannot, however, ascertain from the minutes whether Pierce attended any sessions other than the one in which he was accepted. Although on August 27, 1780, Pierce was appointed—and was probably therefore in attendance—to prepare a declamation for the next meeting, he was absent from this meeting on September 12, 1780, where the discussion centered on whether polygamy was dictated by nature ("Original Phi Beta Kappa Records" 1919, 604).

In the handwritten book where Pierce recorded his character sketches, he included a quotation from Jacques Necker about eloquence, which is cited at greater length in the epigraph of this chapter. Necker described "Words and phrases" as "the interpreters of our sentiments, and the representatives of our thoughts." Speaking was critical for the delegates to the convention who were interested in sharing their own thoughts and sentiments and in persuading other delegates.

On the advice of a rules committee, on May 28, the second day of deliberations, the delegates adopted a number of rules about speaking at the convention. The rules specified, "Every member, rising to speak, shall address the President; and whilst he shall be speaking, none shall pass between them, or hold discourse with another, or read a book, pamphlet or paper, printed or manuscript—and of two members rising at the same time, the President shall name him who shall be first heard." The delegates further decided, "A member shall not speak oftener than twice, without special leave, upon the same question; and not the second time, before every other, who had been silent, shall have been heard, if he choose to speak upon the subject" (Farrand 1966, 11).[1]

Perhaps not surprisingly, Pierce devoted as much critical attention to the speaking styles of the delegates as he did to any other aspect of their characters.[2] He directed most of his comments to public speaking, but, as would be appropriate for a meeting in which delegates might exercise much of their persuasive and negotiating powers in unrecorded private settings, he occasionally also mentioned the delegates' reputations for personal conversation.[3] Pierce sometimes focused on the substance of a delegate's speech, sometimes on points of style, and sometimes on both.[4] When he described a delegate who did not speak much at the convention, for example, Robert Morris, Pierce on occasion referred to the delegate's reputation for speaking in other bodies. In assessing the abilities of delegates he heard,

Pierce had no hesitation in indicating when he thought a delegate's reputation for oratory was inflated or otherwise mistaken.

Although he singled out a number of other delegates for their silence, Pierce was only recorded as speaking on four occasions at the convention (some sources incorrectly cite the number as three), and none of his comments were extensive. This placed him among the bottom half of those who attended in terms of loquaciousness. Although he spoke of other aspects of his character in his own personal sketch, he did not assess his own rhetorical abilities, making it impossible to know from his sketches whether he was judging others from the perspective of a masterful rhetorician or simply one who aspired to be. In Pierce's only known oration, which he gave in commemoration of the Declaration of Independence at Christ Church in Savannah on July 4, 1788, he prefaced what I consider to be a fairly good speech by expressing doubts as to whether he had "abilities or powers equal to" the task. He further observed that "unaccustomed as I am to public speaking, and totally out of the habit of searching after those ornaments that grace and set off style, I cannot but feel a diffidence in entering on the duty which I am called upon this day to perform." It is difficult to know whether to take these reservations completely seriously, in part because Pierce may have been less interested in highlighting his own incapacity than in magnifying the importance of the subject— "the Anniversary of our Independence," which he described as "an event the most important that graces the page of history."

Third-person evidence suggests that Pierce *was* rhetorically gifted. The numerous classical and literary allusions in his letters (as well as some of his comments about fellow delegates' rhetoric) suggest that he was part of the belletristic movement in the eighteenth century. This approach "was based upon the concept that rhetoric and related polite arts, poetry, drama, art, history, biography, philology, and so on should be joined under the broad heading of rhetoric and belles lettres" (Golden and Corbett 1968, 8). Moreover, an obituary that an unnamed friend published in the *Georgia Gazette* positively noted, "His manners [were] polite and obliging, his reasonings precise, his diction perspicuous and eloquent" (Jones 1891, 157).

Pierce's Assessments

A study of the number of times that delegates to the convention spoke identified the following as the most frequent speakers: Gouverneur Morris (173 speeches), James Wilson (168), James Madison (161), Roger Sherman (138), George Mason (136), Elbridge Gerry (119), John Rutledge (47), Pierce Butler (47), John Dickinson

(36), Daniel Carroll (35), Charles Cotesworth Pinckney (35), Luther Martin (31), George Read (27), Alexander Hamilton (23), John Langdon (16), and Benjamin Franklin (16) ("Constitutional Convention, 1787" 1861, 18). Pierce's descriptions of these men's speaking styles were generally more extensive than his descriptions of the styles of other delegates.

The best way to understand Pierce's view of rhetoric is to isolate his comments with respect to the subject delegate by delegate and then look for themes. I have summarized Pierce's assessments by indicating whether they were positive (+), negative (–), or mixed (M), or whether he noted that a delegate was largely silent (S). At times I have also indicated whether the assessment was largely for style or substance.

ABRAHAM BALDWIN (Ga.): "joins in a public debate with great art and eloquence" (+ style)

GUNNING BEDFORD (Del.): "He is a bold and nervous Speaker, and has a very commanding and striking manner;—but he is warm and impetuous in his temper, and precipitate in his judgment" (M style/– substance)

JOHN BLAIR (Va.): "Mr. Blair is however, no Orator" (–)

WILLIAM BLOUNT (N.C.): "He is no Speaker" (–)

DAVID BREARLY (N.J.): "As an Orator he has little to boast of" (–)

JACOB BROOM (Del.): "He is silent in public, but chearful and conversable in private" (S public/+ private)

PIERCE BUTLER (S.C.): "But as a politician or an Orator, he has no pretentions to either" (–)

WILLIAM RICHARDSON DAVIE (N.C.): "a Gentleman of considerable literary talents";[5] "He was silent in the Convention,[6] but his opinion was always respected" (S public/+ private)

JONATHAN DAYTON (N.J.): "he speaks well, and seems desirous of improving himself in Oratory" (+)

JOHN DICKINSON (Del.): "Mr. Dickinson has been famed through all America, for his Farmers Letters"; "When I saw him in the Convention I was induced to pay the greatest attention to him whenever he spoke. I had often heard that he was a great Orator, but I found him an indifferent Speaker. With an affected air of wisdom he labors to produce a trifle,—his language is irregular and incorrect,—his flourishes (for he sometimes attempts them), are like expiring flames, they just shew themselves and go out;—no traces of them are left on the mind to clear or animate it. He is, however, a good writer" (– oratory/differs from reputation and writing)

OLIVER ELLSWORTH (Conn.): "eloquent, and connected in public debate"; "He is very happy in a reply, and choice in selecting such parts of his adversary's arguments as he finds make the strongest impressions,—in order to take off the force of them, so as to admit the power of his own" (+)[7]

WILLIAM FEW (Ga.): "speaks tolerably well in the Legislature" (weak +)

THOMAS FITZSIMONS (Pa.): "speaks very well I am told, in the Legislature of Pennsylvania" (+ reputation)

BENJAMIN FRANKLIN (Pa.): "It is certain that he does not shine much in public Council,—he is no Speaker"; "tells a story in a style more engaging than anything I ever heard" (– public/+ private)

ELBRIDGE GERRY (Mass.): "He is a hesitating and laborious speaker;—possesses a great degree of confidence and goes extensively into all subjects that he speaks on, without respect to elegance or flower of diction. He is connected and sometimes clear in his arguments, conceives well" (– style/+ substance)

NATHANIEL GORHAM (Mass.): "He is eloquent and easy in public debate, but has nothing fashionable or elegant in his style;—all he aims at is to convince, and where he fails it never is from his auditors not understanding him, for no Man is more perspicuous and full"; "has an agreeable and pleasing manner" (M style/+ substance)

ALEXANDER HAMILTON (N.Y.): "To a clear and strong judgment he unites the ornaments of fancy, and whilst he is able, convincing, and engaging in his eloquence the Heart and Head sympathize in approving him. Yet there is something too feeble in his voice to be equal to the strains of oratory;—it is my opinion that he is rather a convincing Speaker, [than] a blazing Orator. Col. Hamilton requires time to think,—he enquires into every part of his subject with the searchings of phylosophy, and when he comes forward he comes highly charged with interesting matter, there is no skimming over the surface of a subject with him, he must sink to the bottom to see what foundation it rests on.—His language is not always equal, sometimes didactic like Bolingbroke's [an English official and political philosopher, 1678–1751] and at others light and tripping like Stern's [probably Laurence Sterne, a cleric and novelist, 1713–1768]. His eloquence is not so defusive as to trifle with the senses, but he rambles just enough to strike and keep up the attention" (M style/+ substance)

WILLIAM HOUSTOUN (Ga.): "He has none of the talents requisite for the Orator, but in public debate is confused and irregular" (–)

JARED INGERSOLL (Pa.): "Mr. Ingersol speaks well, and comprehends his subject fully" (+)

DANIEL OF ST. THOMAS JENIFER (Md.): "He sits silent in the Senate" (S)

WILLIAM SAMUEL JOHNSON (Conn.): "As an Orator in my opinion, there is nothing in him that warrants the high reputation which he has for public speaking. There is something in the tone of his voice not pleasing to the Ear,—but he is eloquent and clear,—always abounding with information and instruction"; "that affectionate style of address with which he accosts his acquaintance" (– style/+ substance)

RUFUS KING (Mass.): "a Man much distinguished for his eloquence and great parliamentary talents"; "a sweet high-toned voice"; "In his public speaking there is something peculiarly strong and rich in his expression, clear and convincing in his arguments, rapid and irresistible at times in his eloquence but he is not always equal [consistent?]. His action is natural, swimming, and graceful, but there is a rudeness of manner sometimes accompanying it" (+)

JOHN LANSING (N.Y.): "He has a hesitation in his speech, that will prevent his being an Orator of any eminence" (–)

WILLIAM LIVINGSTON (N.J.): "His writings teem with satyr and a neatness of style. But he is no Orator" (M)

JAMES MADISON (Va.): "In the management of every great question he evidently took the lead in the Convention, and tho' he cannot be called an Orator, he is a most agreeable, eloquent, and convincing speaker. From a spirit of industry and application which he possesses in a most eminent degree, he always comes forward the best informed Man of any point in debate"; "has a most agreeable style of conversation" (weak + style/high + substance)

ALEXANDER MARTIN (N.C.): "he is not formed to shine in public debate, being no Speaker" (–)

LUTHER MARTIN (Md.): "This Gentleman possesses a good deal of information, but he has a very bad delivery, and so extremely prolix, that he never speaks without tiring the patience of all who hear him" (weak + substance/– style)

GEORGE MASON (Va.): "He is able and convincing in debate" (+)

JAMES MCCLURG (Va.): "He attempted once or twice to speak, but with no great success" (largely S/–)

JAMES MCHENRY (Md.): "nor has he any of the graces of the Orator" (–)

THOMAS MIFFLIN (Pa.): "He is well informed and a graceful Speaker" (+ style)

GOUVERNEUR MORRIS (Pa.): "one of those Genius's in whom every species of talents combine to render him conspicuous and flourishing in public debate:—He winds through all the mazes of rhetoric, and throws around him such a glare that he charms, captivates, and leads away the senses of all who hear him. With an infinite stretch of fancy he brings to view things when he is engaged in deep argumentation, that renders all the labor of reasoning easy and pleasing"; "nor can any one engage the attention more than Mr. Morris" (+)

ROBERT MORRIS (Pa.): "I am told that when he speaks in the Assembly of Pennsylvania, that he bears down all before him. What could have been his reason for not Speaking in the Convention I know not,—but he never once spoke on any point" (+ reputation but S)

WILLIAM PATERSON (N.J.): "an Orator"; "He is very happy in the choice of time and manner of engaging in a debate, and never speaks but when he understands his subject well" (+)

CHARLES PINCKNEY (S.C.): "He speaks with great neatness and perspicuity, and treats every subject as fully, without running into prolixity, as it requires" (+ style/+ substance)

CHARLES COTESWORTH PINCKNEY (S.C.): "When warm in a debate he sometimes speaks well,—but he is generally considered an indifferent Orator" (M)

EDMUND RANDOLPH (Va.): "He came forward with the postulate, or first principles, on which the Convention acted, and he supported them with a force of eloquence and reasoning that did him great honor [if this is a reference to the Virginia Plan, as it appears to be, most commentators believe that James Madison was the force both behind the plan and the speech that introduced it]. He has a most harmonious voice" (+ substance and style)

GEORGE READ (Del.): "his powers of Oratory are fatiguing and tiresome to the last degree;—his voice is feeble, and his articulation so bad that few can have patience to attend to him" (–)

JOHN RUTLEDGE (S.C.): "This Gentleman is much famed in his own State as an Orator, but in my opinion he is too rapid in his public speaking to be denominated an agreeable Orator" (– despite reputation)[8]

ROGER SHERMAN (Conn.): "the oddity of his address, the vulgarisms that accompany his public speaking, and that strange New England cant which runs through his public as well as his private speaking make everything that is connected with him grotesque and laughable;—and yet he deserves infinite praise"; "If he cannot embellish he can furnish thoughts that are wise and useful"; "he turned Almanack maker" (– style/+ substance);

CALEB STRONG (Mass.): "As a Speaker he is feeble, and without confidence" (–)

HUGH WILLIAMSON (N.C.): "He enters freely into public debate from his close attention to most subjects, but he is no Orator" (– style/+ substance)

JAMES WILSON (Pa.): "No man is more clear, copious, and comprehensive than Mr. Wilson, yet he is no great Orator. He draws the attention not by the charm of his eloquence, but by the force of his reasoning" (M style/+ substance)

GEORGE WYTHE (Va.): "He is a neat and pleasing Speaker, and a most correct and able Writer" (+)

ROBERT YATES (N.Y.): "not distinguished as an Orator" (–)

Some Comparisons

As the above survey demonstrates, Pierce provided far more negative and mixed evaluations of the delegates' speaking styles than positive ones. He mitigated his critique in part by crediting some delegates (Sherman, for example) for the substance of their arguments, despite their presentation.

Although Pierce sometimes distinguished his own view from a speaker's reputation, other delegates confirmed some of his observations. After Alexander Hamilton delivered a speech on June 19 that lasted for about six hours, William Samuel Johnson observed that "though he has been much praised by every body, he has been supported by none" (Farrand 1966, 1:36). This suggests that delegates rejected Hamilton's ideas (too pro-British and favoring too strong a national government) rather than reacting negatively to the style in which he delivered them. Similarly, Madison reported (ibid., 1:438, 445) that Luther Martin, who was known for often being inebriated and for giving lengthy, meandering speeches, delivered an extremely long and tedious speech on June 27,[9] which would have been not long before Pierce left the convention. Although it is unclear whether Pierce was present for Gunning Bedford's inflammatory speech of June 30, in which Bedford suggested that smaller states might seek support from a foreign ally, such a speech certainly would have confirmed, if it did not serve as the basis for, Pierce's assessment of his "warm and impetuous . . . temper, and precipitate . . . judgment."

A biographer of Sherman quotes John Adams's observation that Sherman and Eliphalet Dyer (1721–1807, a Connecticut statesman) "speak often and long, but very heavily and clumsily" and, consistent with Pierce's judgment, assessed Sherman as having been "rhetorically handicapped" (Hall 2012, 2–3). Similarly, a study of Madison confirms Pierce's general description of him: "Deliberation for Madison was not a matter of elocutionary flash and rhetorical flourish, the oratorical arts that his era prized and studied," but rather a process of "canvassing alternatives, weighing exigencies, asking what was realistically attainable, forgoing what was not, and being ready to rebut objections and refute fallacies" (Rakove 2009, 349–350). Similarly, Jefferson described Madison's rhetoric by observing that he never wandered "from his subject into vain declamation" but pursued "it closely, in language pure, classical, and copious, soothing always the feelings of his adversaries by civilities and softness of expression" (qtd. by Meacham 2012, 122). By contrast, a biographer of Abraham Baldwin said that Pierce's description of Baldwin as joining "in debate with great art and eloquence" was "an exaggeration." Coulter noted that Baldwin "was neither given to, nor gifted in, much speaking or in involved or flowing language." The biographer did, however, quote an unnamed contemporary as observing that Baldwin's "oratory was simple, forcible, convincing" (Coulter 1987, 264), qualities that would have impressed Pierce.

Pierce was especially complimentary about the rhetoric of Rufus King of Massachusetts. Jeremy Belknap, an observer at the state's ratification convention, confirmed Pierce's judgment: "Rufus King shines among Federalists with a superior lustre. His speeches are clear, cool, nervous, pointed, and conclusive" (qtd. in Heideking 2012, 277).

Good and Bad Qualities of Speaking

Some of Pierce's adjectives were so general as to be of little help. Pierce praised Dayton and Ingersoll for speaking "well"; Few for speaking "tolerably well"; Fitzsimons for speaking "very well"; and Charles Cotesworth Pinckney because "he sometimes speaks well."

Although he used the words "orator" and "oratory" most frequently, Pierce alternated between these terms and "debate" or "public debate," "speaker" or "speaking," which he seemed to use as synonyms. Pierce commended and criticized speakers on at least six somewhat overlapping grounds: their style and eloquence; their command of the facts and logical presentation; their visibility and their effect on the audience; the speakers' manner of delivery; the physical attributes of their voices; and connections between the speakers' speeches and positive elements of their personalities.

People vary as to whether they think oratorical skills are largely innate or learned. Pierce seemed to ally himself with the three leading rhetoricians of the eighteenth century—Hugh Blair, George Campbell, and Richard Whately—who believed that "nurture or training" was required in order "to improve and perfect these inborn traits" (Golden and Corbett 1968, 13). Pierce commented that Dayton "seems desirous of improving himself in Oratory" and suggested that other delegates had allowed their own rhetorical talents to go untested, though they presumably would have improved with a liberal education and/or formal practice or training.

LITERARY STYLE AND ELOQUENCE

Pierce often used terminology that he might just as readily have used with regard to the style of written prose. Pierce frequently mentioned "eloquence," which may also have been intended to identify speaking style. Samuel Johnson defined "oratory" as "[e]loquence; rhetorical skill" (1967, vol. 1), an "oratour" as "a publick speaker; a man of eloquence" (vol. 2), and "eloquence" as "[t]he power of speaking with fluency and elegance; oratory" (ibid.). Johnson further associated eloquence with "fluency" (ibid.).

Pierce found a variety of ways of commending the delegates' rhetoric. He praised Baldwin for his "art and eloquence"; Davie for "considerable literary [writing] talents"; Ellsworth as "eloquent, and connected"; Gorham for being "eloquent and easy"; Hamilton for uniting "the ornaments of fancy" to good judgment and for not being "so defusive as to trifle with the sense" but rambling "just enough to strike and keep up the attention"; Johnson as "eloquent and clear"; King for being "distinguished for his eloquence," "irresistible at times in his eloquence," and "peculiarly strong and rich in his expression"; Madison for being "a most agreeable, eloquent, and convincing Speaker"; Charles Pinckney for speaking "with great neatness and perspicuity"; and Randolph for his "force of eloquence." Pierce also described Hamilton's style as "sometimes didactic" and sometimes "light and tripping"; praised Livingston for his "satyr and a neatness of style"; and identified Mifflin as "a graceful Speaker."

More negatively, Pierce observed that Dickinson was "an indifferent Speaker" whose "language is irregular and incorrect"; Gerry "speaks on, without respect to elegance or flower of diction"; in Gorham's speech there was "nothing fashionable or elegant"; Martin had "a very bad delivery" and was "extremely prolix"; McHenry had no "graces of the Orator"; and Read's speech was "fatiguing and tiresome." Pierce further associated the "oddity" of Sherman's address, which he thought to be both "grotesque and laughable," to "the vulgarisms that accompany his public speaking" and to his "strange New England cant." Almost as though he were describing a fellow artist, Pierce further criticized Sherman for being unable to "embellish."

INFORMATION AND LOGIC

Pierce often associated good speaking with the presentation of relevant information in a comprehensive and logical fashion. Even a speaker with a relatively weak delivery might present compelling arguments. Pierce thus noted that Ellsworth was adept at "selecting such parts of his adversary's arguments as he finds make the strongest impressions,—in order to take off the force of them, so as to admit the power of his own"; Gerry "goes extensively into all subjects that he speaks on," "is connected and sometimes clear in his arguments," and "conceives well"; Gorham aimed "to convince" and promoted "understanding" by being "perspicuous and full"; Hamilton was "able, convincing, and engaging" but more "convincing" than "blazing"; Hamilton further "enquires into every part of his subject with the searchings of phylosophy, and when he comes forward he comes highly charged with interesting manner, there is no skimming over the surface of a subject with him, he must sink to the bottom to see what foundation it rests on"; Ingersoll "comprehends his subject fully"; Johnson was "always abounding with information and instruction"; King was "clear and convincing in his arguments"; Madison relied on "a spirit of industry and application which he possesses in a most eminent degree" to be "the best informed Man of any point in debate"; Mason was "able and convincing in debate"; Gouverneur Morris was "engaged in deep argumentation, that renders all the labor of reasoning easy and pleasing"; Paterson "never speaks but when he understands his subject well"; Charles Pinckney "treats every subject as fully, without running into prolixity, as it requires"; Randolph had a "force of eloquence and reasoning"; Sherman "can furnish thoughts that are wise and useful"; Williamson paid "close attention to most subjects"; Wilson was "clear, copious, and comprehensive" and demonstrated the "force of his reasoning"; and Wythe was a "neat and pleasing Speaker" and "a most correct and able Writer."

By contrast, Pierce believed that Dickinson had "an affected air of wisdom" and "labors to produce a trifle." Similarly, he thought that Houstoun's speech was "confused and irregular."

SPEAKERS' VOICES AND MANNER OF DELIVERY

In addition to the many references to eloquence, Pierce sometimes focused on the speakers' voices and their delivery. He praised Bedford for his "very commanding and striking manner"; Gorham for having "an agreeable and pleasing manner"; Johnson for being "eloquent and clear"; King for having "a sweet high toned voice"; Madison for having "a most agreeable style of conversation"; and Randolph for having "a most harmonious voice." Pierce observed that Gouverneur Morris "winds through all the mazes of rhetoric, and throws around him such a glare that he charms, captivates, and leads away the senses of all who hear him." Pierce also referred to Morris's "infinite stretch of fancy" and to his ability to "engage the attention" of his audience. Robert Morris had a reputation for speaking that "bears down all before him"; Paterson was "very happy in the choice of time and manner of engaging in a debate"; and Charles Pinckney avoided "running into prolixity."

From a more negative perspective, and with considerably greater literary flair, Pierce observed that Dickinson's "flourishes . . . are like expiring flames, they just shew themselves and go out;—no traces of them are left on the mind to clear or animate it." Pierce noted that there was "something too feeble" in Hamilton's voice "to be equal to the strains of oratory" and that he "rambles just enough to strike and keep up the attention"; Gerry's speech was "hesitating and laborious" and lacked "elegance or flower of diction"; and Lansing showed a certain "hesitation" in his speaking. Pierce observed that Martin was so "prolix" that "he never speaks without tiring the patience of all who hear him"; Read's "voice is feeble," his "articulation so bad," and his oratory was "fatiguing and tiresome to the last degree" such that "few can have patience to attend to" it; Rutledge was "too rapid in his public speaking to be denominated an agreeable Orator"; and Strong's voice was "feeble" and "without confidence." Perhaps surprisingly, just as he identified only one individual as an immigrant, Pierce made no direct references to accents (unless he intended to do so when he mentioned Sherman's "strange New England cant"), which must then, as now, have varied considerably, especially between the North and the South.

TIES TO CHARACTER TRAITS

Aristotle stressed the importance of ethical appeals based on the character of the speaker. The Latin rhetorician Quintilian (ca. A.D. 35–100) was known for describing an effective speaker as "a good man speaking" (qtd. in Golden and Corbett 1968, 4). Similarly, Pierce sometimes tied characteristics of delegates' speaking to their personalities. Immediately after describing Bedford's speech, Pierce thus observed that Bedford "was warm and impetuous in his temper, and precipitate in his judgment." Pierce said that Broom's private speech was "chearful and conversable"; Ellsworth was "very happy in a reply"; Franklin's story telling was "engaging"; Johnson had an "affectionate style of address" to his friends; and Gouverneur Morris "charms" and captivates" but was "fickle and inconstant,—never pursuing one train of thinking,—nor ever regular." Pierce also noted that Gerry "possesses a great degree of confidence," whereas Strong was "without confidence." Pierce observed a "rudeness of manner" in King's otherwise exemplary speaking and noted that Wilson's speech depended on "the force of his reasoning" rather than on "the charm of his eloquence."

Summary

While we have notes on what the delegates said, we have fewer reports of how they said it. If Pierce has contributed nothing else to our knowledge of the delegates, his descriptions of their rhetoric are invaluable. Although the proceedings were closed to the public, Pierce's notes suggest that the delegates did not view their task as a mere logical exercise and that they, especially the more accomplished speakers, attempted to appeal not only to the minds but also to the emotions and hearts of their audience.

NOTES

1. "Pierce's Notes on His Constitutional Convention Colleagues." *Colonial Williamsburg* 36 (Spring): 41–45.1. Such rules, designed to promote civility, were similar to and may well have been patterned after rules that Thomas Jefferson drafted for the Continental Congress. Meacham (2012, 111) observes that the rules included the following: "No Member shall read any printed paper in the House during the sitting thereof without Leave of the Congress"; "No Member in coming into the House or in removing from his Place shall pass between the President and the Member then speaking"; and "When the House is sitting no Member

shall speak [or whisper] to another as to interrupt any Member who may be speaking in the Debate."

2. By contrast, John Neal of Maine published short sketches of presidential candidates in an article for *Blackwood's Magazine* of May 1824, "Sketches of the Five American Presidents and of the Five Presidential Candidates," in which he barely mentioned the subject (Daggett 1920, 24–27).

3. It is important to remember that delegates who were not particularly comfortable with public speaking may nonetheless have exerted influence on other delegates by facial expressions, simply by casting their votes (votes were not recorded under individual names at the convention), or in private conversations in their lodgings or at meals that would not be reflected in the notes of the convention itself. Pierce's anecdote about Washington's displeasure when a delegate dropped his notes and Pierce's account of talking to Franklin about his age are not otherwise reflected in the records. Similarly, after Gerry proposed limiting a standing army to 3,000 men, "Washington is alleged to have suggested a counter-motion that 'no foreign enemy should invade the United States at any time, with more than three thousand troops'" (Hutson 1987, 229, quoting Paul Wilstach, *Patriots Off Their Pedestals* [reprint ed., Freeport, N.Y.: Books for Libraries Press, 1970], 29).

4. Eighteenth-century elocutionists put an emphasis on delivery, which sometimes "contributed to the separation of form and content" (Moran 1994, 3).

5. I have been unable to ascertain the basis of Pierce's judgment of Davie's literary talents since he was not, in my mind, associated with any particularly noteworthy public document.

6. The editor of "Notes of Major William Pierce" (1898, 332) observed that Pierce was not completely correct on this point. Indeed, in addition to seconding a number of motions, Davie appears to have spoken on June 30 (Farrand 1966, 1:487–488), July 6 (1:542), and July 12 (1:593). This could be evidence that Pierce's last day at the convention was June 29, although it could also indicate that he simply wrote his sketch of Davie earlier and did not later amend it.

7. In a remarkable parallel, John Leland, a Baptist minister who supported Madison for his advocacy of religious liberty, observed of his speaking style that "after stating, in the clearest manner, the positions and arguments of his opponent, if that opponent had omitted any thing that would strengthen his side of the case, he would add it, and then proceed to meet and answer the whole" (Grau 2008, 30).

8. By way of comparison, in an unattributed quotation about Rutledge, Coleman (1910, 464) reported, "His ideas were clear and strong; his utterance rapid, but distinct; his active and energetic manner of speaking forcibly impressed his sentiments on the mind and heart; and he successfully used both wit and argument in his impassioned style of public address."

9. After observing that the speech on June 27 was "more than three hours," Madison noted that Martin "was too much exhausted . . . to finish his remarks" (Farrand 1966, 1:438). The following day, he observed that Gerry delivered a continuation of the speech "with much diffuseness & considerable vehemence." In an essay first published under the title "The Landholder" on February 29, 1788, Oliver Ellsworth was even more critical of Martin (although he seems to have been incorrect in believing that Martin had given his speech on the day of his arrival at the convention):

> The day you took your seat must be long remembered by those who were present; nor will it be possible for you to forget the astonishment your behavior almost instan-

taneously produced. You had scarcely time to read the proposition which had been agreed to after the fullest investigation, when, without requesting information, or to be let into the reasons of the adoption of what you might not approve, you opened against them in a speech which held during two days, and which might have continued two months, but for those marks of fatigue and disgust you saw strongly expressed on whichever side of the house you turned your mortified eyes. There needed no other display to fix your character and the rank of your abilities, which the Convention would have confirmed by the most distinguished silence, had not a certain similarity in genius provoked a sarcastic reply from the pleasant Mr. Gerry; in which he admired the strength of your lungs and your profound knowledge in the first principles of government; mixing and illustrating his little remarks with a profusion of those hems, that never fail to lengthen out and enliven oratory. This reply (from your intimate acquaintance), the match being so equal and the contrast so comic, had the happy effect to put the house in good humor, and leave you a prey to the most humiliating reflections. But this did not teach you to bound your future speeches by the lines of moderation; for the very next day you exhibited without a blush another specimen of eternal volubility. It was not, however, to the duration of your speeches you owed the perfection of your reputation. (Farrand 1966, 3:271–272)

REFERENCES

Coleman, Nannie McCormick. 1910. *The Constitution and Its Framers*. Chicago: Progress.

"Constitutional Convention, 1787." 1861. *Historical Magazine*, 1st ser., 5 (January):18.

Coulter, E. Merton. 1987. *Abraham Baldwin: Patriot, Educator, and Founding Father*. Arlington, Va.: Vandamer.

Current, Richard Nelson. 1990. *Phi Beta Kappa in American Life: The First Two Hundred Years*. New York: Oxford University Press.

Daggett, Windson. 1920. *A Down-East Yankee from the District of Maine*. Portland, Maine: A. J. Huston.

Farrand, Max, ed. 1966. *The Records of the Federal Convention of 1787*. 4 vols. New Haven, Conn.: Yale University Press.

Golden, James L., and Edward P. J. Corbett. 1968. "Introduction." In *The Rhetoric of Blair, Campbell, and Whatley*, edited by James L. Golden and Edward P. J. Corbett, 1–17. New York: Holt, Rinehart and Winston.

Grasso, Christopher. 1999. *A Speaking Aristocracy: Transforming Public Discourse in Eighteenth-Century Connecticut*. Chapel Hill: University of North Carolina Press.

Grau, Craig. 2008. "More than an Intellectual Scribe: The Political Drives and Traits of James Madison." In *James Madison: Philosopher, Founder and Statesman*, edited by John R. Vile, William D. Pederson, and Frank J. Williams, 21–36. Athens: Ohio University Press.

Hall, Mark David. 2012. *Roger Sherman and the Creation of the American Republic*. New York: Oxford University Press.

Heideking, Jurgen. 2012. *The Constitution before the Judgment Seat: The Prehistory and Ratification of the American Constitution, 1787–1791*. Ed. John P. Kaminski and Richard Leffler. Charlottesville: University of Virginia Press.

Hutson, James H., ed. 1987. *Supplement to Max Farrand's The Records of the Federal Convention of 1787*. New Haven, Conn.: Yale University Press.

Johnson, Samuel. 1967. *A Dictionary of the English Language*. 1755. 2 vols. Reprint, New York: AMS.

Jones, Charles C., Jr. 1891. *Biographical Sketches of the Delegates from Georgia to the Continental Congress*. Boston: Houghton, Mifflin.

Mahaffey, Jerome Dean. 1957. *Preaching Politics: The Religious Rhetoric of George Whitefield and the Founding of a New Nation*. Waco, Tex.: Baylor University Press.

Mahoney, John L. 1958. "The Classical Tradition in Eighteenth Century English Rhetorical Education." *History of Education Journal* 9 (Summer):93–97.

Meacham, Jon. 2012. *Thomas Jefferson: The Art of Power*. New York: Random House.

Moran, Michael G. 1994. *Eighteenth-Century British and American Rhetoric and Rhetoricians: Critical Studies and Sources*. Westport, Conn.: Greenwood.

"Notes of Major William Pierce on the Federal Convention of 1787." 1898. *American Historical Review* 3 (January):310–334.

"The Original Phi Beta Kappa Records." 1919. *Phi Beta Kappa Key* (May):546–554, 599–625.

Rakove, Jack. 2009. *Revolutionaries: A New History of the Invention of America*. New York: Houghton Mifflin Harcourt.

Richard, Carl J. 1994. *The Founders and the Classics: Greece, Rome, and the American Enlightenment*. Cambridge, Mass.: Harvard University Press.

Vile, John R. 2014. "Ridicule, Scorn, and Approbation: Delegate William Pierce's Notes on His Constitutional Convention Colleagues," *Colonial Williamsburg* (Spring 2014): 41–45.

CHAPTER 6

Pierce's Analysis of Military and Public Service, Other Occupations, and Miscellaneous Matters

Power dies away; great Offices disappear; praise itself is transitory; forgetfulness, lassitude, inconstancy, and levity all conspire to disperse it; and nothing will remain with the Minister but faint and melancholy images of the great Offices he filled, if in a happy or at least peaceful private station he cannot recall to his mind some honorable actions which may exalt him in his own Eyes.

—Jacques Necker, *Treatise on the Administration of the Finances of France* (as quoted in *Pierce's Reliques*)

When in *The Old Regime and the French Revolution* (1955, 138–147), Alexis de Tocqueville examined the backgrounds of those who were most influential in the French Revolution, he discovered that few were men of practical experience. By contrast, those who attended the U.S. Constitutional Convention were men of broad political experience, many of whom had developed a nationalistic perspective from their service in the military. Although his observations were far from complete, Pierce, who served in the Revolutionary War and was a member of the Society of the Cincinnati, often made reference to the delegates' military experiences.

Military Service

Wright and MacGregor (1987, 59–130) identified twenty-two of the signers of the Constitution (Abraham Baldwin, Richard Bassett, William Blount, David Brearly, Pierce Butler, Jonathan Dayton, John Dickinson, William Few, Thomas Fitzsimons, Nicholas Gilman, Alexander Hamilton, Rufus King, John Langdon, William Livingston, James McHenry, Thomas Mifflin, Gouverneur Morris, Charles Pinckney, Charles Cotesworth Pinckney, Richard Dobbs Spaight, George Washington, and Hugh Williamson) and the secretary of the convention, William Jackson, as serving either in the Continental or in militia forces. Eight nonsigner participants (270–271) also served (William Richardson Davie, William Churchill Houston, John Lansing, Alexander Martin, James McClurg, John Mercer, William Pierce, and Edmund Randolph). By contrast, Pierce only cited the military service of nine, and one of his comments was negative. It appears that he may have focused chiefly on individuals whom he had personally met during the war.

JONATHAN DAYTON (N.J.): "served with me as a Brother Aid to General Sullivan[1] in the Western expedition of '79"

ALEXANDER HAMILTON (N.Y.): "Col. Hamilton"

DANIEL OF ST. THOMAS JENIFER (Md.): "once served as an Aid de Camp to Major Genl. [Charles] Lee" [1731–1782]

ALEXANDER MARTIN (N.C.): "Mr. Martin was once a Colonel in the American Army, but proved unfit for the field"[2]

JAMES MCHENRY (Md.): "but he afterwards turned Soldier and acted as Aid to Genl. Washington and the Marquis de la Fayette"

THOMAS MIFFLIN (Pa.): "General Mifflin"; "The General"

WILLIAM PIERCE (Ga.): "I am conscious of having discharged my duty as a Soldier through the course of the late revolution with honor and propriety"

CHARLES COTESWORTH PINCKNEY (S.C.): "Mr. Pinckney was an Officer of high rank in the American army, and served with great reputation through the War"

GEORGE WASHINGTON (Va.): "Genl. Washington is well known as the Commander in chief of the late American Army"; "like Cincinnatus he returned to his farm perfectly contented with being only a plain Citizen, after enjoying the highest honor of the Confederacy"; "The General"

Pierce's identification of Jenifer as an aide of Major General Charles Lee was mistaken; Pierce appears to have confused Jenifer with Maryland's John Francis Mercer, one of the two delegates about whom Pierce wrote no sketches (Leffler, Kaminski, and Fore 2012, 48). It seems a bit odd that Pierce did not include his own ranks, which had included both major and captain. Although some delegates, Washington among them, had served during the French and Indian War, Pierce concentrated on those who had served during the Revolution. Pierce's references to the "American army" point away from local and state militias to Continental forces.

Service in Civilian Legislative
or Executive Offices

At the federal level, it is common today to distinguish elected members of the legislative and executive branches from those who are appointed to the judiciary, but under the Articles of Confederation, state legislatures appointed the members of Congress rather than allowing the people to elect them directly. Despite this, legislators at both the state and national levels were involved in the exercise of political skills as were governors and individuals who represented their states in other capacities. Pierce identified the following members as having held legislative or executive offices:

ABRAHAM BALDWIN (Ga.): "has been twice a Member of Congress"

WILLIAM BLOUNT (N.C.): "He has been twice a Member of Congress, and in that office discharged his duty with ability and faithfulness"

PIERCE BUTLER (S.C.): "He has been appointed to Congress, and is now a Member of the Legislature of South Carolina"

WILLIAM FEW (Ga.): "He has been twice a Member of Congress"

THOMAS FITZSIMONS (Pa.): "speaks very well I am told, in the Legislature of Pennsylvania"

NATHANIEL GORHAM (Mass.): "He has been President of Congress, and three years a Member of that Body"

WILLIAM HOUSTOUN (Ga.): "has been Member of Congress for the State of Georgia"

WILLIAM SAMUEL JOHNSON (Conn.): "He was once employed as an Agent for the State of Connecticut to state her claims to certain landed territory before the British House of Commons; this Office he discharged with so much dignity, and made such an ingenious display of his powers, that he laid the foundation of a reputation which will probably last much longer than his own life"

RUFUS KING (Mass.): "He has served for three years in the Congress of the United States with great and deserved applause"

JOHN LANSING (N.Y.): "Mr. Lansing is . . . Mayor of that Corporation [city of Albany]";

WILLIAM LIVINGSTON (N.J.): "Governor Livingston"

JAMES MADISON (Va.): "a character who has long been in public life"; "He has been twice a Member of Congress, and was always thought one of the ablest Members that ever sat in that Council" [Madison had actually served three prior terms in this capacity, and was also a member during the sitting of the convention]

ALEXANDER MARTIN (N.C.): "Mr. Martin was lately Governor of North Carolina, which office he filled with credit"

LUTHER MARTIN (Md.): "is Attorney general for the State of Maryland"

WILLIAM PIERCE (Ga.): "my services in Congress and the Convention were bestowed with the best intention towards the interest of Georgia, and towards the general welfare of the Confederacy"

CHARLES PINCKNEY (S.C.): "He has been a Member of Congress, and served in that Body with ability and eclat"

EDMUND RANDOLPH (Va.): "Mr. Randolph is Governor of Virginia"

JOHN RUTLEDGE (S.C.): "his reputation in the first Congress gave him a distinguished rank among the American Worthies"; "Mr. Rutledge was once Governor of South Carolina"

ROGER SHERMAN (Conn.): "He has been several years a Member of Congress, and discharged the duties of his Office with honor and credit to himself, and advantage to the State he represented"

Service at the Bar or on the Bench

The practice of law provides publicity for attorneys and flexibility in the schedules of practitioners seeking public offices, and a fair number of the delegates to the Constitutional Convention, like many members of contemporary legislatures, were members of the legal profession. Although missing from online versions, Pierce used the terms "Esqr." or "Esquire" to describe delegates from numerous states. Samuel Johnson traced this term to "[t]he armour-bearer or attendant on a knight" and said that it was "[a] title of dignity, and next in degree below a knight" (1967, vol. 1). Although people today sometimes use this term to describe lawyers, Pierce seems to have used it fairly inclusively as a term for gentlemen, while also including more specific references to delegates with legal training or professions:

ABRAHAM BALDWIN (Ga.): "He is a practising Attorney in Georgia"

GUNNING BEDFORD (Del.): "Mr. Bedford was educated for the Bar, and in his profession, I am told, has merit"

JOHN BLAIR (Va.): "He is one of the Judges of the Supreme Court in Virginia, and acknowledged to have a very extensive knowledge of the Laws"

DAVID BREARLY (N.J.): "He is a Judge of the Supreme Court of New Jersey"

GEORGE CLYMER (Pa.): "Mr. Clymer is a Lawyer of some abilities"

WILLIAM RICHARDSON DAVIE (N.C.): "Mr. Davey is a Lawyer of some eminence in his State"

OLIVER ELLSWORTH (Conn.): "Mr. Elsworth is a Judge of the Supreme Court in Connecticut"

WILLIAM FEW (Ga.): "Mr. Few . . . from application has acquired some knowledge of legal matters;—he practices at the bar of Georgia"

ALEXANDER HAMILTON (N.Y.): "He is a practitioner of the Law"

WILLIAM HOUSTOUN (Ga.): "Mr. Houstoun is an Attorney at Law"

JARED INGERSOLL (Pa.): "Mr. Ingersol is a very able Attorney, and possesses a clear legal understanding"

JOHN LANSING (N.Y.): "Mr. Lansing is a practicing Attorney at Albany, and Mayor of that Corporation"

LUTHER MARTIN (Md.): "was educated for the Bar, and is Attorney general for the State of Maryland"

WILLIAM PATERSON (N.J.): "a Classic, a Lawyer, and an Orator"

GEORGE READ (Del.): "Mr. Read is a Lawyer and a Judge;—his legal abilities are said to be very great"

JOHN RUTLEDGE (S.C.): "He was bred to the Law, and now acts as one of the Chancellors of South Carolina"

ROGER SHERMAN (Conn.): "I am told he sits on the Bench in Connecticut, and is very correct in the discharge of his judicial functions"

CALEB STRONG (Mass.): "Mr. Strong is a Lawyer of some eminence"

GEORGE WYTHE (Va.): "Mr. Wythe is the famous Professor of Law at the University of William and Mary"

ROBERT YATES (N.Y.): "Mr. Yates is said to be an able Judge. He is a Man of great legal abilities"

Analysis

In describing delegates, Pierce identified individuals who served as judges on the supreme courts of Connecticut, New Jersey, and Virginia, and others who sat on the bench in Connecticut, Delaware, and South Carolina. He identified Luther Martin as the attorney general of Maryland and John Lansing as the mayor of Albany. Pierce singled out eleven delegates (including himself) as having served in Congress, one of whom (Gorham) had been its president. He identified two delegates as serving as state legislators, one as a state's agent to Great Britain, and four as having been governors.

The delegates in Philadelphia were very politically experienced, and Pierce could have identified many of them as having held far more offices than he indicated. Experience with state constitutions played an important role in providing guidance for the U.S. Constitution (Dinan 2006; Adams 2001; Baum and Fritz 2000; Conley and Kaminsky 1988; Kruman 1997; Levinson 2012). Perhaps because he did not know and had not himself so participated, he did not mention any of their roles in formulating state constitutions and/or declarations of rights—George Mason, for example, was the chief author of the Virginia Declaration of Rights

(Rutland 1961, 49–61)—which might have further supported his positive assessment of the experience and wisdom that the convention embodied.

Other Occupations

Although all the delegates were participating in an event that would affect the future of the nation, not all of them were chiefly known for their actions on the public stage. Pierce identified a number of them for their work as merchants, as doctors, or in other professions. Some delegates combined work in a profession with political service. In language that seems a bit odd, on a number of occasions, Pierce distinguished the profession for which a delegate was "bred," for example, law or medicine, with the occupation the delegate was practicing at the time of the convention.

MERCHANTS OR RELATED TRADES

Pierce did not take the opportunity in his sketches to identify himself as a merchant, but he did cite a number of other delegates in this occupation. All of his descriptions seem positive.

THOMAS FITZSIMONS (Pa.): "Mr. Fitzsimons is a Merchant of considerable talents"

ELBRIDGE GERRY (Mass.): "he has been engaged in the mercantile line and is a Man of property"

NATHANIEL GORHAM (Mass.): "Mr. Gorham is a Merchant in Boston"

GOUVERNEUR MORRIS (Pa.): "He was bred to the Law, but I am told he disliked the profession, and turned merchant. He is engaged in some great mercantile matters with his namesake Mr. Robt. Morris"

ROBERT MORRIS (Pa.): "Robert Morris is a merchant of great eminence and wealth; an able Financier"

Numerous delegates at the convention, including James Wilson and Robert Morris (both of whom ended up in bankruptcy), were engaged in land speculation. Pierce mentioned neither this nor related activities.

COLLEGE PROFESSORS, SCIENTISTS, AND MEDICAL DOCTORS

BENJAMIN FRANKLIN (Pa.): "all the operations of nature he seems to understand,—the very heavens obey him, and the Clouds yield up their Lightning to be imprisoned in his rod"

WILLIAM SAMUEL JOHNSON (Conn.): "Dr. Johnson"

JAMES MCCLURG (Va.): "is a learned physician"; "The Doctor"

JAMES MCHENRY (Md.): "was bred a physician"

GEORGE WYTHE (Va.): "Mr. Wythe is the famous Professor of Law at the University of William and Mary"

Although Pierce identified these five delegates with academic or medical titles or pursuits, Pierce did not mention that fellow Georgian Abraham Baldwin (whom he had incorrectly identified as having graduated from Harvard) had tutored at Yale (his real alma mater) nor that James Wilson, whom he celebrated for his legal knowledge, taught at the University of Pennsylvania. Pierce did not identify Dr. Johnson as having recently accepted the presidency of King's College, nor did he mention that a number of delegates, especially Franklin and Baldwin (though most of his work came later), were associated with the founding of colleges. Pierce did not mention that Hugh Williamson had also been trained and served as a medical doctor and scientist.

FARMERS

JOHN DICKINSON (Del.): "has been famed through all America, for his Farmers Letters"

GEORGE WASHINGTON (Va.): "like Cincinnatus he returned to his farm perfectly contented with being only a plain Citizen"

OTHER OCCUPATIONS

ROGER SHERMAN (Conn.): "In the early part of his life he was a Shoe-maker;—but despising the lowness of his condition, he turned Almanack maker, and so progressed upwards to a Judge"[3]

Analysis

The most remarkable aspect of Pierce's descriptions of occupations was that the only person that he directly associated with agriculture was George Washington (though, as indicated above, Pierce did associate Dickinson with authorship of the Farmers Letters), and one would never know from Pierce's description that Washington's "farm" was a major plantation. Although Pierce described Washington chiefly as a general, he also likened him to Cincinnatus. By contrast, the historian Forrest McDonald (1985) has identified eighteen of the delegates as farmers, and he believes that thirteen of thirty-four who were lawyers chiefly worked with farmers (summarized in Vile 2005, 2:541). David Bernstein identified thirteen of the delegates as planters or large-scale farmers and another two as small farmers (1987, 13).

Pierce clearly knew about the role of agriculture. Not only was he the son of a planter, but he also married a planter's daughter with whom he owned a plantation. Moreover, in his Fourth of July Oration of 1788, he specifically noted that his countrymen who had won the war against Great Britain had been "bred as we were in the toils of agriculture, accustomed only to the reap hook and the plough" (Kaminski and Saladino 1995, 251). In addition, the notebook with his character sketches contains a sophisticated essay on botany. It is possible that Pierce simply did not think that farming skills were especially relevant to the convention's deliberations although this did not prevent him from referring to other occupations, like medicine. Intentionally or otherwise, by omitting any discussion of plantation owners, Pierce did not include the fact that some of the delegates owned slaves, although this was especially common among the landed gentry, particularly in the South. Seventeen to nineteen delegates, including Pierce, were slave owners (Vile 2005, 2:726), and in a letter of July 14, 1785, he wrote to Edward Carrington inquiring as to whether "Negroes can be purchased in Virginia?" and noting that he had much need for "between 20 and 30 Negroes in a rice field about four miles from Savannah" (R693, Manuscript File, National Archives; kindly brought to my attention by Samuel K. Fore). A notice of Pierce's death—doubtless not by one of his slaves (Jones 1891, 158)—observed that he had been an "endearing husband, a kind master." One can only speculate whether slavery was so well known and ubiquitous that Pierce ignored it or whether Pierce sought to enhance the status of the convention delegates by omitting mention of the fact, which would not have reflected positively on the delegates in some quarters.

The only individual whom Pierce identified as an artisan or craftsman was Roger Sherman, who had, according to Pierce, so despised his condition that he raised himself to another. There is a possibility that this passage is somewhat autobiographical. John Singleton Copley, a noted artist writing not quite ten years before Pierce set up his own studio, observed that people tended to regard the art of painting "like that of a Carpenter tailor, or shew [shoe] maker" rather than "as one of the most noble Arts in the World" (qtd. in Rather 1997, 269). It is certainly possible that Pierce was anxious to put what he might have regarded as a humbling role as an artist behind him.

The only two individuals whom Pierce directly associated with ambition were Jonathan Dayton—"a young Gentleman of talents, with ambition to exert them"—and himself: "I possess ambition."[4] Given that he applied the term to himself, it is unlikely that he intended it to denote something negative. It seems more in line with Samuel Johnson's definition of being "desirous of advancement; eager of honours; aspiring" (1967, vol. 1). Perhaps Pierce associated ambition with the more widely attributed desire among the Founding Fathers for fame. Although others did, Pierce did not associate this particular quality with Alexander Hamilton,[5] at least not in his sketches—though such a judgment could account for his reference to Hamilton's vanity.

Work Ethic

Pierce sometimes mentioned that a delegate had done particularly good work, or enhanced his reputation in a job, but he singled out a few for their overall industry. It might be appropriate to tie these comments to those he made about delegates' ambitions.

> JAMES MADISON (Va.): "From a spirit of industry and application which he possesses in a most eminent degree, he always comes forward the best informed Man of any point in debate"
>
> CHARLES PINCKNEY (S.C.): "has a spirit of application and industry beyond most Men"
>
> ROGER SHERMAN (Conn.): "In the early part of his life he was a Shoe-maker;—but despising the lowness of his condition, he turned Almanack maker, and so progressed upwards to a Judge"

As noted previously, Pierce also observed that Dayton "seems desirous of improving himself in Oratory."

Miscellaneous Points and Omissions

At a time when those of European ancestry were encroaching on the lands of Native Americans, when women did not have full participatory rights, and when most Americans of African ancestry were slaves, it is unsurprising that Pierce made no special note of their absence from the convention and may even have attempted to minimize the existence of slavery by not directly identifying convention delegates as planters. One of the issues that the delegates to the convention discussed was the admission of new states into the Union. Pierce's classification of delegates according to states is an indirect indication that frontier areas unaffiliated with such states (unlike today's Tennessee and Kentucky, which were then respectively part of North Carolina and Virginia) were not directly represented.

Although such affiliations might have been widely known, the only delegates that Pierce specifically associated with individual cities were Nathaniel Gorham (Mass.), whose mercantile business he connected with Boston, and Robert Yates (N.Y.), whom he identified as the mayor of Albany. Intentionally or otherwise, by minimizing such associations, Pierce may have downplayed conflicts (such as those in his own state and those that would be revealed during the Federalist/Anti-Federalist debates) between residents of coastal areas and cities and residents in the interior.

Religious Affiliation

Pierce's analysis provides little information to researchers interested in the religious affiliations of the delegates (a particular concern of Bradford 1994), since he only referred directly to the religious connections of two delegates. He described Richard Bassett (Del.) as "a religious enthusiast, lately turned Methodist," and identified John Dickinson (Del.) as having been "bred a Quaker."[6]

Pierce's description of Bassett, which may have been based in part on Bassett's decision to free his slaves and to advocate that others do the same, was probably not a compliment. Samuel Johnson defined "enthusiasm" as "a vain belief of private revelation; a vain confidence of divine favour or communication," as "[h]eat of imagination; violence of passion; confidence of opinion," and as "[e]levation of fancy; exaltation of ideas" (1967, vol. 1). Pierce was an Episcopalian, and it is possible that he intended to damn Bassett with faint praise when he also noted that he "is in high estimation among the Methodists" (implying, perhaps, not among others). Since the term "cant" can refer either to a dialect or to moralizing or excessive piety,[7] Pierce's mention of Sherman's "New England cant" may have been an indirect reference to Sherman's reputation for piety, which Pierce may well have seen as a holier-than-thou old-style Puritanism.[8]

The paucity of religious references suggests that Pierce was either unfamiliar with the religious affiliations of other delegates or that he considered them to be relatively unimportant in this kind of gathering. Had Pierce been more observant, he could have noted the piety of Oliver Ellsworth, the Roman Catholic affiliations of Daniel Carroll and Thomas Fitzsimons, and Abraham Baldwin's service as a chaplain during the Revolutionary War. It is possible that Pierce's failure to be more explicit about such affiliations continues to influence contemporary scholarship on the framers, which tends to focus on the deism of a few leading participants rather than on what may have been the conventional piety of the larger group.[9]

Immigrant Status

Eight of the delegates to the Constitutional Convention were immigrants. Pierce Butler (S.C.), Thomas Fitzsimons (Pa.), James McHenry (Md.), and William Paterson (N.J.) were all from Ireland; William Richardson Davie (N.C.) and Robert Morris (Pa.) came from England; Alexander Hamilton (N.Y.) immigrated from the British West Indies; and James Wilson (Pa.) had been born in Scotland. However, the only delegate that Pierce identified as foreign-born was Butler, whose country of origin Pierce correctly identified. The United States was and remains a nation of immigrants, and it is possible that Georgia, the most recently settled of the thirteen states, had so many immigrants—and/or that, as a merchant, Pierce was so used to dealing with them—that this particular feature did not stand out in his observations. Alternatively, he may have sought to enhance the delegates' reputations by minimizing references to their foreign origins.

Signers of Other Documents

Many treatments of convention delegates specifically identify the individuals who attended who also signed other important founding documents. The delegates to the convention who had signed the Declaration of Independence were George Clymer (Pa.), Benjamin Franklin (Pa.), Elbridge Gerry (Mass.), Robert Morris (Pa.), George Read (Del.), Roger Sherman (Conn.), James Wilson (Pa.), and George Wythe (Va.). Perhaps as notably, John Dickinson, who had opposed British abuses of colonists' liberties leading up to 1776, had refused to sign the Declaration of Independence, which he thought was too precipitate.

Although Pierce made a generic reference to the fact that "many of those illustrious characters" also "grace[d] the scroll of Independence" with their signatures in his oration of July 4, 1788 (Kaminski and Saladino 1995, 251), he did not mention this in his sketches. Similarly, he did not say that John Dickinson (Del.), Elbridge Gerry (Mass.), Gouverneur Morris (then N.Y.), Robert Morris (Pa.), and Roger Sherman (Conn.) had signed the Articles of Confederation—indeed, Dickinson had been the primary author of that document. If Pierce's omission signaled that he did not consider such signatures to be particularly important, this could further illumine his written explanation as to why he made no apparent effort to return to sign the Constitution.

Marital Status and Family

Few delegates to the convention were unmarried; Abraham Baldwin, Nicholas Gilman, Daniel of St. Thomas Jenifer, and Alexander Martin remained so, but at the time, James Madison and Gouverneur Morris were among their ranks. Pierce cited

Nathaniel Gorham, rather than Gouverneur Morris (who had the most notorious reputation as a ladies' man),[10] as being "rather lusty." Almost as though he were defending him against speculation that he might be misogynistic or gay, Pierce noted of Jenifer both that "[f]rom his long continuance in single life, no doubt but he has made the vow of celibacy"[11] and that "[h]e speaks warmly of the Ladies notwithstanding." This was the only time that Pierce mentioned women in his sketches.

Although some wives accompanied their husbands to Philadelphia, Pierce mentioned neither them nor any of the delegates' children.[12] By contrast, Charles Willson Peale, under whom Pierce had studied, was well known for his portraits not only of famous statesmen, but also of their families (Marks 2012).

Issues of Substance at the Constitutional Convention

As indicated by Pierce's account of George Washington's reaction to a delegate's loss of a manuscript, the convention was under a veil of secrecy that most delegates took very seriously.[13] Madison's notes of the convention were not published until after his death. Pierce's own sketches remained unpublished until 1828. Pierce's work revealed almost nothing about the deliberations at the convention or points of substance. He did mention that Washington was unanimously selected as chair of the convention, but that appears to have been common knowledge. Federalist supporters of the Constitution did everything they could to associate Franklin and Washington in the public mind with the new document.

Although Pierce identified Randolph as having come "forward with the postulate, or first principles, on which the Convention acted," Pierce did not specifically identify what these principles were. With a sense for practical politics, he observed of James Madison, "In the management of every great question he evidently took the lead in the Convention." But Pierce did not mention the controversies between small states and large states over representation and between northern and southern states over slavery, nor did he mention the debates over terms of office, the method of selecting the president, and the like.

Pierce reported the rumor that Yates, who left the convention on July 10, was an Anti-Federalist. Although Pierce did not believe the rumor to be true (thus indicating that he probably wrote his sketches before the Federalist/Anti-Federalist debates during which Yates's position would have been obvious), Yates confirmed it in a critical report about the convention that he and Lansing wrote to the New York governor (Farrand 1966, 3:244–247).

Summary

Here is a summary of the types of information that Pierce provided about each delegate:

ABRAHAM BALDWIN (Ga.) [Pierce had limited time to observe at the convention]: abilities, speaking, education, occupation, political office, age

RICHARD BASSETT (Del.): religious affiliation, personal characteristics, silence, reputation, age

GUNNING BEDFORD (Del.): education, occupation, speaking, temperament, age, weight

JOHN BLAIR JR. (Va.): reputation, family and wealth, occupation, knowledge, speaking, character, age

WILLIAM BLOUNT (N.C.) [Pierce had limited time to observe at the convention]: character, political office, speaking, talents, age

DAVID BREARLY (N.J.): abilities, public office, reputation, speaking, virtues, age

JACOB BROOM (Del.): abilities, speaking, age

PIERCE BUTLER (S.C.): reputation, character, speaking, political abilities, wealth, office, age, national origin

DANIEL CARROLL (Md.) [Pierce was unable to observe at the convention]: fortune, influence, abilities, reputation

GEORGE CLYMER (Pa.): occupation, reputation, age

WILLIAM RICHARDSON DAVIE (N.C.): occupation, education, abilities, silence, reputation, age

JONATHAN DAYTON (N.J.) [Pierce had limited time to observe at the convention]: talents, ambition, education, speaking, character, reputation, age, military service

JOHN DICKINSON (Del.): reputation, writing, knowledge, speaking abilities, reputation, age, religious upbringing

OLIVER ELLSWORTH (Conn.): office, learning, speaking abilities, age, reputation, personal qualities

WILLIAM FEW (Ga.): abilities, knowledge, profession, speaking skills, office, reputation, age

THOMAS FITZSIMONS (Pa.): occupation, talents, speaking skills, office, age

BENJAMIN FRANKLIN (Pa.): reputation, knowledge, political abilities, speaking abilities, virtues, chronological and mental ages

ELBRIDGE GERRY (Mass.): character, speaking abilities, patriotism, occupation, property, age

NICHOLAS GILMAN (N.H.): [Pierce was unable to observe at the convention]: personal characteristics, virtues, age

NATHANIEL GORHAM (Mass.): occupation, reputation, education, speaking abilities, office, age, personal characteristics

ALEXANDER HAMILTON (N.Y.): reputation, talents, occupation, education, speaking abilities, age, physical characteristics, personality

WILLIAM CHURCHILL HOUSTON (N.J.) [Pierce had limited time to observe at the convention]: no report

WILLIAM HOUSTOUN (Ga.): profession, offices, family, place of education, political knowledge, physical characteristics, speaking abilities, age, temperament, principles

JARED INGERSOLL (Pa.): occupation, understanding, education, speaking abilities, character, age

DANIEL OF ST. THOMAS JENIFER (Md.): fortune, personality, silence, political skills, marital status, age, military service

WILLIAM SAMUEL JOHNSON (Conn.): knowledge, education, speaking abilities, office, age, temperament

RUFUS KING (Mass.): political skills, education, knowledge, office, age, physical characteristics, speaking abilities, reputation

JOHN LANGDON (N.H.) [Pierce did not observe at the convention]: wealth, knowledge, age

JOHN LANSING (N.Y.): occupation, office, speaking abilities, knowledge, education, personal qualities, age

WILLIAM LIVINGSTON (N.J.): talents, education, speaking abilities, political abilities, age, health

JAMES MADISON JR. (Va.): office, reputation, political skills, speaking abilities, work ethic, information, age, temperament

ALEXANDER MARTIN (N.C.): office, knowledge, political skills, speaking abilities, military service, age

LUTHER MARTIN (Md.): education, occupation, office, information, public speaking, age

GEORGE MASON (Va.): abilities, knowledge, speaking abilities, principles, political skills, age, health

JAMES MCCLURG (Va.): occupation, political skills, speaking skills, education, age, reputation, character

JAMES MCHENRY (Md.) [Pierce had limited time to observe at the convention]: occupational training, military service, talents, political skills, speaking skills, reputation, age

JOHN FRANCIS MERCER (Md.) [Pierce did not observe at the convention]: no report

THOMAS MIFFLIN (Pa.): title, talents, speaking abilities, age, physical characteristics

GOUVERNEUR MORRIS (Pa.) [Pierce had limited time to observe at the convention, although, given Morris's loquaciousness, Pierce probably heard him speak more than most delegates about whom he reported]: talents, speaking abilities, knowledge, legal training, occupation, age, physical characteristics

ROBERT MORRIS (Pa.): occupation, reputation and wealth, patriotism, knowledge, education, speaking abilities, silence, association with Robert Morris, age

WILLIAM PATERSON (N.J.): talents, personal qualities, education, profession, speaking abilities, reputation, knowledge, age, height

WILLIAM PIERCE (Ga.): military service, patriotism, office, ambition

CHARLES PINCKNEY (S.C.): talents, age, knowledge, work habits, speaking abilities, office

CHARLES COTESWORTH PINCKNEY (S.C.): family and fortune, education, knowledge, speaking abilities, military service, age

EDMUND RANDOLPH (Va.): office, education, political skills, speaking abilities, personal characteristics, age

GEORGE READ (Del.): occupation, office, knowledge, speaking abilities, character, age, height, health

JOHN RUTLEDGE (S.C.): reputation, education, offices, speaking skills, other abilities, fortune, age

ROGER SHERMAN (Conn.): oddity of character, thinking, public speaking, reputation, political skills, offices, occupations, age

RICHARD DOBBS SPAIGHT (N.C.): character, abilities, fortune, age

CALEB STRONG (Mass.): occupation, reputation, education, speaking abilities, age

GEORGE WASHINGTON (Va.): reputation, military service, comparison to other world leaders, patriotism, virtues, unanimous selection by convention, age

HUGH WILLIAMSON (N.C.): education, talents, information, speaking abilities, character, age

JAMES WILSON (Pa.): knowledge, understanding, speaking abilities, age

GEORGE WYTHE (Va.) [Pierce had limited time to observe at the convention]: occupation, learning, reputation, principles, political skills, speaking abilities, age

ROBERT YATES (N.Y.): office, legal abilities, speaking abilities, Anti-Federalist reputation, age, health

Analysis

Although Pierce surveyed all but two of the delegates, he generally devoted more analysis to individuals at the convention who played key roles or those who stood out for unique speaking styles. As noted earlier, Pierce listed the delegates by state and almost always reported on their age. He frequently commented on general abilities and education, but rarely about formal degrees. Pierce's references to reputation indicate that he often based his overall evaluation on the opinions of contemporaries, although he was willing to differ when it came to evaluating the strength of their reasoning or the persuasiveness of their rhetoric.

The most disappointing aspect of Pierce's portraits, and the reason that they must almost always be supplemented by notes of the deliberations, is their failure (consistent with the delegates' vow of secrecy) to identify the substantive positions that the delegates and the states they represented took during the convention. By contrast, a salutary aspect of Pierce's portraits is that one can read them in a single sitting. Moreover, by providing information about so many of the participants, he indicated that the result of the convention was a collective product rather than the work of a single delegate or handful of delegates.

Among some researchers, it has been common to identify James Madison, the presumed primary author of the Virginia Plan, as "The Founder" (see, for example, Meyers 1973; for a study of this phenomenon, see Vile 2008). Madison's role was certainly as important as that of anyone there, but to designate him as *the* founder is simply inconsistent with the facts (see Hobson 1979 for a discussion of some of Madison's defeats at the convention). When a correspondent referred to Madison in 1834 as "the writer of the Constitution of the U.S.," consistent with his own republicanism Madison responded that the Constitution "was not, like the fabled Goddess of Wisdom, the offspring of a single brain. It ought to be regarded as the work of many heads & many hands" (qtd. in Rutland 1984, 23). In so doing, Madison affirmed Benjamin Franklin's observations in his concluding speech to the convention. Having observed that "when you assemble a number of men to have the advantage of their joint wisdom, you inevitably assemble with those men, all their prejudices, their passions, their errors of opinion, their local interest, and their selfish views," Franklin proceeded to express pleasure in finding "this system approaching so near to perfection as it does" (Farrand 1966, 2:642). Although Pierce did not mention the specific issues and compromises in which the delegates engaged, it seems clear that in addition to their division into states and regions, the delegates' varied personalities and temperaments would have been a barrier to unanimity.

Pierce's Self-Assessment

This review of Pierce's assessments of fellow delegates prepares the ground for an examination of what Pierce told readers about himself. Because people tend to remember things that they have seen or heard first and last, good writers typically use the principles of primacy (early placement) and recency (placement at the end) to emphasize aspects of their narratives that they most want their audience to remember. Although listing delegates from north to south has other justifications that have already been cited, by placing himself last in the narrative, Pierce gained the advantages of appearing humble and of leaving readers with his own portrait as their last impression.

Having previously mentioned that Jonathan Dayton had been a "Brother Aid" to General Sullivan during the Revolutionary War, Pierce described himself as follows:

> My own character I shall not attempt to draw, but leave those who may choose to speculate on it, to consider it in any light that their fancy or imagination may depict. I am conscious of having discharged my duty as a Soldier through the course of the late revolution with honor and propriety; and my services in Congress and the Convention were bestowed with the best intention towards the interest of Georgia, and towards the general welfare of the Confederacy. I possess ambition, and it was that, and the flattering opinion which some of my Friends had of me, that gave me a seat in the wisest Council in the World, and furnished me with an opportunity of giving these short Sketches of the Characters who composed it.

Given Charles Willson Peale's expressed belief in a letter of September 4, 1775, that Pierce was not yet "a perfect Master of the Drawing" (Peale 1983, 2:509–510), it is possible that Pierce was making an intentional pun when he refused to "draw" a picture of his own character. So interpreted, it is almost as though Pierce, after sketching most of the other delegates, was refusing to sit for his own self-portrait.

Whether he intended this as a pun or not, Pierce's offer to allow readers the opportunity to consider his character "in any light that their fancy or imagination may depict" seems less than frank, given the positive information that he subsequently supplied. Students of Greek and Roman rhetoric call this a *praeteritio*, or paraleipsis, which Pierce may well have learned during his college education. Francisca Henkemans explains, "The principle [*sic*] characteristic of praeteritio is that the speaker announces that he will omit something, but mentions it nonetheless" (2009, 242). Writers and speakers typically use this mechanism to call greater attention to something that readers might otherwise miss.

In Pierce's case, he followed his offer to readers to fill in the blanks of his character by mentioning his devotion to "duty" as exemplified in the "honor and propriety" with which he served his country as a soldier. One commentator observes that a "remarkable sense of duty" appeared to "separate the Founders from others" (Kaminski 2008, xiv). Not surprisingly, Pierce described his service both as a member of Congress and at the convention as part of his dual service to his state and his nation while minimizing his early departure from his convention duties. He legitimized his own "ambition" by indicating that others had "flattering" opinions of him and his ability to sit in such wise councils.

One would certainly expect that Pierce would be proud of his service during the Revolutionary War and that he would stress his own good intentions—character traits that others cannot gauge directly but have to ascertain by looking at actions. Pierce's emphasis on the dual nature of his service to his state and country might indirectly hint at conflicts in the convention over how states would be represented in Congress or how to handle issues like slavery, where the interests of individual states and the Union as a whole arguably diverged. Such conflicts would, however, also be present if he were speaking as a modern member of Congress or, indeed, of another constitutional convention. Pierce's reference to "the general welfare of the Confederacy," which echoed the language of the preamble to the new Constitution, suggests that he believed that changing the Articles of Confederation was the only way to save them.

Douglass Adair (1974) has emphasized the role that the desire for fame played in spurring some American founders to great achievements. Although Pierce did not in his sketches refer to fame, he did tie his "ambition" to public service and to the approbation of his friends. He ended his narrative by stressing his role as an eyewitness to the characters he described.[14]

As a comparison with the summary above indicates, Pierce did not provide some key information about himself that he sometimes presented about others. Although one can learn much from what he valued in others, one cannot know simply from his personal sketch about his own formal education, his age, his occupation, his family, his financial situation, his place of birth, the city where he did most of his business, his religious beliefs and affiliation, his political principles and connections, his marital status, his physical qualities, or his health. These omissions and Pierce's early death undoubtedly contributed to the mistakes that earlier chroniclers of the convention made with respect to him.

Commentators have often noted that (with the help of Madison) Benjamin Franklin, whose model speech on constitutional ratification (Farrand 1966, 2:641–643) was somewhat eclipsed by those of delegates explaining their decisions *not* to sign the Constitution, thrust himself back into prominence by expressing the winsome hope during the signing of the document that the sun painted on the back of the president's chair was rising on a new day for America (ibid., 2:648). Pierce's strategy in his character sketches appears to have been similar. Beginning his narrative with the businesslike words "From New Hampshire," he ended by linking his opportunity to share the sketches with what he believed to have been "the wisest

Council in the World."[15] By calling the Philadelphia meeting a "council" rather than a "convention," Pierce might well have intended to emphasize its deliberative, as opposed to its purely representational, aspect.[16] He both glowed in and wanted to be remembered for contributing to the luster of this gathering.

Pierce's Date of Departure

As indicated earlier, Rossiter (1966) has concluded that Pierce left the convention near the end of June, but the exact date is difficult to ascertain simply by reading his character sketches because Pierce did not limit his comments to delegates whom he observed. Unfortunately, I cannot narrow this date further. Pierce's comments on Bedford's "warm and impetuous" temper and "precipitate judgment" suggest that he might have listened to Bedford's impassioned speech of June 30,[17] whereas his reference to Davie's silence at the convention suggests that he was not there to hear his comments, which came somewhat earlier on the same day. As suggested above, he might also have heard Davie and simply failed to revise his notes.

Pierce's decision to include descriptions of the two New Hampshire delegates who had not arrived—if made during the convention itself (a point that remains unknown)—could be a clue that he expected them to come. This might, in turn, have been prompted by attending the June 30 session, since David Brearly (from New Jersey, one of the small states eager for reinforcements) had at the beginning of that day's meeting requested the president to write to the state's executive informing him that he should send the delegates. The motion failed out of apparent fear that it might cause alarm (Farrand 1966, 1:481–482).

NOTES

1. John Sullivan was an American Revolutionary War general (1740–1795), who later became governor of New Hampshire, where he was allied against John Langdon, a convention delegate whom Pierce described but who did not arrive until after Pierce had left the convention.
2. Martin had been charged, but not convicted, of cowardice at the battle of Germantown.
3. For eighteenth-century prejudices against shoemakers, see Rather 1997, 270.
4. In a letter to Nathanael Greene dated October 15, 1782, Pierce observed, after convalescing from malaria: "Idleness, is of all things, the most disagreeable to me, because it occasions the mind to be sluggish and inactive; and it has been my misfortune to have been in this state for upwards of four Months. The hours have passed away in gloom and mortification; scarcely a pleasing moment has crept in to rouze the natural chearfulness of my disposition. . . . I have a degree of ambition to excel in whatever I undertake" (Greene 1991–2005, 12:65).

   In another letter to Greene dated June 24, 1784, Pierce revisited the issue of ambition while reflecting on his newly married state: "My ambition has made a pause, not to stop forever, but to look around for a worthy pursuit, before I put it again in motion." He went on,

"Human life is chequered by a prodigious variety of fortune, a croud of incidents pass along with it and make our calculations very dubious and uncertain" (ibid., 13:337).

5. At the age of fourteen, Hamilton had written to his friend Edward Stevens: "my ambition is [so] prevalent that I contemn the groveling and conditions of a clerk or the like to which my fortune &c. condemns me and would willingly risk my life, tho' not my character, to exalt my station" (qtd. in Chernow 2004, 30–31).

6. Although Quakers had a general reputation for pacifism and loyalism, John Dickinson fought on the patriot side. Similarly, General Nathanael Greene, under whom Pierce had served during the Revolutionary War, had been raised as a Quaker. In a reference to a letter of St. George Tucker that I have been unable to find, Pierce responded on February 6, 1782, by observing that he had received "[y]our Quaker epistle of the 30th of December" and that "[i]t groaned exceedingly under the weight of the spirit, and had you not dated it at your ordinary dwelling place I should have sworn that you had written it in a religious fit at some Quaker meeting house, or at the council board upon Shockho Hill, at Richmond. But, be that as it may, I sincerely congratulate you on the discovery of your admirable talents for the character of Simon Pure. God grant that you may be happy under the influence of the spirit, and that all your days may roll away in pleasantness and peace" (Pierce 1881, 436–437). Pierce's mocking tone certainly suggests that he was not enamored with Quakers. "Simon Pure," whose name came to stand for someone either genuinely pure or superficially virtuous, was a character in a play by Susanna Centlivre (1669–1723), *A Bold Stroke for a Wife.*

7. Johnson (1967, vol. 1) associated it with "a corrupt dialect" (definition 1); "a particular form of speaking peculiar to some certain class or body of men" (definition 2); or "a whining pretension to goodness, in formal and affected terms" (definition 3).

8. As noted above, in the notebook with his character sketches, Pierce included two examples of restrictive Connecticut laws about keeping the Sabbath and suppressing luxury.

9. Hall 2012, 9, notes that while scholars frequently cite Madison, Jefferson, and other deists when describing the faiths of the Founding Fathers, there were numerous founders (some at the convention) who were in the Reformed (Calvinist) tradition. His list: "Samuel Adams, Isaac Backus, Abraham Baldwin, Elias Griswold, John Hancock, Benjamin Huntington, Samuel Huntington, Richard Law, Joseph Montgomery, William Paterson, Tapping Reeve, Jesse Root, Ezra Stiles, Richard Stockton, John Treadwell, Jonathan Trumbull, William Williams, John Witherspoon, and Oliver Wolcott."

Lest it be thought that Pierce was a skeptic, his handwritten notebook contained the following proposed inscription (Pierce did not list a source so it is possible that he wrote it) for a statute of the French skeptic Voltaire (François-Marie Arouet, 1694–1778). The inscription seems to mock his agnosticism, although Pierce may simply have admired the poem for its wit:

> Behold Voltaire! Deserving of a Stone!
> Who in poetry was great,
> In history little;
> Still last in Phylosophy;
> And in religion,
> Nothing at all.
> His wit was acute,
> His judgment precipitate,

> His dishonesty extreme.
> Loose Women smiled upon him;
> The half learned applauded him,
> And the profane patronized him.
> Though he spared neither God nor Man,
> A junto of Atheists,
> Who call themselves philosophers,
> Scraped some Money together,
> And raised this Statue
> To his memory.

10. This reputation has been highlighted in Brookhiser 2003. For a far more sympathetic portrait, see the remarks of Madame de Damas in Sparks 1832, 1:506–512.

11. The phrase "vow of celibacy" might have been an indirect way of referencing the fact that Carroll, whose younger brother John was a bishop, was a Roman Catholic.

12. Unfortunately, McKenney's (2013) book on the wives of delegates, while otherwise quite useful in filling gaps in earlier treatments, limits coverage to those who were married to signers of the Constitution and thus provides no additional information about Pierce.

13. On May 29, the convention adopted a rule "[t]hat nothing spoken in the House be printed, or otherwise published or communicated without leave" (Farrand 1966, 1:37).

14. Although Pierce was not an attorney, such testimony is especially valued in court, which, consistent with the confrontation clause of the Sixth Amendment, permits hearsay only in limited and closely defined occasions. Some of the writers of the gospels in the New Testament cited their roles as eyewitnesses to bolster the believability of their accounts. See Luke 1:1–3 and John 21:24.

15. Pierce had twice before referred to wisdom, once in reference to John Dickinson's (Del.) "affected air of wisdom" and then to Roger Sherman's "wise and useful" thoughts.

16. Although Wood (1969) stressed how the framers often associated conventions with the will of the people, almost as though they were referenda, this might have been truer of the conventions called to ratify the Constitution than to the Constitutional Convention of 1787 that proposed it. For an examination of the convention mechanism, see Natelson 2012.

17. Yates reported that Read, who as a delegate from a small state was making a case for equal representation for less populous states and had threatened to seek help from foreign countries, said: "*I do not, gentlemen, trust you.* If you possess the power, the abuse of it could not be checked; and what then would prevent you from exercising it to our destruction?" (Farrand 1966, 1:500).

REFERENCES

Adams, Willi Paul. 2001. *The First American Constitutions: Republican Ideology and the Making of the State Constitutions in the Revolutionary Era.* Expanded ed. Lanham, Md.: Rowman and Littlefield.

Adair, Douglass. 1974. "Fame and the Founding Fathers." In *Fame and the Founding Fathers: Essays,* edited by Trevor Bolbourn, 3–26. New York: Norton.

Baum, Marsha L., and Christian G. Fritz. 2000. "American Constitution-Making: The Neglected State Constitutional Sources." *Hastings Constitutional Law Quarterly* 27 (Winter):199–242.

Bernstein, David. 1987. "The Constitutional Convention: Facts and Figures." *History Teacher* 21, no. 1 (November):11–19.

Bradford, M. E. 1994. *Founding Fathers: Brief Lives of the Framers of the United States Constitution.* 2nd ed. Lawrence: University Press of Kansas.

Brookhiser, Richard. 2003. *Gentleman Revolutionary: Gouverneur Morris, the Rake Who Wrote the Constitution.* New York: Free Press.

Chernow, Ron. 2004. *Alexander Hamilton.* New York: Penguin Press.

Conley, Patrick T., and John P. Kaminski, eds. 1988. *The Constitution and the States: The Role of the Original Thirteen in the Framing and Adoption of the Federal Constitution.* Madison, Wis.: Madison House.

Dinan, John J. 2006. *The American State Constitutional Tradition.* Lawrence: University Press of Kansas.

Farrand, Max, ed. 1966. *The Records of the Federal Convention of 1787.* 4 vols. New Haven, Conn.: Yale University Press.

Greene, Nathanael. 1991–2005. *The Papers of General Nathanael Greene.* Vols. 6–13. Ed. Dennis M. Conrad. Chapel Hill: University of North Carolina Press for the Rhode Island Historical Society.

Hall, Mark David. 2012. *Roger Sherman and the Creation of the American Republic.* New York: Oxford University Press.

Henkemans, Francisca Snoeck. 2009. "The Contribution of Praeteritio to Arguers' Confrontational Strategic Manoeuveres." In *Examining Argumentation in Context: Fifteen Studies on Strategic Maneuvering,* edited by Frans H. Van Eemeren, 241–255. Philadelphia: John Benjamins.

Hobson, Charles F. 1979. "The Negative on State Laws: James Madison, the Constitution, and the Crisis of Republican Government." *William and Mary Quarterly,* 3rd ser., 36 (April):214–235.

Johnson, Samuel. 1967. *A Dictionary of the English Language.* 1755. 2 vols. Reprint, New York: AMS.

Jones, Charles C., Jr. 1891. *Biographical Sketches of the Delegates from Georgia to the Continental Congress.* Boston: Houghton, Mifflin.

Kaminski, John P., ed. 2008. *The Founders on the Founders: Word Portraits from the American Revolutionary Era.* Charlottesville: University of Virginia Press.

Kaminski, John P., and Gaspare J. Saladino, eds. 1995. *Commentaries on the Constitution, Public and Private,* vol. 6: *10 May to 13 September 1788.* Madison: State Historical Society of Wisconsin.

Kruman, Marc W. 1997. *Between Authority and Liberty: State Constitution Making in Revolutionary America.* Chapel Hill: University of North Carolina Press.

Leffler, Richard, John P. Kaminski, and Samuel K. Fore, eds. 2012. *William Pierce on the Constitutional Convention and the Constitution.* Dallas, Tex.: Harlan Crow Library.

Levinson, Sanford. 2012. *Framed: America's Constitutions and the Crisis of Governing.* New York: Oxford University Press.

Marks, Arthur S. 2012. "Private and Public in the Peale Family: Charles Willson Peale as Pater and Painter." *Proceedings of the American Philosophical Society* 156 (June):109–187.

McDonald, Forrest. 1985. *Novus Ordo Seclorum: The Intellectual Origins of the Constitution.* Lawrence: University Press of Kansas.

McKenney, Janice E. 2013. *Women of the Constitution: Wives of the Signers.* Lanham, Md.: Scarecrow Press.

Meyers, Marvin, ed. 1973. *The Mind of the Founder: Sources of the Political Thought of James Madison.* Indianapolis: Bobbs-Merrill.

Natelson, Robert G. 2012. "James Madison and the Constitution's 'Convention for Proposing Amendments.'" *Akron Law Review* 45:431–448.

Peale, Charles Willson. 1983. *The Selected Papers of Charles Willson Peale and His Family.* 2 vols. Ed. Lillian B. Miller. New Haven, Conn.: Yale University Press for the National Portrait Gallery, Smithsonian Institution.

Pierce, William. 1881. "Southern Campaign of General Greene 1781–2: Letters of Major William Pierce to St. George Tucker." Ed. Charles Watson Coleman Jr. *Magazine of American History* 7 (December):431–445.

Rather, Susan. 1997. "Carpenter, Tailor, Shoemaker, Artist: Copley and Portrait Painting around 1770." *Art Bulletin* 79 (June):269–290.

Rossiter, Clinton. 1966. *1787: The Grand Convention.* New York: Norton.

Rutland, Robert. 1961. *George Mason: Reluctant Statesman.* New York: Rinehart and Winston.

———. 1984. "The Virginia Plan of 1787: James Madison's Outline of a Model Constitution." *This Constitution* 4 (Fall):23–30.

Sparks, Jared. 1832. *The Life of Gouverneur Morris, with Selections from His Correspondence and Miscellaneous Papers.* 3 vols. Boston: Gray and Bowen.

Tocqueville, Alexis de. 1955. *The Old Regime and the French Revolution.* New York: Doubleday.

Vile, John R. 2005. *The Constitutional Convention of 1787: A Comprehensive Encyclopedia of America's Founding.* 2 vols. Santa Barbara, Calif.: ABC-CLIO.

———. 2008. "James Madison and Constitutional Paternity." In *James Madison: Philosopher, Founder, and Statesman*, edited by John R. Vile, William D. Pederson, and Frank J. Williams, 37–62. Athens: Ohio University Press.

Wood, Gordon S. 1969. *The Creation of the American Republic, 1776–1787.* Chapel Hill: University of North Carolina Press.

Wright, Robert W., Jr., and Morris J. MacGregor Jr. 1987. *Soldier-Statesmen of the Constitution.* Washington, D.C.: Center of Military History, United States Army.

CHAPTER 7

Comparing Pierce's Descriptions with
Those of a French Diplomat

*The voice and scepter of France lose their prominence
in the United States about 1784 until the middle
years of Washington's administration.*

—Ralph Ketcham, "France and American Politics"

The charm and distinctiveness of Pierce's portraits rest largely on the range of their coverage (all but two of the convention delegates), their pithiness, their humor, and their composition by an eyewitness. They are not, however, unique. In *The Records of the Federal Convention*, Max Farrand (1966, 3:232–238) included character sketches from a manuscript found in the correspondence archives of the French Ministry of Foreign Affairs. Although it specifically focused on the members and officers of Congress in 1788 (placing its composition fairly close to the time of Pierce's sketches—and still prior to the French Revolution), it included portraits of twenty-one of the delegates who participated in the Constitutional Convention.

The sketches appear to have been composed by the French minister Louis-Guillaume Otto (1754–1817),[1] who served as the secretary to the Chevalier de la Luzerne, the French minister to the United States from 1779 to 1784 and then returned as chargé d'affaires in America from 1785 to 1792 (O'Dwyer 1964, 408–409). Otto received his education at the University of Strasbourg. He married into the Livingston family; after his first wife's death, he then married the daughter of Saint John de Crèvecoeur, the New York consul, in a ceremony attended by Thomas Jefferson (Hill 1988, 10–11). Known as "an able and acute observer of American political life" (O'Dwyer 1964, 410), Otto did not, of course, have access to the proceedings of the Constitutional Convention, which had been secret, but his portraits of leading members of Congress exhibit similar wit to that of Pierce and make for a fascinating comparison (for an English version of a 1785 report that Otto wrote to Foreign Minister Charles Gravier, Count of Vergennes, see Sifton 1965).

To my knowledge, a complete English version of these sketches has not been previously published. Like Pierce, Otto examined the representatives from north to south, but his notes did not have any portraits of representatives from Rhode Island or Delaware. Not surprisingly, Otto was especially interested in the congressmen's sentiments toward his country and its rival Great Britain. By contrast to Pierce, Otto rarely mentioned the representatives' ages but put particular emphasis on their political alignments. Although the minister did not address rhetorical issues with the same breadth as Pierce did, those observations that he did make provide useful comparisons and contrasts.

Because the minister's report focused on congressional, rather than on convention, service, it does not illumine the dynamics of the convention in the same way that Pierce's portraits do. Rather than providing the same scrutiny to it, I will provide Otto's full description of each delegate (translated into English) and then highlight the similarities and differences between his view and that of Pierce.

Abraham Baldwin (Ga.)

Otto: "Reasonable and well-intentioned, but never had the opportunity to distinguish himself. Congress just gave him the means to do so by nominating him as one of the commissaries to settle accounts with the states."

Perhaps in part because Pierce was a fellow Georgia delegate, the minister's sketch is not as detailed as Pierce's. Although Pierce incorrectly identified Baldwin as having been educated at Harvard rather than Yale, Pierce gave considerably more attention to Baldwin's intellectual gifts. Pierce described Baldwin as more of an established attorney and statesman whereas the minister (who had an additional bit of information—a recent congressional appointment) described him as a virtual unknown. Otto did not mention Baldwin's service at the Constitutional Convention.

Jonathan Dayton (N.J.)

Otto: "Not well known; has the sole merit to be the son of a good patriot and benefactor of Mr. d'Anteroches; this is why we can presume he likes the French. There are in this state several individuals that we need to treat considerately because they are our friends and because they are very influential."

Pierce had the advantage of having known Dayton because of their military service together. The French minister is referring to Louis Joseph D'Anterroches (1753–1814), a Frenchman who initially served on the side of the British during the American Revolution but on whose behalf Lafayette and others intervened after his capture. Pierce went into greater detail than Otto about Dayton's education, character traits, speaking abilities, and ambition.

John Dickinson (Del.)

Otto: "Author of the letters of the farmer from Pennsylvania; very rich man who was a member of the anti-Anglican party at the beginning of the revolution without however favoring independence against which he publicly voted. He is old, weak and has no influence."

Like Pierce, the French minister highlighted Dickinson's famed authorship of *Letters from a Farmer in Pennsylvania*, but added, perhaps because Americans would have been more likely to know this than would the French minister, that Dickinson had failed to sign the Declaration of Independence. The minister's description of Dickinson as "old" and "weak" may help account for Pierce's judgment, which he consciously posed against the judgment of others, that Dickinson had been "an indifferent Speaker" at the convention.

Oliver Ellsworth (Conn.)

Otto: "Mr. Ellsworth, a current member of Congress, is a man of the absolute same bearing and dispositions [as Benjamin Huntington]. . . . the people of this state, in general, possess a national character that can scarcely be found in the other parts of the continent. They are closer to the republican simplicity: they live comfortably without knowing opulence. Rural economy and home industry are pushed very far in Connecticut. People live happy there."

This portrayal suffers from the fact that Max Farrand did not include Otto's description of Benjamin Huntington (1736–1800), Ellsworth's fellow Connecticut representative who had graduated from Yale, pursued law, and held a variety of offices, including serving in the Continental Congress. Whereas Pierce linked Sherman to a "strange New England cant," the French minister clearly believed that all three Connecticut representatives (Huntington, Ellsworth, and Sherman) embodied values of simplicity, economy, and industry that were peculiar to the culture of the state.

William Few (Ga.)

Otto: "Even though he is no great genius, he possesses more knowledge than his name or his looks seem to indicate. Still quite young, he has constantly been employed during the war. His colleagues have a good opinion of him. He is very shy and embarrassed in society except when one talks to him about business."

Whereas Pierce said that Few possessed "a strong natural Genius," Otto thought that "he is no great genius." Pierce thought Few, who was thirty-nine, was thirty-five, and a year later, the French minister identified him as "Still quite young." This probably indicates that Few was aging well. Pierce focused on Few's legal occupation and knowledge, but the minister associated him with "business," although this may be a generic reference to work in general rather than to commerce or industry. The minister portrayed a man of far greater reticence than one sees in Pierce's version.

Benjamin Franklin (Pa.)

Otto: "Dr. Franklin, current President of this state, is too well-known to be in need for the praises we owe him. He senses, more than any other American, that to be a true patriot, one needs to be a friend of France. Unfortunately, this philosopher who managed to brave anathema and the wrath of the Parliament of England, will not fight for much longer old age infirmities. It is our regret that immortality only belongs to his name and his writings."

Because Benjamin Franklin had served as a popular diplomat to France, it is not surprising that the French minister identified him as a "friend." The minister correctly listed Franklin as the president of his state and recounted his drubbing in Parliament (see Penegar 2011), both facts that Pierce omitted. Both Pierce and Otto identified Franklin as a philosopher.

Elbridge Gerry (Mass.)

The minister's description of Elbridge Gerry grew from his portrayal of Nathan Dane: "In Congress, he [Dane] has always sided with Mr. Gerry,* who does not like us and has been mainly opposed to the ratification of our Consular Convention. He possesses more talents than Mr. Gerry and is less duplicitous." Otto continued the description of Gerry, in more dramatic fashion, in a footnote:

*Mr. Elb. Gerry is a small, very scheming man full of niceties, which so far, have profited him quite well. He is, of all members of Congress, the one who has officiated the longest time. He has acquired there a great knowledge in public affairs which he uses to impress upon his fellow citizens. In 1782, he delivered quite a good speech in the legislature of Boston in which he urged not to permit the ratification of the Consular Convention. He pretends to like Sir de La Luzerne[2] but one should be suspicious of all his great protestations. In general, we have very few friends among the powerful men of Massachusetts; our commerce is of no interest to them and our fisheries put them out. Mr. Bowdoin [James Bowdoin, a fellow Massachusetts political leader], Mr. King, Mr. Sam. Adams etc., draw all of their political notions from the writings or the conversations of Mr. Jay and Mr. J. Adams. In general, people like the French for they have often seen our fleets and they remember the services we rendered them.

Pierce's portrait of Gerry and Otto's portrait vary considerably. Whereas Pierce viewed Gerry as a man of "integrity and perseverance," the minister viewed him as "very scheming." The French minister noted that he was small (contemporaries sometimes compared him to a bird), but Pierce did not. Pierce examined Gerry's speaking style in detail, and the minister noted that he had given a "good speech" to the Massachusetts legislature. What is fascinating is that Otto identified a major fissure in early American politics, which seems to be largely absent from Pierce's character sketches: the schism between those who favored France and those who favored England.

Prior to the Constitutional Convention, John Jay of New York had attempted to negotiate a treaty with the Spanish minister plenipotentiary, Don Diego de Gardoqui, in which Jay indicated a willingness (counter to his instructions from Congress) to cede navigation of the Mississippi River in exchange for the right to open the Spanish market to American grain and fish (Merritt 1991). Although southern states successfully formed a block in opposition to this, the incident appears to have influenced the convention's decision to require the approval of two-thirds of the Senate for the ratification of treaties (Vile 2005, 2:371).

The French minister's list of New England leaders that he believed to be tepid toward France corresponds with the primary leadership of the Federalist Party, which emerged in Washington's first administration. In a possible foreshadowing of the Genet incident,[3] Otto distinguished the general public's attitude toward France from that of the leadership.

Nicholas Gilman (N.H.)

Otto: "Young man with pretensions; not much liked by his colleagues; mockingly nicknamed 'the Congress.' He however has the advantage to have represented his state at the Great Convention of Philadelphia and to have signed the Constitution. Such circumstance proves that choices are scarce in that state or that to the least, the most sensible and skillful men are not wealthy enough to accept a public position. Mr. G. served during the war as a camp aid."

Although he included Gilman's character sketch among his descriptions, Pierce did not have an opportunity to observe him at the convention and included only the barest details: a set of positive character qualities and his age. Noting his youth and military service (something Pierce omitted), Otto included a mocking nickname ("the Congress") that colleagues gave to Gilman and cited his selection for the Constitutional Convention not as a testament to Gilman's abilities or reputation but as proof of the financial inability of more qualified individuals to accept such a post.

Alexander Hamilton (N.Y.)

The French minister devoted greater attention to Hamilton than to any of the other members of Congress who had attended the Constitutional Convention.

> Great orator: intrepid in public debates. A zealous partisan and besides, outraged by the new Constitution,[4] he is a declared enemy of the Clinton government which he courageously and publicly attacked in the newspapers, without any incitement. He is one of those rare men who has distinguished himself equally at the battlefield and to the bar. He owes everything to his talents. An indiscretion caused him to be on bad terms with General Washington for whom he was the trustworthy secretary. Other indiscretions led him to leave Congress in 1783. He has too many pretentions and possesses too little prudence.
>
> Here is what Sir de La Luzerne said about him in 1780: "Mr. Hamilton: one of General Washington's camp aids who has the most influence over him. He is a witty man of a mediocre probity. Estranged from the English because he is of low birth from one of their colonies, he fears to return to his former state. He is a peculiar friend of Mr. de La Fayette. Mr. Conway thinks that Hamilton hates the French, that he is fundamentally corrupt and that the ties he pretends to have with us will never be anything else than misleading."
>
> Mr. Hamilton hasn't done anything that could justify the last comment. He is simply too impetuous and because he wants to control everything, he misses his target. His eloquence is often out of place during public debates as precision and clarity are preferred to a brilliant imagination. It is believed that Mr. Hamilton is the author of a pamphlet entitled "the Federalist." His purpose was again lost in it. This piece of work is of no use to the educated people, and it is too scholarly and too long to the ignoramuses.
>
> Nevertheless, it made him famous; a small frigate pulled on the streets of New

York during the great federal procession was named the "Hamilton" after him. However, whether displayed here or elsewhere, these types of parades are only but ephemeral impressions. Since the party of the anti-federalists was the most numerous in the state, Mr. Hamilton lost more than he won because of the zeal he displayed during this event.

Estranged in this state where he has been brought up by charity, Mr. Hamilton found a way to abduct the daughter of General Schuyler,[5] a wealthy and very influential landowner. Since his reconciliation with the family, he currently lives off his father-in-law's money.

As in the case of New Hampshire, Otto identified political divisions in the state (between supporters of Hamilton and of Governor George Clinton, who would become a Democratic-Republican); Pierce was either unaware or chose to ignore this. Both mentioned Hamilton's role as an attorney and veteran. The French minister focused on a dispute between Hamilton and Washington (perhaps in the hope of exploiting it for advantage?), and used much more negative terms to describe Hamilton's character. Long before Hamilton would die in a duel, the minister referenced Hamilton's willingness to incite others. The minister's reference to Hamilton's "pretentions" is similar to Pierce's observations about his vanity. Although Otto noted the observation of Thomas Conway (who was born in Ireland and fought as a general on the American side before fighting for royalist forces in France and eventually returning to Ireland) that Hamilton hated France, the minister was inclined to attribute this judgment to Hamilton's impetuousness and, in a comment later echoed by John Adams (who called Hamilton "the bastard brat of a Scotch peddler"), seemed to suggest that he might even harbor some ill will because of his "low birth from one of their colonies."

With the benefit of another year having passed, the minister identified Hamilton with one of the processions that was tied to the celebration of the ratification of the Constitution (for details, see Rigal 1996). Otto speculated that Hamilton was the author (rather than one of three) of *The Federalist Papers*, which he incorrectly called a "pamphlet"; it actually began as a series of newspaper articles and ended up as a two-volume work. In a colossal misjudgment, Otto thought that the work, now recognized as perhaps the epitome of American political thought, was fairly useless and associated Hamilton with excessive zeal on behalf of the Constitution, which the minister believed had undercut his reputation in his home state of New York.

In some final gossip, the French minister accused Hamilton of kidnapping his wife. As juicy as the story is, it is inaccurate. Indeed, Hamilton's wife, Elizabeth (Eliza), was the only one of five sisters who did *not* elope (Chernow 2004, 129).

Similarly, although acknowledging Hamilton's leading place at the bar, the French minister associated Hamilton's wealth with his father-in-law's money rather than with Hamilton's substantial prowess in the courtroom (Ely 2001).

John Langdon (N.H.)

Perhaps because he had no opportunity to observe him at the Constitutional Convention, Pierce noted little about Langdon other than his fortune, his mind and understanding, and his age. By contrast, the French minister went into much greater detail:

> One of the most interesting and amiable men in the United States; current Governor of New Hampshire and head of a powerful party, he is in opposition to General Sullivan.
> Mr. L. made a great fortune in commerce; he is the Rob. Morris of his state for he spends a lot of money and he has a lot of citizens on his side because of his liberalities. He was one of the main members of the Philadelphia Convention but he only sat in Congress for a few days. Even though his colleagues offered him the presidency, he did not want to stay because his intentions were to be reelected as Governor of New Hampshire, and because his business did not allow him to stay away from it for too long. He is sincerely attached to France and is even predisposed to our customs and manners. In order to spread people's taste for our furniture, he has had very beautiful pieces shipped from Paris. The rumor goes that he is jealous of his wife, which is something quite uncommon in America. Several French officers sadly realized that this jealousy had no foundation.

There are two fascinating aspects of this sketch. One is its discussion of the political differences in New Hampshire between Langdon and Sullivan, under whom Pierce had served for a time during the Revolutionary War (and whom he mentioned in passing in his character sketch of Jonathan Dayton). Otto mentioned Langdon's office as governor (and his chance to be the "president" of Congress at a time when the Articles of Confederation were still in effect) whereas Pierce did not. Although Pierce did identify Langdon as "a Man of considerable fortune," he did not, like the French minister, present this as reflecting a division in the state between gentlemen and those of lesser means.

The other fascinating aspect of the minister's sketch is its gossipy tone, designating Langdon as the Robert Morris of his state, mentioning his taste for fine furniture, and even discussing his misplaced jealousy of his wife. The minister attributed to Langdon far more influence at the Constitutional Convention than he actually had there.

William Livingston (N.J.)

As in the case of Langdon, the French minister's description provided more information about Livingston's status in his home state of New Jersey than did Pierce's sketch.

Otto: "*William Livingston*, Esq., governor since the beginning of the revolution, he is well learned, firm, patriotic and prefers the public good to his own popularity and has often risked his position as governor to prevent the legislature to adopt bad laws. Even though he does not cease to satirize the people, he is always reelected, for even his enemies agree that he is one of the most skillful and virtuous men in the continent. He is the father of Madame Jay and of Mr. Broc. Livingston."

In contrast to Pierce, who used the term fairly freely, Livingston was one of the few individuals whom the French minister (perhaps with a greater sense of aristocratic differences?) identified as an esquire. Otto gave higher testimony to Livingston's patriotism. Both Pierce and Otto noted his reputation for satire. By mentioning two of his children (one of whom was married to John Jay), the French minister did a better job than Pierce of tying Livingston to a political dynasty.

James Madison (Va.)

Otto:

Learned, wise, moderate, docile and studious; may be more profound than Mr. Hamilton but less brilliant; close friend of Mr. Jefferson and sincerely attached to France. He was very young when he first started working at Congress and he seems to have devoted himself specifically to public affairs. He may one day become the governor of his state if his modesty allows him to accept the position. He recently declined the position of President of Congress. He is a man one needs to scrutinize for a long time before being able to conceive a just opinion of him.

The fact that Otto was already associating Madison with Jefferson,[6] with whom he had a lifelong political friendship (see Koch 1950), and comparing Madison to Hamilton suggests that the minister had already sensed the divisions that would later develop in Washington's cabinet and lead to the first two political parties. Both Pierce and Otto took note of Madison's attention to public affairs. Both mentioned his "modesty." Only Pierce discussed his rhetoric. The reference to Madison declining the position of president of Congress is a reminder that the new Constitution had yet to go into effect. The French minister's thought that Madison might one day become Virginia's governor, rather than the nation's fourth president, seems to confirm, rather than contradict, his further observation that one should "scrutinize" him for some time before being able to estimate his potential.

Luther Martin (Md.)

The French minister, writing during the Federalist/Anti-Federalist debates, had some information about Luther Martin that was not available to Pierce. He observed: "Distinguished lawyer who wrote a lot on the resolutions of the Philadelphia Convention and of which he was a member."

It seems odd that Otto identified Martin as a delegate to the Constitutional Convention without indicating that his writings were directed not to supporting, but to opposing, the Constitution that it proposed. Both observers identified Martin as an attorney. The minister's lack of comment on Martin's rhetoric suggests that the author never witnessed one of his harangues.

Thomas Mifflin (Pa.)

Unlike Pierce, the French minister mentioned that Mifflin was an "officer" without giving his military rank; he did, however, identify him as a lawyer whereas Pierce did not: "*Tho. Mifflin.* Current General, President of Congress, orator of the assembly, etc. Proclaimed and proven friend of France. He is very popular and he handles with a surprising ease the one hundred headed monster named the people. He is a good lawyer, a good officer, a good patriot, and he is of a very agreeable society. Whatever he does, he does it well because he takes after nature and he can but only overcome by showing who he really is." In referring to members of the public as a multiheaded monster, Otto revealed his fears about republican rule.

Gouverneur Morris (Pa., N.Y.)

Unlike Pierce, the French minister noted that Gouverneur Morris had on various occasions represented both New York (his home state) and Pennsylvania (his state of business): "*Gouv. Morris.* A citizen of the state of New York, he is still in touch with Mr. Rob. Morris and has represented Pennsylvania many times. Famous lawyer; one of the most organized head in the continent but has no morals and according to his enemies, no principles either; infinitely interesting in a conversation, he studied with peculiar care the field of finances. He constantly works with Mr. Rob. Morris. He is more feared than admired but few people respect him."

Both Pierce and Otto connected Gouverneur Morris to Robert Morris. Both agreed that Gouverneur Morris's principles were questionable, with the minister elaborating in somewhat greater detail. Pierce went into far more detail about Morris's speaking abilities and added information about his physical deformities that Otto omitted. Interestingly, the minister did not assess Morris's position vis-à-vis France, even though Morris would soon be serving there as an ambassador.

Robert Morris (Pa.)

The minister's description of Robert Morris put heavier emphasis on his role as superintendent of finance during the Revolutionary War, including reference to a contract with France that had gone awry: "Superintendent of Finances during the war, he is a powerful negotiator in his state. He owes everything to his good looks and to his experiences and very little to his education. His relationship with France cooled off ever since Mr. de Marbois [a former French diplomat to America] took to the party of Mr. Hotker [whom I have been unable to identify] with so much passion and since we disapproved of his contract with the farm. It will however be easy to gain it by using good methods. He is a very influential man and we shall not be indifferent to his friendship."

Both observers noted that Morris had risen to prominence without formal education. Unlike Pierce, the minister commented favorably on Morris's physical appearance but did not mention either his reputation for or his excellence in speaking.

Edmund Randolph (Va.)

Although placing Randolph higher in reputation than where Pierce ranked him, the French minister had a jaundiced view of Randolph, largely based on his part in previous negotiations with France:

> [C]urrent governor, he is one of the most distinguished men in America for his talents and his influence; he has however lost a part of his consideration when he opposed the ratification of the new Constitution with too much violence. He

was a member of Congress in 1780 and in 1781, and judging from all the difficulties Sir de La Luzerne faced while negotiating with him our Consular Convention, we must consider him to be at least very indifferent to the French cause. All the objections that are recorded on file by Mr. Jay had been made by Mr. Randolph and the French Secretary only succeeded thanks to the moderation of the other members of the Committee.

Although Randolph refused to sign the Constitution at the convention, he later contributed to its ratification by supporting it at the Virginia Ratifying Convention. Although Otto noted Martin's writings on the Constitution without indicating that they had opposed ratification, he clearly associated Randolph with too much opposition to the document.

John Rutledge (S.C.)

Whereas Pierce criticized Rutledge for speaking too rapidly, the French minister, who misspelled the representative's name, associated his speech with excessive pride. "*J. Ruthledge*. Governor during the war, member of Congress, of the Convention and in general employed at all the important events. He is the most eloquent, but the proudest and the most imperious man in the United States. He takes advantage of his great influence and of his knowledge of the law to not pay his debts, which greatly exceed his fortune. His son travels in France for his education."

Otto contributed additional information about what he considered to be Rutledge's profligate spending habits and the French education of his son.

Roger Sherman (Conn.)

The French minister's discussion of Roger Sherman cannot be separated from that of Oliver Ellsworth, of the same state: "Mr. Ellsworth, a current member of Congress, is a man of the absolute same bearing and dispositions [as Benjamin Huntington]. The same thing can be said of Mr. Sherman—the people of this state, in general, possess a national character that can scarcely be found in the other parts of the continent. They are closer to the republican simplicity: they live comfortably without knowing opulence. Rural economy and home industry are pushed very far in Connecticut. People live happy there."

Otto substituted a description of the virtues of the state for those of the men who represented it.

Hugh Williamson (N.C.)

Neither Pierce nor the French minister provided much information about Williamson who, by most accounts, was the leader of his state's delegation at the convention. Otto: "Physician and currently professor in astronomy. Excessively bizarre, he likes to perorate but speaks with wit. It is difficult to know his character well; it is even possible that he doesn't have any but his occupation has recently given him a lot of influence at Congress."

Otto correctly identified Williamson as both a medical doctor and an astronomer, but considered him to be bizarre—perhaps not altogether different from the way in which someone today might refer to intellectuals as living in "ivory towers" or as "nerds" or "eggheads." Pierce mentioned Williamson's "humour" and the French minister his "wit," which suggests that this must have been a fairly noticeable aspect of his character.

James Wilson (Pa.)

Otto was familiar with Wilson from the legal services that Wilson had previously rendered to France, but he was far less enamored with Wilson than was Pierce. Otto: "Distinguished legal adviser. It is he who was designated by Mr. Gerard to be the lawyer of the French nation, a position that has been since then, recognized as useless. He is a haughty man, an intrepid aristocrat, active, eloquent, profound, secretive, and known as 'James the Caledonian,' a nickname given to him by his enemies. He disturbed his fortune with great enterprises that public affairs did not permit him to follow. Attached to France rather badly."

Whereas Pierce downplayed foreign birth and ancestry, the minister highlighted it by mentioning Wilson's nickname, a Latin term for someone from northern Scotland. Nor did Pierce associate Wilson with the aristocracy or with the financial mismanagement and possible conflicts of interest that would follow him to his grave. Both observers recognized Wilson's legal skills, which Wilson would later exercise on the U.S. Supreme Court, although Pierce put greater emphasis on the effectiveness of his rhetoric.

Comparative Analysis

Of the two sets of character sketches, Pierce covered more delegates and put greater focus on their rhetoric and their intellectual abilities. Not surprisingly, the

French minister focused more on how representatives were likely to regard the interests of his nation and of the representative's likelihood of favoring Britain or France in international affairs. Perhaps because he had an additional year of observation, the French minister was more cognizant of intrastate political dynamics. Given the pending revolution in France, which would forever change international dynamics, the French report might be seen to confirm what a narrow window of opportunity the delegates seized by formulating a Constitution when they did.[7] Although Pierce sometimes engaged in backhanded compliments, Otto truly played hardball, sometimes (most notably in the case of Alexander Hamilton) mixing false rumors with candid assessments. Considered in their totality, Pierce's overall assessments were arguably more "diplomatic" than those of Otto.

NOTES

1. Kaminski 2008, for example, attributes the portraits to Otto.
2. This is a reference to Anne-César de la Luzerne (1741–1791), the first official French ambassador to the United States.
3. The French minister to the United States, Edmond-Charles Genêt, had antagonized his host by attempting to raise privateers against the British, contrary to U.S. declarations of neutrality in the conflict between England and France. Although Washington demanded his recall, Genet faced death from the revolutionaries at home, and he chose to marry an American woman and remain in the country.
4. This would appear to be a reference to the constitution of the state of New York rather than to that of the United States.
5. Almost as though he were explaining an exotic tribe, the French minister added, perhaps with a bit of irony: "Abductions are more common in America than in France. Parents get angry first, and then they are moved by the situation and patch things up after a few months. Everybody is interested in these types of marriage because they seem to conform to the first impulsion of nature."
6. I believe that Otto's comparison between Madison's profundity and Hamilton's brilliance would apply equally to a comparison between Madison and Jefferson.
7. Robertson 2012 notes that this view was widely shared by delegates to the convention: "Many delegates also believed that there never would be a better moment to change the nation's path and create a more effective, durable national government. The United States was at a critical turning point, and political support for replacing the Articles of Confederation would never be stronger" (16). Focusing specifically on France, Ralph Ketcham said that "the voice and scepter of France lose their prominence in the United States from about 1784 until the middle years of Washington's administration" (1963, 217).

REFERENCES

Chernow, Ron. 2004. *Alexander Hamilton*. New York: Penguin.
Ely, James W., Jr. 2001. "Hamilton, Alexander." In *Great American Lawyers: An Encyclopedia*, edited by John R. Vile, 1:318–324. 2 vols. Santa Barbara, Calif.: ABC-CLIO.

Farrand, Max, ed. 1966. *The Records of the Federal Convention of 1787*. 4 vols. New Haven, Conn.: Yale University Press.

Hill, Peter P. 1988. *French Perceptions of the Early American Republic 1783–1793*. Philadelphia: American Philosophical Society.

Kaminski, John P., ed. 2008. *The Founders on the Founders: Word Portraits from the American Revolutionary Era*. Charlottesville: University of Virginia Press.

Ketcham, Ralph L. 1963. "France and American Politics, 1763–1793." *Political Science Quarterly* 78, no. 2 (June):198–223.

Koch, Adrienne. 1950. *Jefferson and Madison: The Great Collaboration*. New York: Knopf.

Merritt, Eli. 1991. "Sectional Conflict and Secret Compromise: The Mississippi River Question and the United States Constitution." *American Journal of Legal History* 35 (April):117–171.

O'Dwyer, Margaret M. 1964. "A French Diplomat's View of Congress, 1790." *William and Mary Quarterly*, 3rd ser., 21 (July):408–444.

Penegar, Kenneth Lawing. 2011. *The Political Trial of Benjamin Franklin: A Prelude to the American Revolution*. New York: Algora.

Rigal, Laura. 1996. "'Raising the Roof': Authors, Spectators and Artisans in the Grand Federal Procession of 1788." *Theatre Journal* 48, no. 3:253–277.

Robertson, David Brian. 2012. *The Original Compromise: What the Constitution's Framers Were Really Thinking*. New York: Oxford University Press.

Sifton, Paul G. 1965. "Otto's Mémoire to Vergennes, 1785." *William and Mary Quarterly*, 3rd ser., 22 (October):626–645.

Vile, John R. 2005. *The Constitutional Convention of 1787: A Comprehensive Encyclopedia of America's Founding*. 2 vols. Santa Barbara, Calif.: ABC-CLIO.

CHAPTER 8

Comparing Pierce's Descriptions
with Those of His Son

With exultation we hold
Each lofty name by fame enroll'd.
Statesman, hero, patriot, sage,
Of other and a happier age;
But ah! Their laurell'd brows proclaim
The father's worth and offspring's shame.

—William Leigh Pierce, *The Year* (1813)

It is common to observe with respect to offspring that an apple rarely falls far from the tree. As Pierce was dying, his wife was carrying a child who would bear his name. Whereas Pierce had come of age during the American Revolution, this son would reach maturity and seek his literary fame on the eve of the War of 1812, during which he authored *The Year: A Poem, in Three Cantoes.* David Longworth of New York's Shakespeare Gallery, which chiefly specialized in literary works, published the poem in 1813. "Cantos" are divisions often used in epic poems. Although Pierce's poem concentrated on a single year, he clearly believed that the year he described had epic significance for the fate of the nation.

The son's publication is important because it sheds additional light on his father and the legacy that he left. The son's publication provides remarkable points of comparison and contrast to the writings of his father and his assessment of early American leaders. An understanding of the son's views reinforces the idea, mentioned in the previous chapter, that the Constitutional Convention may have been held at a propitious time—before party politics might have made constitutional compromises much less possible.

William Leigh Pierce's Life

In part because it was so brief (1790–1814), the son's life story is about as elusive as that of his father. William Leigh Pierce was born to Charlotte Fenwick Pierce. Pierce's stepfather, Ebenezer Jackson, was a Revolutionary War veteran, a businessman, and a member of the Society of the Cincinnati. Indeed, this son of Brigadier Michael Jackson (1734–1801) was one of five sons (some underage) who served with their father in this conflict.

According to the website of the Litchfield Historical Society, Pierce graduated from the College of New Jersey (a favorite school for southerners) in 1808,[1] and attended the Litchfield Law School in 1809. Tapping Reeve (1744–1823), another graduate of the College of New Jersey, who was elected to the Supreme Court of Connecticut, founded the school, which was the first of its kind in America. Reeve's first student was his brother-in-law Aaron Burr. In the 1780s and 1790s, Reeve was educating ten to fifteen students a year, and at its peak in the first quarter of the nineteenth century, the school housed forty to fifty students at a time (Denning 2001, 587). The school, a proprietary institution in which James Gould, one of Reeve's former students, also took a hand, educated individuals from throughout the nation. In an article comparing the town of Litchfield with that of Williamsburg, Meeks noted that in addition to Aaron Burr and John C. Calhoun, Litchfield graduated "six cabinet officers; twenty-six United States senators; ninety members of Congress and many others" (1951, 20). A typical course of study was fourteen months. The school was a Federalist stronghold that cautioned against "mobocracy" and stressed Federalist values of "order, hierarchy, and benevolency" (qtd. in Denning 2001, 587). Pierce also earned a master of arts degree at the College of New Jersey in 1811 (*General Catalogue* 1908, 121).

It must have been a heady inheritance to have not one, but two, fathers (and a grandfather) who had fought in the Revolutionary War, and Pierce was clearly proud of his heritage.[2] After referring in his second canto (1813, 113) to "Shade of my father," he added a footnote to his memory, which explained who his father was: "Major William Leigh Pierce, of the Virginia continental line in the revolutionary war, an aid-de-camp of major-general Nathanael Greene, and one of the delegates from the state of Georgia in the convention which formed the federal constitution, where, to use his own language, 'his best exertions were bestowed for the welfare of the confederacy at large, and that state in particular whose interest he represented'" (ibid.).[3] The quotation, although imprecise, indicates that the son had access to and possible custody of his father's character sketches prior to their publication in 1828. The son followed with further details about his birth father:

> For major Pierce's military character and career while fighting for the freedom of his country, the generous reader will indulge the filial pride of the author while he states, that during a long term of service, of trial, and successive hardships, he steadfastly retained the confidence of his general, the friendship of the virtuous, the good opinion of the world, and above all, the affections of his country. He accompanied Greene throughout his noble series of military operations at the south, and was active, vigilant, and faithful to his duty; his gallantry was particularly marked at the battle of Eutaw, and won him tokens of approbation from his general and his country: but he was my father, and I may not say all that my feelings would dictate. (ibid.)

Rather than continuing in the first person, Pierce cited his father's commendation from Congress.[4] He further indicated that he possessed the sword that Congress gave to his father and said, "though it shall leap indignantly from its scabbard to oppose an invading foe, yet it sleeps, deaf to the call of that mad ambition which would urge it to be drawn in the fields of conquest" (114).[5]

Somewhat later in his cantos, Pierce referenced not his stepfather, who had also served in the Revolution, but his step-grandfather Brigadier Michael Jackson, who had lived in Newton, Massachusetts. Pierce thus noted in another footnote (151), "Under the roof of this excellent man the author's juvenile years were spent; and it is with pleasure he embraces this opportunity to testify [to] his respect for the memory of the worthy veteran." Earlier in the notes he observed, "This firm patriot and excellent officer of the revolution, was a major at the battle of Bunker's-hill, and by his coolness, good conduct, and intrepidity on that occasion, contributed not a little to the safety of our troops in the retreat of that celebrated and well-fought day" (ibid.). He also described other engagements in which his step-grandfather had participated, including one near West Point in which thirty-three of forty-two men who participated were killed or wounded.

In the preface to his poem, Pierce wrote that he "has scarce attained his twenty second year" (11). Pierce may have indicated something about his education and his general proclivity for the arts over the sciences in his introduction to the first canto:

> Soft, magic poesy! To thee
> My tender youth was votary;
> Early won by soothing measure,
> I eager grasp'd the mystic treasure;
> Stealing oft from Euclid's rules,

From close, dry, logic of the schools,
My fancy drank the witching lore,
While vision'd rose the days of yore. (14-15)

Under "Communicated," the *Ontario Repository* of December 20, 1814 (12, no. 36:3, reported that Pierce had been "the only surviving son of Maj. William Pierce, a distinguished patriot and Soldier of the Revolution." Mentioning that he was a native of Savannah and a Princeton graduate, the article further observed (in language reminiscent of his father's confessed ambition in his character sketches): "With talents uncommonly brilliant, and an ambition that bore him an expectation far above mediocricy [*sic*] in life, he selected the profession of Law as best adopted to his genius and inclination. He entered upon his profession with most ardent and sanguine hopes of future eminence, and had just qualified himself for admittance at the bar, when he was arrested by a premature and lamented death." The obituary mentioned his mother's and friends' loss and, somewhat conventionally, compared his life to that of a blossom whose stem had been prematurely snapped. The *Geneva Gazette* reported on December 21, 1814, that "William Leigh Pierce, Esq." had died "in Canandaigua, on Sunday, the 18th inst., after a short illness of the Typhus fever."[6] A letter sent to a Princeton archivist in 1993 reported that Pierce was buried "in the town cemetery [in Canandaigua] near the Historical Society" and that "[h]e has an approx. 2' x 5' stone, with his name [and] 'Savannah 1790–December 1814," followed by an approximately ten-line poem. At the bottom appears "T. Morgan [otherwise unidentified], Jun. Albany" (letter to Ben Primer from "Leonard," June 15, 1993, provided by Princeton University Library). Although his commonplace book contains many musings about romantic love, Pierce appears to have died unmarried and childless. Most other biographical information about Pierce must be gleaned from the perspective that he took in his cantos and in other written works.

Dedication of the Cantos

The most notable aspect of the cantos and the fairly extensive accompanying notes is that they were written by a twenty-two-year-old. Although such literary accomplishments are not unknown,[7] it is impressive both that the work was an extended poem on current events and that it abounded with the kinds of classical and literary references that one finds in the writings of Pierce's birth father and that evidenced a good classical education.[8] The father who most dominated the poem, however, was neither Pierce's birth father nor his stepfather, but George Washington, the father of the country. Like Pierce's birth father, Washington had been a delegate to the Constitutional Convention. The son thus evoked Washington frequently in his narrative and dedicated his poem "to The Washington Benevolent Society of the City of New York," whose members he praised for their "devotion to freedom, love of country, and integrity of political principle."

In his preface, dated May 10, 1813, Pierce indicated that he wrote from "Canandaigua, county of Ontario, state of New-York" (12), but he did not say what he was doing there. In "Introduction to Canto I" (13), Pierce dedicated the first canto of his poem "to JOHN GREIG, esquire of Canandaigua." As the term "esquire" might suggest, Greig (1779–1858) was a lawyer who had been born in Scotland, immigrated to the United States in 1797, and was admitted to the bar in 1804. He helped to found the Ontario Female Seminary and was elected as a Whig to the House of Representatives, where he served from May 21, 1841, to September 25, 1841 (*Biographical Directory of the South Carolina House of Representatives* 1974). Greig devoted most of his practice to serving as a land agent for wealthy clients, including the son of Robert Morris, but he also appears to have had a literary bent that would have appealed to Pierce.[9] Having attended the Litchfield Law School and being designated as "Esq." on the title page of his poem, Pierce was probably working with or for Greig.[10] Although it might be a mere literary flourish, Pierce certainly seems to have had law on his mind. In the preface to his cantos, he wrote: "Without asking a favor from society, this first offspring of my fancy is submitted to their hands: I depend upon the decision of the bench; the jury may exercise mercy, but rigid justice and a strict annunciation of the law rests with the judge: it were however unworthy myself, and indecorous to the public, to say that I view with indifference the verdict, but I may say with truth, I am prepared for any result" (12).

Pierce dedicated his second canto to George Washington Parke Custis, whom he identified as an "esquire, of Arlington" (65). Custis (1781–1857) was the stepgrandson of Martha Washington, and she and George adopted him. A noted orator and playwright, he delivered a speech in 1812 titled "Oration by Mr. Custis, of Arlington; with an Account of the Funeral Solemnities in Honor of the Lamented Gen. James M. Lingan," which covered much of the subject of Pierce's second canto and from which Pierce probably drew.

Pierce dedicated his third canto to Stephen Van Rensselaer (1764–1839), whom he also called an "esquire, of Albany" and whom he further identified as a "late major general in the New York state line, and commander in chief of the American forces in the attack upon the heights of Queenston, on the 16th October, A.D. 1812" (124). He was also one of the heroes that Pierce celebrated in the third canto. Given Rensselaer's extensive land holdings, it is likely that he did business with John Greig.

Pierce's dedication of his overall poem to a Washington Benevolent Society was an immediate clue that he was allied with the Federalist Party, which used the Washington Benevolent Societies to oppose Democratic-Republican policies. The New York chapter was the first such organization, designed in part to counteract the Democratic-Republican Tammany Society ("Washington Benevolent Society" 1915–1916, 276; also see Ballard 1900). Washington Benevolent Societies were particularly known for holding processions on Washington's birthday, the anniversary of Washington's first inauguration, or the Fourth of July, which were often accompanied by orations ("Washington Benevolent Society" 1915–1916, 282). Chiefly based in New England, these societies were especially associated with opposition to the War of 1812.

The author of an article on the Washington Benevolent Societies observed that the writings and speeches of the society "are all distinguished by pessimism and distrust in American institutions. They look backward, not to the future" ("Washington Benevolent Society" 1915–1916, 283). The preamble of the Boston branch of the society, probably typical of others, evoked a golden age when "the people were prosperous in their industry, the government was respected by foreign nations, and the commercial prosperity, the wealthy and the power of the United States were augmented to a degree without precedent and beyond the most sanguine expectation" (qtd. ibid., 278).

Pierce reflected such sentiments in the introduction to his first canto:

> With exultation we hold
> Each lofty name by fame enroll'd.
> Statesman, hero, patriot, sage,
> Of other and a happier age;
> But ah! Their laurell'd brows proclaim
> The father's worth and offspring's shame. (17)

In the preface to his poems, Pierce expressed concern about the state of poetry in the United States—"the first of the fine arts which flourishes in a country, and the first also which declines" (7). This concern seems extraordinary for a man his age. Although he cited Joel Barlow (1754–1812), Timothy Dwight (1752–1817), and John Trumbull (1750–1831),[11] he thought only the latter was of real consequence (11). He further acknowledged that "the subject-matter," the political events of a single year, was somewhat "transient," and said that he had composed his work in three months. He reported that he intended for "the miscellaneous cast" of characters to be similar to that which Sir Walter Scott (1771–1832) employed in his poem *Marmion*, published in 1808 (ibid.). Pierce ended his preface, much as his birth father had ended his self-description in the character sketches, by professing, "if there is a chord wound around my heart, as durable as the spring of life itself, it is that which feelingly vibrates to the name of country" (12).

Outline of Pierce's Cantos

Pierce is perhaps best known for his vivid journalistic descriptions of the great earthquake of 1811, which he experienced on a flatboat on the Mississippi while taking a tour from Pittsburgh to New Orleans (notes to Canto I, 8). His account was published in the *New-York Evening Post*, copied by the *Weekly Messenger* of Boston, and later published in a rare pamphlet, William Leigh Pierce et al., *An Account of the Great Earthquakes, in the Western States, Particularly on the Mississippi River, December 16–23, 1811: Collected from Facts* (Newburyport, 1812) (Ross 1968, 93).[12]

Pierce continued his theme of catastrophe in Canto I, "The Review," where he used this earthquake, a similar event in Caracas, and a theater fire in Richmond, Virginia, on December 26, 1811, in which many were killed (detailed in Baker 2012), as portents of the following terrible year, which would include the beginning of an American war against Great Britain.[13] Whereas the earthquakes and fire he described were largely effects of nature, wise statesmen could have avoided war. Pierce sadly contrasted the leaders of the early republic with those, most notably Thomas Jefferson and James Madison, whom he believed were responsible for unwise policies that resulted in war. As a man with ties to both North and South, he was clearly more comfortable with the negative attitude toward the war of the former rather than the general support for the war, which he observed in the latter (63).

Pierce entitled his second canto "The Mob." He devoted most of this canto to a vivid description of a mob attack against Alexander Contee Hanson, the virulent Federalist publisher of the *Federal-Republican* in Baltimore, that resulted in many injuries and at least one death (that of General James M. Lingan, a Revolutionary War veteran) among Hanson's defenders; Hanson was the president of Baltimore's Washington Benevolent Society (Cassell 1975, 243). Pierce tied such mob behavior, which modern scholars believe was a departure from the more controlled riots that had been so important in the American Revolution (see Gilje 1980), to faction[14] and to the influence of the revolution in France, both common themes in Federalist literature of the period (Roth 1960). He believed these had largely led to the war against Britain, which he treated in his third canto. The most fascinating aspect of the second canto may be that it enabled Pierce to emerge as a defender of "liberty of speech, and the freedom of the press," both of which he described (notes to Canto II, 52–53) as "so radically interwoven with the federal constitution."[15]

Pierce was distraught over the partisan nature of the contemporary press. James T. Callender (1758–1803), the Jeffersonian propagandist who later turned on Jefferson and publicized his sexual relationship with his slave Sally Hemings, was a favorite target. In his notes to Canto III, Pierce wrote:

> It is degrading to the good sense of community, that in the United States the editorial columns of most of the public prints are not only used as the vehicle of virulent invective, but are seized with avidity by a large class of readers as firmly established political doctrine. Although devotedly attached to "the freedom of the press"; although I view it as one of the principal palladiums of liberty, and would more cheerfully draw in its defence; yet I cannot but feel mortified and humbled as an American, when I see it so much abused by men whom nature has not qualified to adorn it. (69)

Observing that "An honest fame directs an honest heart; / That man is blest who plays a virtuous part," Pierce further opined, "Sublime that love which warms at country's name, / And greets her glories with a loud acclaim" (136). In a passage quoted in at least one literary anthology of the period (Kettell 1829),[16] Pierce continued:

> In all the vary'd change and state of life,
> The calm of solitude, or noisy strife,
> Man still is man, and read him as you will,
> Unstript, he stands the child of interest still. (139)

Pierce elaborated:

> The wandering tartar, and the swarthy moor;
> The Parthian archer, and Norwegian boor;
> The booted pole, whose birthright is his sword;
> The bearded saxon, bart'd by his lord;
> The stubborn russ, devoted to his czar;
> The crafty Frenchman, clamorous for war;
> The whisker'd Spaniard, solemn, grave and sad;
> The highland soldier, in his tartan plaid;
> The soft Italian, studious of wile;
> The generous Briton, faithful to his isle;
> The brave columbian, freedom's favor'd son;
> All, all alike, the race of interest run. (138)

Not only do these lines rely chiefly on racial and cultural stereotypes, but the canto as a whole reflects deep nativist sentiments, with particular antagonism toward the French, the Irish, and Albert Gallatin (Switzerland), all of which contemporaries associated with the Democratic-Republican Party (144–146). Although Pierce clearly believed the war of 1812 to be a mistake,[17] his third canto celebrated the American forces who sought to invade Canada as well as those, including the crew of the U.S.S. *Constitution*, who distinguished themselves in battles at sea.

Pierce's Descriptions of the Convention Delegates

Pierce was, of course, more interested in the chief political characters of 1812 rather than the delegates to the Constitutional Convention, which his father had previously described, but the portraits of those delegates that the younger Pierce did include are worth comparing. Notably, many of the individuals about whom the son commented were already dead, so he could not have observed them personally, and his accounts thus lacked the immediacy of those of his father. Sadly, even Pierce's description of his birth father and his exploits were hearsay since the father had passed away before the son was born.

GEORGE WASHINGTON

Pierce's most numerous tributes were to George Washington as father of the country. Pierce chiefly used Washington as a symbol for those who recognized the need for ordered liberty:

> Well did he know, that freedom uncontrol'd
> Was fierce, oppressive, virulent and bold:
> That passion, like old ocean's raging waves,
> Lashes the strand; along its landmarks raves:
> Disdains restraint,—with loud tumultuous roar,
> And breaks in thunder on the sounding shore. (36)[18]

Pierce further cited the first president as "the name of freedom's loved, her darling son, / The great, the wise, the virtuous Washington" (82) and referred to "His country's savior, godlike Washington!" (190).

In his notes to Canto I, Pierce observed, "There probably never existed a man who was deeper versed in the study of human nature, than the lamented founder of American freedom, George Washington, and certainly the annals of the world exhibit no brighter instance of public and private virtue" (23).

JAMES MADISON

Pierce clearly conceived of President James Madison (who had also served as secretary of state under Jefferson) as the author of America's participation in the War of 1812. Notwithstanding the positive portrayals of Madison by his birth father, the junior Pierce suggested that he regarded Madison as continuing under what he considered to be the spell of Jefferson, whom he in turn associated with James Callender and other scurrilous propagandists. It is not clear whether Pierce's reference to Madison's pen was to his work on the Virginia Plan, the Constitution, *The Federalist Papers*, or another work:

> Eight years thus roll'd away their baneful flight,
> Chill, drear, and heavy, closed the shades of night;
> When crafty Madison arose to rule,
> Opinion's weathercock, a party's tool;
> Shaped with the times, and true alone to Gaul [France],
> He watch'd her wishes, to obey them all!
> And could that man, whose pen in early age,
> Impress'd so deep a stamp upon the page,
> That man, who, leagued with wisdom's sons
>   [Hamilton and Jay] to twine,
> Around the Fed'ralist a wreath divine,
> Could he consent to play a minor part,
> The puppet fashion'd by a master's art? (41–42)

Pierce further affirmed in the notes to his first canto: "The course of policy pursued by James Madison since he was first elected president of the United States, has been bottomed upon the Jeffersonian system, notwithstanding the continued experience of its futility and inefficacy, and notwithstanding his assertions in black and white, in express contradiction of its leading principles; he carried however his subserviency to France, yet further than his predecessor" (28–29).

PIERCE'S APPRECIATION OF
SKILLFUL RHETORIC

Pierce occasionally praised Randolph, but the Randolph he had in mind was not Edmund Randolph, who, as governor, had represented Virginia at the Constitutional Convention of 1787 and went on to serve as attorney general and secretary of state, but the quirky John Randolph, who, as a member of Congress, eventually abandoned Jefferson because he believed he had grown soft on states' rights (see Johnson 1929; Johnson 2012) and became a tertium quid (a third something). Randolph was known for opposing the War of 1812.

The most fascinating aspect of Pierce's comments on John Randolph is that Pierce, as his father had done with so many of the delegates, focused on Randolph's language, which Pierce correctly identified as among the most notable in U.S. history for its invective:

Randolph has oft pour'd elocution's stream,
And for a moment broke delusion's dream;
Oft his keen satire, with resistless sway,
Has flash'd on folly all the light of day;
That galling lash, who of the suitor train,
Has not experienced and writhed with pain? (54)

Some other lines also indicate that Pierce shared his father's appreciation of good rhetoric. Referring to Fisher Ames (1758–1808), the one-time leader of the Federalist Party in the House of Representatives, Pierce observed:

What tongue like thine, mellifluous streams distill'd,
Touch'd every soul, and trembling passion thrill'd?
"The thoughts that breathe, and words that burn," we find
In every effort of thy godlike mind. (49)

CHARLES COTESWORTH PINCKNEY

Pierce referenced Charles Cotesworth Pinckney, whom Madison had defeated in the presidential election of 1808. Pierce largely focused this portrait, however, not on Pinckney's work at the Constitutional Convention but on his role (with John Marshall and Elbridge Gerry) in the xyz Affair, in which they had resisted French pleas for a bribe in return for access and influence:

What friend of freedom, sees, nor sees with pain,
Her Pinckney wise, and great, and good, in vain?
That man, the glory of our public weal,
Forgotten in wild party's frantic zeal;
That man, whose eye with more than lightning glance,
Shot its own terrors through the court of France.
How look'd the wily Talleyrand amazed,
When Pinckney's virtues in his presence blazed?
When from her stately hall, with splendors hung,
France heard aghast the thunders of his tongue? (47–48)

OLIVER ELLSWORTH

Although Connecticut's Oliver Ellsworth, whom his father had also admired, was dead, Pierce evoked his memory:

Who feels not, in this dark and dismal day,
The want of learned Ellsworth's vigorous ray?
Ellsworth, whose bold, sublime and nervous mind,
Unravell'd art, and gave to sight the blind;
Guided by reason's strong, unyielding clue,

Through the dark labyrinth he fearless flew;
Like lightning, pierced the deep recess of wile,
Delusion stript, and made the desert smile;
Intrigue shrunk back and fled his searching sight;
In vain she shrunk, he dragg'd her into light.
His mind, unmoved by the soft syren's tale,
With forceful grasp asunder rent her veil. (50)

WILLIAM PATERSON

Pierce mentioned the connection of William Paterson of New Jersey, a former governor and delegate to the Constitutional Convention, with Stephen Van Rensselaer of Albany, who had married Paterson's daughter and whom Pierce admired. Pierce's misspelling of Paterson's name, while common, reflects that of his father and might thus be another indication that he consulted the earlier sketches while writing his poem:

Well chose the virtuous Patterson,
In thee a bosom friend and son,
Gave to thine arms a darling child,
And while he gave his daughter, smiled. (125)

Pierce followed this with a note: "The honorable judge Patterson, one of the justices of the supreme court of the United States, and among the most illustrious names in the annals of our confederacy" (135).[19]

ALEXANDER HAMILTON

In addition to Washington, another hero of Pierce appears to be Alexander Hamilton, who would have been especially admired in New York. As in the cases of Ames and Randolph, Pierce's praise, which centered on Hamilton's role in Washington's administration rather than at the Constitutional Convention, included specific reference to Hamilton's rhetoric:

There was a time, an ever glorious time,
When men beheld our councils tower sublime.
When wisdom touch'd the lips of her fond son,
The world's great wonder, matchless Hamilton.
His was the hero's hand and statesman's head,
The field to rule, the cabinet to lead;
His was the mind, intuitively great.
To form and shape the credit of a state;
To teach the stream of eloquence to roll,
Rouse, nerve, expand, and overwhelm the soul;

> To save his country, and expound her laws,
> And hear unmoved the thunder of applause. (49)

Critiquing Albert Gallatin, who had served as secretary of the treasury, Pierce asked: "What has the artful, upstart-favorite done, / But filch'd some springs from godlike Hamilton?" (146).

FRANKLIN, MASON, AND OTHERS

Some individuals who had served as delegates to the Constitutional Convention received little more than passing mention. In his preface, Pierce included a number of these delegates in a list of worthies: "the names of WASHINGTON in the camp and cabinet, of HAMILTON on the forum, of FRANKLIN in the study, of [Benjamin] WEST, STEWART [Gilbert Stuart?] and [John] TRUMBULL, in the gallery, of [Benjamin] RUSH, [George] MASON, [James] SMITH, [John] MARSHALL, WALSH [whom I've been unable to identify], and the illustrious author of McFingal [John Trumbull] are positive contradictions to the assertion so often made, that 'there is a constitutional-phlegm and dullness in the American character'" (9).

It seems worthy of note that Pierce did not include his birth father's mentor Charles Willson Peale (perhaps because of his high regard among Democratic-Republicans) among the artists that he listed. Many other convention luminaries—including Gouverneur Morris, James Wilson, and Roger Sherman—go unmentioned in Pierce's poem.

CONNECTICUT

As discussed in the previous chapter, when Louis-Guillaume Otto portrayed various members of Congress, he viewed the leaders of Connecticut not as epitomizing their own particular attributes but as the reflection of the wholesome character of the state's people. In his third canto, William Leigh Pierce employed a similar strategy when defending the honor of the New England states, whose patriotism had been called into question because of their opposition to the War of 1812. His characterization of Connecticut is similar in theme to that of Otto:

> First, where Connecticut without a stain
> Rears her fair front, and overlooks the main;
> A land where industry pleads virtue's cause,
> Whose moral purity defends its laws;
> A land whose shores the pilgrim patriot trod,
> When tyrants crush'd the altars of his god. (152)

Pierce's Conclusion

At the end of his third canto, William Leigh Pierce included a final reference to the "Land of my sires! To whom my early youth / Fond and devoted pledged its sacred truth" (190). The poet ended (a literary convention or a premonition of Pierce's early death?) with an epitaph for himself:

> When in the grave the child of song shall sleep,
> And some few friends in fond remembrance weep;
> O may the stone to feeling strangers tell.
> "Here lies a man, who loved his country well;
> "Here lies the bard, who shed compassion's tear
> "O'er freedom's fall, and mad delusion's year." (191)

Much like his birth father, Pierce wanted to be remembered, first and foremost, as a patriot, yet his vision was far less hopeful for the future than his father's had been. Instead of the triumph of reason and compromise that the elder Pierce associated with the Constitutional Convention, the younger Pierce beheld a catastrophe that he believed had resulted from the presence of self-interest and faction. Despite his high regard for patriotism and virtue and for those citizens who embodied them, it is as though his earlier words were proven true: "Man still is man, and read him as you will, / Unstript, he stands the child of interest still" (139).

Fourth of July Oration

There remains one additional work of Pierce to consider, an oration that he gave on the Fourth of July 1812. Pierce delivered this speech before the Savannah Volunteer Guard, a group formed by John Cumming, a Savannah businessman, in 1802, largely of former Revolutionary War veterans, to defend the state ("Savannah Volunteer Guard" n.d.). The title page of the published work identified Pierce as a member, and the War of 1812 would be among the engagements in which it participated. The speech is significant both because it makes for a fascinating comparison to the speech that Pierce's father gave during the controversy over ratification of the U.S. Constitution in 1788 and because the tone of the speech was more optimistic than that of the poem and seems to be in partial tension with it.

The title page cites a verse from an otherwise unidentified "New-Year's Address for 1812." It reads in whole:

> A People here, who Freedom's altars sought,
> Possess that Land, for which their Fathers fought;

In union blest, they wear no tyrant's chain,
They fear no Lodi, dread no Wagram's plain—
If to their country's sacred banner true,
They want not splendor, need no empty shew.[20]

Several themes unite Pierce's Fourth of July oration with his poem. The speech, like the poem, expressed a great deal of filial piety. As in the poem, Pierce used his speech to indicate proudly that his father participated in the Revolution (7). Although Pierce did not specifically mention his father's or his stepfather's exploits, as in the poem, he praised "our own *Washington*, the friend of man—the savior of liberty—the father of his country" (8). Pierce further described Washington as "the preserver of our rights; the bulwark of our liberties" (ibid.). He particularly praised Washington for giving up his command at the end of the conflict (10) and for helping to bring about "the halcyon days of freedom—days of happy prosperity, and honorable peace" (11). As in his poem, Pierce lauded the memory "of his friend and companion in arms, the intelligent and accomplished *Hamilton*" (12).

Pierce associated both Washington and Hamilton with a glorious Constitution and with progress. Calling the "federal constitution, an everlasting monument of enlightened virtue," he rhetorically posed: "Under the auspices of that noble instrument what limit has man in his progress towards the goal of political prosperity?" (14). Moreover, in a vision that many Democratic-Republican advocates of westward expansion would also have shared, Pierce observed that the Constitution had fostered national prosperity and expansion:

Wherever you turn your eyes, you behold, "all full of courage and strength." In the east, the nerves and sinews of war, industry, commerce and wealth; in the south, a luxuriant agriculture; in the west a wide and spacious domain, abounding with every convenience and luxury of life; there the honest and industrious farmer, with little labor, produces plenty; and the ploughshare has already opened the glebe on the banks of the beautiful Ohio. The hum of business is heard along the majestic shores of the great Parent of waters—our adventurous countrymen, penetrating into the wilds of the west, have made them "to blossom as the rose." (15)

Pierce then offered a much more balanced view of Britain and France than he would present in his poem the following year.

Pierce offered a foretaste of the theme of faction that would emerge with greater vigor in his poem: "The hour has arrived to chain the inexorable demon of party, and rally with fraternal harmony around the altars of freedom" (18). Perhaps because of his audience, Pierce seemed to counsel defense of the nation rather than defiance of its policies: "In such a moment, I see the American matrons like their prototypes of Sparta, assist in arming their sons for battle; I see the father once more unsheathe that sword which in days of his youth had flashed amid the ranks of an insulting foe" (ibid.). Pierce further noted that some of his comrades were "already toiling on the tented field, ready to display the intrepidity of freemen; their gallant spirits shall find a friend in every honest bosom; their example shall arouse, where it slumbers, the dormant fire of martial emulation" (21). In a footnote, Pierce explained that he was referring to "East-Florida," where even prior to the War of 1812, forces from Georgia had invaded with the unrealistic hope of wresting the territory from Spain (see Cusick 2007).

It seems appropriate that Pierce ended his speech with a reference to a metaphor that his father had used in letters defending the Constitution. He called for the help of providence in helping "to launch our peaceful BARQUE [ship]" (22).

Although not as directly relevant to his father's character sketches as the poem is, the speech raises a number of questions, which will, for now, remain unanswered. Did Pierce's opposition to the war increase with time? Did he present a somewhat different character before his fellow Savannah Volunteer Guards, some of whom were in active service, than he did to the general public? Was he perhaps conflicted over what he considered the folly of American policy and the hope of imperialistic gains (especially in Florida, which bordered his state of birth)?

What Does a Reading of William Leigh Pierce
Add to His Father's Sketches?

The speech and poem by William Leigh Pierce contain limited information about his birth father and the son's circumstances since his death, but they show some remarkable parallels. Like his birth father, Pierce was a gifted writer with a keen ear, deep appreciation for the liberal arts, and deep pride in his country.

The contrast between the works of the father and son remain palpable, however. Although the former could be brutally candid about the strengths and weaknesses of the characters he described, even his backhanded descriptions do not have the partisan or gossipy tone that both Otto and his son sometimes did. This suggests that part of what made the Constitutional Convention and the document that emerged so remarkable was that the work was done at a time before leading national figures were clearly identified as members of one of two major political parties in the United States or with the rival foreign policies of the French and the English. The framers, of course, had to work through compromises involving the large and small states, the free and slave states, the coastal states and new states that would be created in the interior, and those that depended chiefly on commerce and industry and those that relied chiefly on farming. The framers, most notably James Madison in his classic Federalist No. 10 essay (Hamilton, Madison, and Jay 1961, 76–84), had suggested that the new nation would have to work with factions rather than attempting to eliminate them, and yet perhaps not even he fully expected the fissures that developed during Washington's first administration. Although Madison had worked closely with Hamilton and Jay in writing *The Federalist Papers*, he soon differed with them on the constitutionality of a national bank (and accompanying issues of constitutional interpretation) and with respect to attitudes toward Britain and France.

These fissures were heightened during the historic presidential and congressional elections of 1800 and were rarely more evident than during the period leading up to and including the War of 1812, during which William Leigh Pierce wrote. Delegates from the New England states met at the Hartford Convention from December 1814 to January 1815 to discuss whether they should even remain in the Union. Gouverneur Morris was among those who were willing to consider breaking up the nation (Brookhiser 2003, 205–206). While the victory over the British at New Orleans, the coming of peace, and the election of James Monroe ushered in a brief "era of good feelings," these fissures—especially those between states that were free and those that permitted slavery—would become even more evident in the disputes that led to the Civil War.

Otto's descriptions of congressmen in 1788 suggest that the convention's compromises might have been difficult even a year later. William Leigh Pierce's extended poem likewise suggests that it would have been very difficult to tailor compromises like those that the members of the Constitutional Convention achieved in 1787 against the backdrop of the War of 1812. Catherine Drinker Bowen named her account of the Constitutional Convention *Miracle at Philadelphia* (1966), and Otto's and Pierce's reflections seem to concur. Steven D. Smith observed that the framers considered "their own situation as in some important sense uniquely privileged," and this assessment may not have been far from the mark (1998, 42–43). The true genius of the men who met in Philadelphia in 1787 may not have been so much the specific solution that they crafted (however wise and enduring it has been) but their recognition that the time to act was at hand, and if they failed to act, the opportunity may well have been lost for many years.

NOTES

1. School records show that Pierce joined the Clio Society, a literary and debating club, in 1807. Revived from the earlier Plain Dealing Club and Well Meaning Club by William Paterson, the Whig society and the Clio societies (now joined under one rubric) were respectively

founded by James Madison and Aaron Burr. See "The American Whig Cliosophic Society: History," http://whigclio.princeton.edu/history. The Clio Society likely served a similar function for William Leigh Pierce that Phi Beta Kappa had served for his father when he was in Williamsburg.

2. At the end of Pierce's commonplace book (375), there were several seals, including the U.S. artillery seal of Colonel John H. Fenwick, the seal of Ebenezer Jackson, his own, and others. Most are difficult to decipher, but his appears to be a colonial gentleman in relief.

3. Although he used quotation marks as if he were referring to his father's character sketches, the younger Pierce was paraphrasing since his father had actually stated that "my services in Congress and the Convention were bestowed with the best intention towards the interest of Georgia, and towards the general welfare of the Confederacy."

4. Pierce also praised his father's commander, Nathanael Greene:

> In fame's immortal temple, where is seen
> A name more glorious than the name of Greene?
> Oft did he face the cannon's Levin jaws,
> Oft draw his sword in freedom's holy cause;
> Yet mourn we not that o'er Columbia's shore
> Peace scarce had triumph'd ere he was no more.
> How had it grieved that hero to behold
> His country duped, her independence sold;
> To see her shameless, base ingratitude,
> To those who shed in freedom's cause their blood. (42–43)

5. Based on the rest of the poem, the "fields of conquest" is almost surely a reference to the War of 1812.

6. This information is in "Marriage and Death Notices from Early Geneva Newspapers," http://ontario.nygenweb.net/earlygenevanewsmarriagedeath.htm.

7. Simon Willard Jr. (1795–1874), the son of a famous clockmaker, wrote an extended call for constitutional reform in a book that he published in Albany, New York, in 1815 when he was only about twenty. Like Pierce, Willard referred to the United States as "Columbia." A narrative rather than a poem, Willard's work makes for laborious reading. For an analysis, see Vile 2010, 2:541–545.

8. Pierce's descriptions of earthquakes and natural disasters further evidenced a strong emphasis on the natural sciences. In the notes to his first canto (17), Pierce differed with those who thought the earthquake was caused by electrical forces and hypothesized instead that it was caused by steam. He also seemed to associate the earthquake with the weather. While this was not scientifically correct, it shows a mind that was oriented to connecting possible causes and effects.

9. McNall summarized Greig's life: "John Greig—patron of education in Canandaigua and elsewhere, long-term member of the Board of Regents of the State of New York, supporter and patron of libraries, churches, and charities, champion of internal improvements, leader in agricultural organizations, hospitable host to a score of literary travelers, Lafayette and Louis Philippe in Paris, benefactor of numerous Scottish connections in the homeland and in the United States, and briefly a member of Congress, in short an immigrant boy who made good in 'the new land o' cakes'" (1959, 534).

10. Pierce, however, used this same designation for the two other individuals to whom he dedi-

cated his cantos, neither of whom was a lawyer. This suggests that, like his birth father, he used the term "esquire" as a more general title of esteem.

11. All three were among the group, associated with Yale, known as the Connecticut Wits. See Howard 1943.

12. Noting that no nineteenth-century writers appear to have cited this work, Ross (1968, 93) believed that it "was lost in the obscurity of newspaper and pamphlet publication." She found the account to be "the most interesting," in part because it was written in Arkansas and in part because it was written so contemporaneously with the event (Christmas Day 1812).

13. In a similar vein, Arthur Joseph Stansbury, a Presbyterian minister, published a sermon entitled *God Pleading with America* (1813) likening God's judgment on America to that on Sodom and Gomorrah. As if drawing from the same playbook, Stansbury asked: "Have we forgotten the catastrophe at Richmond? How suddenly were the haunts of sinful pleasure turned into a furnace of judgment, and the temple of folly with all her thoughtless votaries made a smouldering ruin! After the fires came storms upon our sea-board; and scarcely had these finished their commission by strewing our coast with the wrecks of ships and the dead bodies of their crews, when they were followed by earthquakes along all our southern and western border" (19).

14. There is irony in the fact that Pierce supported a Benevolent Society, which was tied to a faction and a party, while criticizing another. Richard Hofstader (1972) is among those historians who have noted that it took a while before early Americans recognized the legitimacy and patriotism of members of rival parties.

15. By contrast, modern historians are far more likely to link Federalists to the repressive Alien and Sedition Acts of 1798, which made it a crime to criticize the president or the government of the United States, while linking Republicans to the defense of the First Amendment. Donald R. Hickey (1976) wrote an account of the Baltimore riots in which he concluded "that neither the party nor the people were as enlightened as republican ideologues liked to believe. The Republicans in 1812 were very much a part of their age, and like the Federalists in 1798, they found it difficult to tolerate dissent to their war policy" (14–15).

16. Kettell (1829) said that Pierce displayed "considerable talent, for one of his age." The editor also observed, "Party prejudices and antipathies, in which he seems to have participated deeply, will account for the harshness of his invectives, and the gloomy and distorted picture which in many cases he has drawn of the state of affairs" (http://www.bartleby.com/96/194. html).

17. This was a common view among New England Federalists. See Lawrence Delbert Cress, "'Cool and Serious Reflection': Federalist Attitudes toward War in 1812," *Journal of the Early Republic* 7 (Summer 1987):123–145.

18. By contrast, although Pierce recognized John Adams's important contributions to the American Revolution, he was highly critical of his presidency:

> Unhappy man! Hadst thou but early died,
> We yet had hail'd thee with an honest pride:
> Thy name rank'd high among our greatest men,
> And paid due homage to thy logic pen!
> Now gray in years, that pen with frothy rage
> Distils the licensed petulance of age;
> Securely daring, meanly strives to shed
> Its dastard slanders on the mighty dead [Hamilton].

Alas! Betray'd by power's insatiate lust,
Behold thy honors prostrate in the dust!
Behold thyself now call'd "a doting fool."
Dark knavery's bolster, and convenient tool.
Art thou that man, who erst in happier times
Bearded the despot and reproved his crimes? (38)

This criticism is consistent with Pierce's praise of Alexander Hamilton, who, although he was a fellow Federalist, also had little faith in Adams.

19. The use of the term "confederacy" seems, at least indirectly, to point back to the Articles of Confederation, which Paterson's New Jersey Plan would have more closely followed than did the Virginia Plan and the Constitution that emerged from the convention.

20. This may have been taken from a newspaper carrier's address, which were common in this era, although I have been unable to identify the specific paper that might have printed this one. See "Carriers' Addresses: New Year's Greetings" n.d.

REFERENCES

Baker, Meredith Henne. 2012. *The Richmond Theater Fire: Early America's First Great Disaster*. Baton Rouge: Louisiana State University Press.

Ballard, Harlan H. 1900. "A Forgotten Fraternity." *Collections of the Berkshire Historical and Scientific Society* 3:279–298.

Bowen, Catherine Drinker. 1966. *Miracle at Philadelphia: The Story of the Constitutional Convention, May to September 1787*. Boston: Little, Brown.

Brookhiser, Richard. 2003. *Gentleman Revolutionary: Gouverneur Morris, the Rake Who Wrote the Constitution*. New York: Free Press.

"Carriers' Addresses: New Year's Greetings." n.d. Special Collections, Brown University Library. http://dl.lib.brown.edu/repository2/repoman.php?verb=render&id=1078233105841778&v.

Cassell, Frank A. 1975. "The Great Baltimore Riot of 1812." *Maryland Historical Magazine* 70, no. 3 (Fall):241–259.

Cusick, James G. 2007. *The Other War of 1812: The Patriot War and the American Invasion of Spanish East Florida*. Athens: University of Georgia Press.

Denning, Brannon. 2001. "Reeve, Tapping." In *Great American Lawyers: An Encyclopedia*, edited by John R. Vile, 2:583–588. 2 vols. Santa Barbara, Calif.: ABC-CLIO.

Ernst, Nan Thompson. 2007. *Ebenezer Jackson: A Register of His Papers in the Library of Congress*. Washington, D.C.: Manuscript Division, Library of Congress.

General Catalogue of Princeton University, 1746–1906. 1908. Princeton, N.J.: Princeton University.

Gilje, Paul A. 1980. "The Baltimore Riots of 1812 and the Breakdown of the Anglo-American Mob Tradition." *Journal of Southern History* 13, no. 4 (Summer):547–564.

"Greig, John." n.d. *Biographical Directory of the United States Congress*. http://bioguide.congress.gov/scripts/biodisplay.pl?index=G000449.

Hamilton, Alexander, James Madison, and John Jay. 1961. *The Federalist Papers*. New York: New American Library.

Hickey, Donald R. 1976. "The Darker Side of Democracy: The Baltimore Riots of 1812." *Maryland Historian* 7, no. 2 (Fall):1–19.

Hofstader, Richard. 1972. *The Idea of a Party System: The Rise of Legitimate Opposition in the United States, 1780–1840*. Berkeley: University of California Press.

Howard, Leon. 1943. *The Connecticut Wits*. Chicago: University of Chicago Press.

Johnson, David. 2012. *John Randolph of Roanoke*. Baton Rouge: Louisiana State University Press.

Johnson, Gerald W. 1929. *Randolph of Roanoke: A Political Fantastic*. New York: Minton, Balch.

Kettell, Samuel, ed. 1829. *Specimens of American Poetry, with Critical and Biographical Notices*. 3 vols. Boston: S. G. Goodrich.

McNall, Neil A. 1959. "John Greig: Land Agent and Speculator." *Business History Review* 33, no. 4 (Winter):524–534.

Meeks, Carroll L. V. 1951. "Lynx and Phoenix: Litchfield and Williamsburg." *Journal of the Society of Architectural Historians* 10 (December):18–23.

Pierce, William Leigh. 1812. *Oration on American Independence Delivered in the Presbyterian Church, Savannah, Georgia, on the Fourth of July, 1812, by Appointment of the Savannah Volunteer Guards, and Published at Their Request*. Savannah, Ga.: John J. Evans.

———. 1813. *The Year: A Poem, in Three Cantoes*. New York: David Longworth.

Ross, Margaret. 1968. "The New Madrid Earthquake." *Arkansas Historical Quarterly* 27, no. 2 (Summer):83–104.

Roth, George L. 1960. "Verse Satire on 'Faction,' 1790–1815." *William and Mary Quarterly*, 3rd ser., 17, no. 4 (October):473–485.

"The Savannah Volunteer Guard." n.d. http://www.savannahvolunteerguard.org/home.htm.

Smith, Steven D. 1998. *The Constitution and the Pride of Reason*. New York: Oxford University Press.

Stansbury, Arthur Joseph. 1813. *God Pleading with America: A Sermon Delivered on the Late Fast Day, Recommended by the American Churches and by the President of the U. States*. Goshen, N.Y.: T. B. Crowell.

Starr, Frank Farnsworth. 2012. *The Edward Jackson Family of Newton, Massachusetts, in the Lines of Commodore Charles Hunter Jackson, United States Navy, Middletown, Connecticut*. 1895. Reprint, Charleston, S.C.: Nabu Press.

Vile, John R. 2010. *Encyclopedia of Constitutional Amendments, Proposed Amendments, and Amending Issues, 1789–2010*. 3rd ed. 2 vols. Santa Barbara, Calif.: ABC-CLIO.

"The Washington Benevolent Society in New England: A Phase of Politics during the War of 1812." 1915–1916. *Proceedings of the Massachusetts Historical Society*, 3rd. ser., 49 (October–June):274–286.

Willard, Simon, Jr. 1815. *The Columbian Union, Containing General and Particular Explanations of Government, and the Columbian Constitution, Being an Amendment to the Constitution of the United States: Providing a Yearly Revenue to Government of About Forty Millions of Dollars, and the Inevitable Union of the People by a Rule of Voting, and Exemption from Unnecessary Taxation, Consequently Their Permanent and Perpetual Freedom*. Albany, N.Y.: printed for the author.

CODA

My own character I shall not attempt to draw, but leave
those who may choose to speculate on it, to consider it in
any light that their fancy or imagination may depict.

—William Pierce Jr.'s Character Sketches

Jacob Broom of Delaware is the only one of the thirty-nine signers of the Constitution for whom no contemporary portrait, painting, or sketch is known to exist.
Louis Glanzman's 1987 painting of the signing of the Constitution, which greets
visitors to Independence Hall, sought to overcome this problem by portraying
Broom signing the document with his back to viewers (Vile 2005, 1:37).

William Churchill Houston, William Houstoun, Robert Yates, and William
Pierce are the only four nonsigning delegates for whom no picture remains.[1] It
seems ironic that Pierce, who studied under a portrait artist, is part of this group.
His presence among them likely stems from the fact that Pierce died so shortly after
the convention that he was not accessible to those interested in commemorating
the delegates who had attended the event. Although today's scholars know that the
work of the convention largely endured, the participants could not be sure that it
would. On the day after the delegates signed the Constitution, George Washington
noted in a letter to Lafayette that the Constitution "is a Child of fortune, to be fostered by some and buffeted by others" (St. John 1990, ix).

Pierce's sketches of the delegates are, to my knowledge, the first attempt at a
collective portrait of them ever published,[2] and thus may have exerted far greater
influence on subsequent understandings of the Constitutional Convention than is
generally thought. The next collective set of what would later be a torrent of such
biographies appears to be that of Hampton L. Carson, but his work was not published until 1889, just after the centennial celebration of the Constitution.

In his brief sketch of Benjamin Franklin, Pierce invited "his Biographer" to
"finish his character." Pierce remains one of the lesser known participants in part
because he has *not* been the subject of an extended biography and in part because
reports of such basic information as the year and place of his birth are often con-

tradictory. Researchers must rely on their own observations and analyses of his writings to ascertain his character. Such observations reveal a sharp wit and a willingness to compare his judgments (especially on assessments of rhetorical abilities) against those of others. Although Pierce's attendance at the convention was limited, his portraits indicate that he gave relatively close and careful attention to the debates. Pierce's observations suggest that he strongly valued a classical education and the virtues typically associated with it. His focus on the legal backgrounds of the delegates seems somewhat excessive, especially when coupled with the little attention that he devoted to those with landed wealth (though this may have partly been subsumed under his use of the word "gentleman"). Pierce projected himself as an individual of ambition who valued political skills, but he sometimes believed that the skills of certain delegates were overrated.

Pierce invited readers to consider his character "in any light that their fancy or imagination may depict," but although there is no complete portrait, an analysis of his sketches, including his comments about himself, hardly leaves his readers with a blank canvas. In my judgment, there are times, like his description of William Livingston of New Jersey, when Pierce's sketches are as notable for "a sportiveness of wit" as for their "strength of thinking"; they remain classics. Given that Pierce made relatively few comments about delegates' physical characteristics, the central strength of his sketches stems not from Pierce's artist-trained eye but from the acuity of his ear for speaking mannerisms and styles. The sketches' strengths are further highlighted when Pierce's portraits are compared with those of his contemporaries and those of his namesake. Pierce generally portrayed characters as individuals, rather than as symbols for larger political parties or movements. Even after adding these comparisons to previously gathered facts, however, one's imagination must still fill in some gaps in the verbal portrait of Pierce.

NOTES

1. The last of six prefatory pages to Coleman 1910 (picture 12 on the bottom of the right side) has a sketch of a man with long hair and a prominent mustache and beard, who is identified as Pierce, but Coleman does not identify the source, and the absence of pictures of Pierce in similar volumes suggests that the identification is conjectural. Similarly, the artist Alonzo Chappel (1828–1887), who was best known for his battle scenes, did an engraving published by Johnson, Fry and Co. in New York in 1858 titled *The Battle of Eutaw Springs* in which he depicted a man on horseback next to General Greene who apparently represents Pierce. Chappel could not, of course, have seen Pierce, and while his engraving is not quite "all hat and no cattle," the image of Pierce derives its force more from the battle cap and uniform than from any specific features of his face.
2. John Sanderson, Robert Wain, and Henry D. Gilpin (1823–1827) did publish a nine-volume work, *Biography of the Signers to the Declaration of Independence*, near its fiftieth anniversary.

It seems possible that this series, as well as the nation's celebration of the fiftieth anniversary of the writing of the Declaration of Independence, served as an impetus for the publication of Pierce's sketches. For a discussion of the celebrations surrounding the jubilee of the Declaration of Independence, see Burstein 2001.

REFERENCES

Burstein, Andrew. 2001. *America's Jubilee: How in 1826 a Generation Remembered Fifty Years of Independence*. New York: Knopf.

Carson, Hampton L. 1889. "Biographies of the Members of the Federal Convention." In *History of the Celebration of the One Hundredth Anniversary of the Promulgation of the Constitution of the United States*, edited by Hampton L. Carson, 1:135–237. 2 vols. Philadelphia: Lippincott.

Coleman, Nannie McCormick. 1910. *The Constitution and Its Framers*. Chicago: Progress.

Sanderson, John, Robert Wain, and Henry D. Gilpin. 1823–1827. *Biography of the Signers to the Declaration of Independence*. 9 vols. Philadelphia: R. W. Pomeroy.

St. John, Jeffrey. 1990. *A Child of Fortune: A Correspondent's Report on the Ratification of the U.S. Constitution and the Battle for a Bill of Rights*. Ottawa, Ill.: Jameson Books.

Vile, John R. 2005. *The Constitutional Convention of 1787: A Comprehensive Encyclopedia of America's Founding*. Santa Barbara, Calif.: ABC-CLIO.

APPENDIX 1

William Pierce's Character Sketches of
Delegates to the Federal Convention

From Farrand, *Records of the Federal Convention of 1787* (1966, appendix CXIX, 3:87–97), who got them from the *American Historical Review* (1898, 3:325–334). The Connecticut State Library provided me with a copy of the original *Pierce's Reliques*.

FROM NEW HAMPSHIRE
Jno. Langdon Esqr. and Nichs. Gilman Esquire

Mr. Langdon is a Man of considerable fortune, possesses a liberal mind, and a good plain understanding.—about 40 years old.

Mr. Gilman is modest, genteel, and sensible. There is nothing brilliant or striking in his character, but there is something respectable and worthy in the Man.—about 30 years of age.

FROM MASSACHUSETTS
Rufus King, Natl. Gorham, [Elbridge] Gerry and
Jno. [Caleb] Strong Esquires

Mr. King is a Man much distinguished for his eloquence and great parliamentary talents. He was educated in Massachusetts, and is said to have good classical as well as legal knowledge. He has served for three years in the Congress of the United States with great and deserved applause, and is at this time high in the confidence and approbation of his Country-men. This Gentleman is about thirty three years of age, about five feet ten Inches high, well formed, an handsome face, with a strong expressive Eye, and a sweet high toned voice. In his public speaking there is something peculiarly strong and rich in his expression, clear and convincing in his arguments, rapid and irresistible at times in his eloquence but he is not always equal. His action is natural, swimming, and graceful, but there is a rudeness of manner sometimes accompanying it. But take him *tout en semble*, he may with propriety be ranked among the Luminaries of the present Age.

Mr. Gorham is a Merchant in Boston, high in reputation, and much in the esteem of his Country-men. He is a Man of very good sense, but not much improved in his education. He is eloquent and easy in public debate, but has nothing fashionable or elegant in his style;—all he aims at is to convince, and where he fails it never is from his auditors not understanding him, for no Man is more perspicuous and full. He has been President of Congress, and three years a Member of that Body. Mr. Gorham is about 46 years of age, rather lusty, and has an agreeable and pleasing manner.

Mr. Gerry's character is marked for integrity and perseverance. He is a hesitating and laborious speaker;—possesses a great degree of confidence and goes extensively into all subjects that he speaks on, without respect to elegance or flower of diction. He is connected and sometimes clear in his arguments, conceives well, and cherishes as his first virtue, a love for his Country. Mr. Gerry is very much of a Gentleman in his principles and manners;—he has been engaged in the mercantile line and is a Man of property. He is about 37 years of age.

Mr. Strong is a Lawyer of some eminence,—he has received a liberal education, and has good connections to recommend him. As a Speaker he is feeble, and without confidence. This Gentn. is about thirty five years of age, and greatly in the esteem of his Colleagues.

FROM CONNECTICUT

Saml. Johnson, Roger Sherman, and
W. [Oliver] Elsworth Esquires

Dr. Johnson is a character much celebrated for his legal knowledge; he is said to be one of the first classics in America, and certainly possesses a very strong and enlightened understanding.

As an Orator in my opinion, there is nothing in him that warrants the high reputation which he has for public speaking. There is something in the tone of his voice not pleasing to the Ear,—but he is eloquent and clear,—always abounding with information and instruction. He was once employed as an Agent for the State of Connecticut to state her claims to certain landed territory before the British House of Commons; this Office he discharged with so much dignity, and made such an ingenious display of his powers, that he laid the foundation of a reputation which will probably last much longer than his own life. Dr. Johnson is about sixty years of age, possesses the manners of a Gentleman, and engages the Hearts of Men by the sweetness of his temper, and that affectionate style of address with which he accosts his acquaintance.

Mr. Sherman exhibits the oddest shaped character I ever remember to have met with. He is awkward, un-meaning, and unaccountably strange in his manner. But in his train of thinking there is something regular, deep and comprehensive; yet the oddity of his address, the vulgarisms that accompany his public speaking, and that strange New England cant which runs through his public as well as his private speaking make everything that is connected with him grotesque and laughable;—and yet he deserves infinite praise,—no Man has a better Heart or a clearer Head. If he cannot embellish he can furnish thoughts that are wise and useful. He is an able politician, and extremely artful in accomplishing any particular object;—it is remarked that he seldom fails. I am told he sits on the Bench in Connecticut, and is very correct in the discharge of his Judicial functions. In the early part of his life he was a Shoe-maker;—but despising the lowness of his condition, he turned Almanack maker, and so progressed upwards to a Judge. He has been several years a Member of Congress, and discharged the duties of his Office with honor and credit to himself, and advantage to the State he represented. He is about 60.

Mr. Elsworth is a Judge of the Supreme Court in Connecticut;—he is a Gentleman of a clear, deep, and copious understanding; eloquent, and connected in public debate; and always attentive to his duty. He is very happy in a reply, and choice in selecting such parts of his adversary's arguments as he finds make the strongest impressions,—in order to take off the force of them, so as to admit the power of his own. Mr. Elsworth is about 37 years of age, a Man much respected for his integrity, and venerated for his abilities.

FROM NEW YORK

*Alexander Hamilton, [Robert] Yates, and
W. [John] Lansing Esquires*

Colo. Hamilton is deservedly celebrated for his talents. He is a practitioner of the Law, and reputed to be a finished Scholar. To a clear and strong judgment he unites the ornaments of fancy, and whilst he is able, convincing, and engaging in his eloquence the Heart and Head sympathize in approving him. Yet there is something too feeble in his voice to be equal to the strains of oratory;—it is my opinion that he is rather a convincing Speaker, [than] a blazing Orator. Colo. Hamilton requires time to think,—he enquires into every part of his subject with the searchings of philosophy, and when he comes forward he comes highly charged with interesting matter, there is no skimming over the surface of a subject with him, he must sink to the bottom to see what foundation it rests on.—His language is not always equal, sometimes didactic like Bolingbroke's and at others light and tripping like Stern's. His eloquence is not so defusive as to trifle with the senses, but he rambles just enough to strike and keep up the attention. He is about 33 years old, of small stature, and lean. His manners are tinctured with stiffness, and sometimes with a degree of vanity that is highly disagreeable.

Mr. Yates is said to be an able Judge. He is a Man of great legal abilities, but not distinguished as an Orator. Some of his Enemies say he is an anti-federal Man, but I discovered no such disposition in him. He is about 45 years old, and enjoys a great share of health.

Mr. Lansing is a practicing Attorney at Albany, and Mayor of that Corporation. He has a hesitation in his speech, that will prevent his being an Orator of any eminence;—his legal knowledge I am told is not extensive, nor his education a good one. He is however a Man of good sense, plain in his manners, and sincere in his friendships. He is about 32 years of age.

Wm. Livingston, David Brearly, Wm. Patterson,
and Jonn. Dayton, Esquires

Governor Livingston is confessedly a Man of the first rate talents, but he appears to me rather to indulge a sportiveness of wit, than a strength of thinking. He is however equal to anything, from the extensiveness of his education and genius. His writings teem with satyr and a neatness of style. But he is no Orator, and seems little acquainted with the guiles of policy. He is about 60 years old, and remarkably healthy.

Mr. Brearly is a man of good, rather than of brilliant parts. He is a Judge of the Supreme Court of New Jersey, and is very much in the esteem of the people. As an Orator he has little to boast of, but as a Man he has every virtue to recommend him. Mr. Brearly is about 40 years of age.

M. Patterson is one of those kind of Men whose powers break in upon you, and create wonder and astonishment. He is a Man of great modesty, with looks that bespeak talents of no great extent,—but he is a Classic, a Lawyer, and an Orator;—and of a disposition so favorable to his advancement that every one seemed ready to exalt him with their praises. He is very happy in the choice of time and manner of engaging in a debate, and never speaks but when he understands his subject well. This Gentleman is about 34 ys. of age, of a very low stature.

Capt. Dayton is a young Gentleman of talents, with ambition to exert them. He possesses a good education and some reading; he speaks well, and seems desirous of improving himself in Oratory. There is an impetuosity in his temper that is injurious to him; but there is an honest rectitude about him that makes him a valuable Member of Society, and secures to him the esteem of all good Men. He is about 30 years old, served with me as a Brother Aid to General Sullivan in the Western expedition of '79.

Benja. Franklin, Thos. Mifflin, Robt. Morris,
Geo. Clymer, Thomas Fitzsimons, Jared Ingersol[l],
James Wilson, Go[u]verneur Morris

Dr. Franklin is well known to be the greatest phylosopher of the present age;—all the operations of nature he seems to understand,—the very heavens obey him, and the Clouds yield up their Lightning to be imprisoned in his rod. But what claim he has to the politician, posterity must determine. It is certain that he does not shine much in public Council,—he is no Speaker, nor does he seem to let politics engage his attention. He is, however, a most extraordinary Man, and tells a story in a style more engaging than anything I ever heard. Let his Biographer finish his character. He is 82 years old, and possesses an activity of mind equal to a youth of 25 years of age.

General Mifflin is well known for the activity of his mind, and the brilliancy of his parts. He is well informed and a graceful Speaker. The General is about 40 years of age, and a very handsome man.

Robert Morris is a merchant of great eminence and wealth; an able Financier, and a worthy Patriot. He has an understanding equal to any public object, and possesses an energy of mind that few Men can boast of. Although he is not learned, yet he is as great as those who are. I am told that when he speaks in the Assembly of Pennsylvania, that he bears down all before him. What could have been his reason for not Speaking in the Convention I know not,—but he never once spoke on any point. This Gentleman is about 50 years old.

Mr. Clymer is a Lawyer of some abilities;—he is a respectable Man, and much esteemed. Mr. Clymer is about 40 years old.

Mr. Fitzsimons is a Merchant of considerable talents, and speaks very well I am told, in the Legislature of Pennsylvania. He is about 40 years old.

Mr. Ingersol is a very able Attorney, and possesses a clear legal understanding. He is well educated in the Classics, and is a Man of very extensive reading. Mr. Ingersol speaks well, and comprehends his subject fully. There is a modesty in his character that keeps him back. He is about 36 years old.

Mr. Wilson ranks among the foremost in legal and political knowledge. He has joined to a fine genius all that can set him off and show him to advantage. He is well acquainted with Man, and understands all the passions that influence him. Government seems to have been his peculiar Study, all the political institutions of the World he knows in detail, and can trace the causes and effects of every revolution from the earliest stages of the Greecian commonwealth down to the present time. No man is more clear, copious, and comprehensive than Mr. Wilson, yet he is no great Orator. He draws the attention not by the charm of his eloquence, but by the force of his reasoning. He is about 45 years old.

Mr. Governeur Morris is one of those Genius's in whom every species of talents combine to render him conspicuous and flourishing in public debate:—He winds through all the mazes of rhetoric, and throws around him such a glare that he charms, captivates, and leads away the senses of all who hear him. With an infinite stretch of fancy he brings to view things when he is engaged in deep argumentation, that renders all the labor of reasoning easy and pleasing. But with all these powers he is fickle and inconstant,—never pursuing one train of thinking,—nor ever regular. He has gone through a very extensive course of reading, and is acquainted with all the sciences. No Man has more wit,—nor can any one engage the attention more than Mr. Morris. He was bred to the Law, but I am told he disliked the profession, and turned merchant. He is engaged in some great mercantile matters with his namesake Mr. Robt. Morris. This Gentleman is about 38 years old, he has been unfortunate in losing one of his Legs, and getting all the flesh taken off his right arm by a scald, when a youth.

John Dickinson, Gunning Bedford, [George Read],
Geo. Richd. Bassett, and Jacob Broom Esquires

Mr. Dickinson has been famed through all America, for his Farmers Letters; he is a Scholar, and said to be a Man of very extensive information. When I saw him in the Convention I was induced to pay the greatest attention to him whenever he spoke. I had often heard that he was a great Orator, but I found him an indifferent Speaker. With an affected air of wisdom he labors to produce a trifle,—his language is irregular and incorrect,—his flourishes (for he sometimes attempts them), are like expiring flames, they just shew themselves and go out;—no traces of them are left on the mind to clear or animate it. He is, however, a good writer and will ever be considered one of the most important characters in the United States. He is about 55 years old, and was bred a Quaker.

Mr. Bedford was educated for the Bar, and in his profession I am told, has merit. He is a bold and nervous Speaker, and has a very commanding and striking manner;—but he is warm and impetuous in his temper, and precipitate in his judgment. Mr. Bedford is about 32 years old, and very corpulant [*sic*].

Mr. Read is a Lawyer and a Judge;—his legal abilities are said to be very great, but his powers of Oratory are fatiguing and tiresome to the last degree;—his voice is feeble, and his articulation so bad that few can have patience to attend to him. He is a very good Man, and bears an amiable character with those who know him. Mr. Read is about 50, of a low stature, and a weak constitution.

Mr. Bassett is a religious enthusiast, lately turned Methodist, and serves his Country because it is the will of the people that he should do so. He is a Man of plain sense, and has modesty enough to hold his Tongue. He is a Gentlemanly Man, and is in high estimation among the Methodists. Mr. Bassett is about 36 years old.

Mr. Broom is a plain good Man, with some abilities, but nothing to render him conspicuous. He is silent in public, but chearful and conversable in private. He is about 35 years old.

Luther Martin, Jas. Mc.Henry,
Daniel of St. Thomas Jenifer, and Daniel Carrol[l] Esquires

Mr. Martin was educated for the Bar, and is Attorney general for the State of Maryland. This Gentleman possesses a good deal of information, but he has a very bad delivery, and so extremely prolix, that he never speaks without tiring the patience of all who hear him. He is about 34 years of age.

Mr. Mc.Henry was bred a physician, but he afterwards turned Soldier and acted as Aid to Genl. Washington and the Marquis de la Fayette. He is a Man of specious talents, with nothing of genious to improve them. As a politician there is nothing remarkable in him, nor has he any of the graces of the Orator. He is however, a very respectable young Gentleman, and deserves the honor which his Country has bestowed on him. Mr. Mc.Henry is about 32 years of age.

Mr. Jenifer is a Gentleman of fortune in Maryland;—he is always in good humour, and never fails to make his company pleased with him. He sits silent in the Senate, and seems to be conscious that he is no politician. From his long continuance in single life, no doubt but he has made the vow of celibacy. He speaks warmly of the Ladies notwithstanding. Mr. Jenifer is about 55 years of Age, and once served as an Aid de Camp to Major Genl. Lee.

Mr. Carrol is a Man of large fortune, and influence in his State. He possesses plain good sense, and is in the full confidence of his Countrymen. This Gentleman is about ___ years of age.

FROM VIRGINIA

Genl. Geo. Washington, Geo. Wythe, Geo. Mason,
Jas. Maddison junr., Jno. Blair, Edmd. Randolph,
and James Mc.Lurg

Genl. Washington is well known as the Commander in chief of the late American Army. Having conducted these States to independence and peace, he now appears to assist in framing a Government to make the People happy. Like Gustavus Vasa, he may be said to be the deliverer of his Country;—like Peter the Great he appears as the politician and the States-man; and like Cincinnatus he returned to his farm perfectly contented with being only a plain Citizen, after enjoying the highest honor of the Confederacy,—and now only seeks for the approbation of his Country-men by being virtuous and useful. The General was conducted to the Chair as President of the Convention by the unanimous voice of its Members. He is in the 52d. year of his age.

Mr. Wythe is the famous Professor of Law at the University of William and Mary. He is confessedly one of the most learned legal Characters of the present age. From his close attention to the study of general learning he has acquired a compleat knowledge of the dead languages and all the sciences. He is remarked for his exemplary life, and universally esteemed for his good principles. No Man it is said understands the history of Government better than Mr. Wythe,—nor any one who understands the fluctuating condition to which all societies are liable better than he does, yet from his too favorable opinion of Men, he is no great politician. He is a neat and pleasing Speaker, and a most correct and able Writer. Mr. Wythe is about 55 years of age.

Mr. Mason is a Gentleman of remarkable strong powers, and possesses a clear and copious understanding. He is able and convincing in debate, steady and firm in his principles, and undoubtedly one of the best politicians in America. Mr. Mason is about 60 years old, with a fine strong constitution.

Mr. Maddison is a character who has long been in public life; and what is very remarkable every Person seems to acknowledge his greatness. He blends together the profound politician, with the Scholar. In the management of every great question he evidently took the lead in the Convention, and tho' he cannot be called an Orator, he is a most agreeable, eloquent, and convincing Speaker. From a spirit of industry and application which he possesses in a most eminent degree, he always comes forward the best informed Man of any point in debate. The affairs of the United States, he perhaps, has the most correct knowledge of, of any Man in the Union. He has been twice a Member of Congress, and was always thought one of the ablest Members that ever sat in that Council. Mr. Maddison is about 37 years of age, a Gentleman of great modesty,—with a remarkable sweet temper. He is easy and unreserved among his acquaintance[s], and has a most agreeable style of conversation.

Mr. Blair is one of the most respectable Men in Virginia, both on account of his Family as well as fortune. He is one of the Judges of the Supreme Court in Virginia, and acknowledged to have a very extensive knowledge of the Laws. Mr. Blair is however, no Orator, but his good sense, and most excellent principles, compensate for other deficiencies. He is about 50 years of age.

Mr. Randolph is Governor of Virginia,—a young Gentleman in whom unite all the accomplishments of the Scholar, and the States-man. He came forward with the postulate, or first principles, on which the Convention acted, and he supported them with a force of eloquence and reasoning that did him great honor. He has a most harmonious voice, a fine person and striking manners. Mr. Randolph is about 32 years of age.

Mr. Mc.Lurg is a learned physician, but having never appeared before in public life his character as a politician is not sufficiently known. He attempted once or twice to speak, but with no great success. It is certain that he has a foundation of learning, on which, if he pleases, he may erect a character of high renown. The Doctor is about 38 years of age, a Gentleman of great respectability, and of a fair and unblemished character.

NORTH CAROLINA

Wm. Blount, Richd. Dobbs Spaight, Hugh Williamson,
Wm. Davey, and Jno. [Alexander] Martin Esquires

Mr. Blount is a character strongly marked for integrity and honor. He has been twice a Member of Congress, and in that office discharged his duty with ability and faithfulness. He is no Speaker, nor does he possess any of those talents that make Men shine;—he is plain, honest, and sincere. Mr. Blount is about 36 years of age.

Mr. Spaight is a worthy Man, of some abilities, and fortune. Without possessing a Genius to render him brilliant, he is able to discharge any public trust that his Country may repose in him. He is about 31 years of age.

Mr. Williamson is a Gentleman of education and talents. He enters freely into public debate from his close attention to most subjects, but he is no Orator. There is a great degree of good humour and pleasantry in his character; and in his manners there is a strong trait of the Gentleman. He is about 48 years of age.

Mr. Davey is a Lawyer of some eminence in his State. He is said to have a good classical education, and is a Gentleman of considerable literary talents. He was silent in the Convention, but his opinion was always respected. Mr. Davey is about 30 years of age.

Mr. Martin was lately Governor of North Carolina, which office he filled with credit. He is a Man of sense, and undoubtedly is a good politician, but he is not formed to shine in public debate, being no Speaker. Mr. Martin was once a Colonel in the American Army, but proved unfit for the field. He is about 40 years of age.

SOUTH CAROLINA
Jno. Rutledge, Chs. Cotesworth Pinckney,
Charles Pinckney, and Pierce Butler Esquires

Mr. Rutledge is one of those characters who was highly mounted at the commencement of the late revolution;—his reputation in the first Congress gave him a distinguished rank among the American Worthies. He was bred to the Law and now acts as one of the Chancellors of South Carolina. This Gentleman is much famed in his own State as an Orator, but in my opinion he is too rapid in his public speaking to be denominated an agreeable Orator. He is undoubtedly a man of abilities, and a Gentleman of distinction and fortune. Mr. Rutledge was once Governor of South Carolina. He is about 48 years of age.

Mr. Chs. Cotesworth Pinckney is a Gentleman of Family and fortune in his own State. He has received the advantage of a liberal education, and possesses a very extensive degree of legal knowledge. When warm in a debate he sometimes speaks well,—but he is generally considered an indifferent Orator. Mr. Pinckney was an Officer of high rank in the American army, and served with great reputation through the War. He is now about 40 years of age.

Mr. Charles Pinckney is a young Gentleman of the most promising talents. He is, altho' only 24 ys. of age, in possession of a very great variety of knowledge. Government, Law, History and Phylosophy are his favorite studies, but he is intimately acquainted with every species of polite learning, and has a spirit of application and industry beyond most Men. He speaks with great neatness and perspicuity, and treats every subject as fully, without running into prolixity, as it requires. He has been a Member of Congress, and served in that Body with ability and eclat.[1]

Mr. Butler is a character much respected for the many excellent virtues which he possesses. But as a politician or an Orator, he has no pretentions to either. He is a Gentleman of fortune, and takes rank among the first in South Carolina. He has been appointed to Congress, and is now a Member of the Legislature of South Carolina. Mr. Butler is about 40 years of age; an Irishman by birth.

FROM GEORGIA

Wm. Few, Abraham Baldwin, Wm. Pierce,
and Wm. Houstoun Esqrs.

Mr. Few possesses a strong natural Genius, and from application has acquired some knowledge of legal matters;—he practices at the bar of Georgia, and speaks tolerably well in the Legislature. He has been twice a Member of Congress, and served in that capacity with fidelity to his State, and honor to himself. Mr. Few is about 35 years of age.

Mr. Baldwin is a Gentleman of superior abilities, and joins in a public debate with great art and eloquence. Having laid the foundation of a compleat classical education at Harvard College, he pursues every other study with ease. He is well acquainted with Books and Characters, and has an accommodating turn of mind, which enables him to gain the confidence of Men, and to understand them. He is a practising Attorney in Georgia, and has been twice a Member of Congress. Mr. Baldwin is about 38 years of age.

Mr. Houstoun is an Attorney at Law, and has been Member of Congress for the State of Georgia. He is a Gentleman of Family, and was educated in England. As to his legal or political knowledge he has very little to boast of. Nature seems to have done more for his corporeal than mental powers. His Person is striking, but his mind very little improved with useful or elegant knowledge. He has none of the talents requisite for the Orator, but in public debate is confused and irregular. Mr. Houstoun is about 30 years of age of an amiable and sweet temper, and of good and honorable principles.

My own character I shall not attempt to draw, but leave those who may choose to speculate on it, to consider it in any light that their fancy or imagination may depict. I am conscious of having discharged my duty as a Soldier through the course of the late revolution with honor and propriety; and my services in Congress and the Convention were bestowed with the best intention towards the interest of Georgia, and towards the general welfare of the Confederacy. I possess ambition, and it was that, and the flattering opinion which some of my Friends had of me, that gave me a seat in the wisest Council in the World, and furnished me with an opportunity of giving these short Sketches of the Characters who composed it.

NOTE

1. "In reference to this part of his life, Mr. Pinckney frequently spoke of the deep diffidence and solemnity which he felt, being the youngest member of the body, whenever he addressed the Federal Convention." J. B. O'Neall, *Biographical Sketches of the Bench and Bar of South Carolina* (Charleston, 1859), 2:140.

APPENDIX 2

French Minister's Sketches

List of Members and Officers of Congress, 1788

Included are notes on the most interesting persons from the various states.

Nich[olas] Gillman

Young man with pretensions; not much liked by his colleagues; mockingly nicknamed "the Congress." He however has the advantage to have represented his state at the Great Convention of Philadelphia and to have signed the Constitution. Such circumstance proves that choices are scarce in that state or that to the least, the most sensible and skillful men are not wealthy enough to accept a public position. Mr. G. served during the war as a camp aid.

John Langdon

One of the most interesting and amiable men in the United States; current Governor of New Hampshire and head of a powerful party, he is in opposition to General Sullivan.[1]

Mr. L. made a great fortune in commerce; he is the Rob. Morris of his state for he spends a lot of money and he has a lot of citizens on his side because of his liberalities. He was one of the main members of the Philadelphia Convention but he only sat in Congress for a few days. Even though his colleagues offered him the presidency, he did not want to stay because his intentions were to be reelected as Governor of New Hampshire, and because his business did not allow him to stay away from it for too long. He is sincerely attached to France and is even predisposed to our customs and manners. In order to spread people's taste for our furniture, he has had very beautiful pieces shipped from Paris. The rumor goes that he is jealous of his wife, which is something quite uncommon in America. Several French officers sadly realized that this jealousy had no foundation.

MASSACHUSETTS
[Elbridge Gerry]

In Congress, he [Nathan Dane] has always sided with Mr. Gerry,[2] who does not like us and has been mainly opposed to the ratification of our Consular Convention. He possesses more talents than Mr. Gerry and is less duplicitous.

CONNECTICUT
[Oliver Ellsworth and Roger Sherman]

Mr. Ellsworth, a current member of Congress, is a man of the absolute same bearing and dispositions [as Benjamin Huntington]. The same thing can be said of Mr. Sherman—the people of this state, in general, possess a national character that can scarcely be found in the other parts of the continent. They are closer to the republican simplicity: they live comfortably without knowing opulence. Rural economy and home industry are pushed very far in Connecticut. People live happy there.

NEW YORK
Alex[ander] Hamilton

Great orator: intrepid in public debates. A zealous partisan and besides, outraged by the new Constitution, he is a declared enemy of the Clinton government which he courageously and publicly attacked in the newspapers, without any incitement. He is one of those rare men who has distinguished himself equally at the battlefield and to the bar. He owes everything to his talents. An indiscretion caused him to be on bad terms with General Washington for whom he was the trustworthy secretary. Other indiscretions led him to leave Congress in 1783. He has too many pretentions and possesses too little prudence.

Here is what Sir de La Luzerne said about him in 1780: "Mr. Hamilton: one of General Washington's camp aids who has the most influence over him. He is a witty man of a mediocre probity. Estranged from the English because he is of low birth from one of their colonies, he fears to return to his former state. He is a peculiar friend of Mr. de La Fayette. Mr. Conway thinks that Hamilton hates the French, that he is fundamentally corrupt and that the ties he pretends to have with us will never be anything else than misleading."

Mr. Hamilton hasn't done anything that could justify the last comment. He is simply too impetuous and because he wants to control everything, he misses his target. His eloquence is often out of place during public debates as precision and clarity are preferred to a brilliant imagination. It is believed that Mr. Hamilton is the author of a pamphlet entitled "the Federalist." His purpose was again lost in it. This piece of work is of no use to the educated people, and it is too scholarly and too long to the ignoramuses.

Nevertheless, it made him famous; a small frigate pulled on the streets of New York during the great federal procession was named the "Hamilton" after him. However, whether displayed here or elsewhere, these types of parades are only but ephemeral impressions. Since the party of the anti-federalists was the most numerous in the state, Mr. Hamilton lost more than he won because of the zeal he displayed during this event.

Estranged in this state where he has been brought up by charity, Mr. Hamilton found a way to abduct the daughter of General Schuyler,[3] a wealthy and very influential landowner. Since his reconciliation with the family, he currently lives off his father-in-law's money.

NEW JERSEY
[Jonathan] Dayton

Not well known; has the sole merit to be the son of a good patriot and benefactor of Mr. d'Anteroches; this is why we can presume he likes the French. There are in this state several individuals that we need to treat considerately because they are our friends and because they are very influential.

[William Livingston]

William Livingston, Esq., governor since the beginning of the revolution, he is well learned, firm, patriotic and prefers the public good to his own popularity and has often risked his position as governor to prevent the legislature to adopt bad laws. Even though he does not cease to satirize the people, he is always reelected, for even his enemies agree that he is one of the most skillful and virtuous men in the continent. He is the father of Madame Jay and of Mr. Broc. Livingston.

PENNSYLVANIA
[Benjamin Franklin]

Dr. Franklin, current President of this state, is too well-known to be in need for the praises we owe him. He senses, more than any other American, that to be a true patriot, one needs to be a friend of France. Unfortunately, this philosopher who managed to brave anathema and the wrath of the Parliament of England, will not fight for much longer old age infirmities. It is our regret that immortality only belongs to his name and his writings.

[Thomas Mifflin]

Current General, President of Congress, orator of the assembly, etc. Proclaimed and proven friend of France. He is very popular and he handles with a surprising ease the one hundred headed monster named the people. He is a good lawyer, a good officer, a good patriot, and he is of a very agreeable society. Whatever he does, he does it well because he takes after nature and he can but only overcome by showing who he really is.

[Robert Morris]

Superintendent of Finances during the war, he is a powerful negotiator in his state. He owes everything to his good looks and to his experiences and very little to his education. His relationship with France cooled off ever since Mr. de Marbois took to the party of Mr. Hotker with so much passion and since we disapproved of his contract with the farm. It will however be easy to gain it by using good methods.[4] He is a very influential man and we shall not be indifferent to his friendship.

[Gouverneur Morris]

A citizen of the state of New York, he is still in touch with Mr. Rob. Morris and has represented Pennsylvania many times. Famous lawyer; one of the most organized head in the continent but has no morals and according to his enemies, no principles either; infinitely interesting in a conversation, he studied with peculiar care the field of finances. He constantly works with Mr. Rob. Morris. He is more feared than admired but few people respect him.

James Wilson

Distinguished legal adviser. It is he who was designated by Mr. Gerard to be the lawyer of the French nation, a position that has been since then, recognized as useless. He is a haughty man, an intrepid aristocrat, active, eloquent, profound, secretive, and known as "James the Caledonian," a nickname given to him by his enemies. He disturbed his fortune with great enterprises that public affairs did not permit him to follow. Attached to France rather badly.

John Dickinson

Author of the letters of the farmer from Pennsylvania; very rich man who was a member of the anti-Anglican party at the beginning of the revolution without however favoring independence against which he publicly voted. He is old, weak and has no influence.

MARYLAND
Mr. Luther Martin

Distinguished lawyer who wrote a lot on the resolutions of the Philadelphia Convention and of which he was a member.

VIRGINIA
James Madison

Learned, wise, moderate, docile and studious; may be more profound than Mr. Hamilton but less brilliant; close friend of Mr. Jefferson and sincerely attached to France. He was very young when he first started working at Congress and he seems to have devoted himself specifically to public affairs. He may one day become the governor of his state if his modesty allows him to accept the position. He recently declined the position of President of Congress. He is a man one needs to scrutinize for a long time before being able to conceive a just opinion of him.

[Edmund Randolph]

Edmund Randolph, current governor, he is one of the most distinguished men in America for his talents and his influence; he has however lost a part of his consideration when he opposed the ratification of the new Constitution with too much violence. He was a member of Congress in 1780 and in 1781, and judging from all the difficulties Sir de La Luzerne faced while negotiating with him our Consular Convention, we must consider him to be at least very indifferent to the French cause. All the objections that are recorded on file by Mr. Jay had been made by Mr. Randolph and the French Secretary only succeeded thanks to the moderation of the other members of the Committee.

NORTH CAROLINA

Hugh Williamson

Physician and currently professor in astronomy. Excessively bizarre, he likes to perorate but speaks with wit. It is difficult to know his character well; it is even possible that he doesn't have any but his occupation has recently given him a lot of influence at Congress.

SOUTH CAROLINA

J[ohn] Ruthledge [Rutledge]

Governor during the war, member of Congress, of the Convention and in general employed at all the important events. He is the most eloquent, but the proudest and the most imperious man in the United States. He takes advantage of his great influence and of his knowledge of the law to not pay his debts, which greatly exceed his fortune. His son travels in France for his education.

GEORGIA

Abrah[am] Baldwin

Reasonable and well-intentioned, but never had the opportunity to distinguish himself. Congress just gave him the means to do so by nominating him as one of the commissaries to settle accounts with the states.

William Few

Even though he is no great genius, he possesses more knowledge than his name or his looks seem to indicate. Still quite young, he has constantly been employed during the war. His colleagues have a good opinion of him. He is very shy and embarrassed in society except when one talks to him about business.

NOTES

Vilay Lyxuchouky, who is pursuing a Ph.D. in French and teaching at Middle Tennessee State University, translated this appendix from Max Farrand, *The Records of the Federal Convention*

(1966, 3:232–238). It is from a French archive labeled "Ministère des Affaires Estragères, Archives, Etats-Unis, Correspondence, supp., 2nd ser., vol. 15, 314ff." Farrand observed (232n1), "Although this document strictly does not belong to the records of the Federal Convention, it contains such interesting characterizations of so many of the delegates to that body, that it has seemed worth while to print it."

1. This opposition is only but personal and does not pertain to their political sentiments. Both antagonists are equally attached to their country, to the revolution and to France but Sullivan is a man of the people whereas Langdon is the protégé of *gentlemen*. One has countrymen on his side while the other, business men. However successful their intrigues are, the nation [*La chose publique*, equivalent to the Latin *res republica—trans.*]. will never be the ruin of it and the governing principles shall remain the same. In society, Mr. Langdon is by far ahead of his opponent. However, one should see Sullivan to the bar or at the head of the militia.

2. Mr. Elb. Gerry is a small, very scheming man full of niceties, which so far, have profited him quite well. He is, of all members of Congress, the one who has officiated the longest time. He has acquired there a great knowledge in public affairs which he uses to impress upon his fellow citizens. In 1782, he delivered quite a good speech in the legislature of Boston in which he urged not to permit the ratification of the Consular Convention. He pretends to like Sir de La Luzerne but one should be suspicious of all his great protestations. In general, we have very few friends among the powerful men of Massachusetts; our commerce is of no interest to them and our fisheries put them out. Mr. Bowdoin, Mr. King, Mr. Sam. Adams etc., draw all of their political notions from the writings or the conversations of Mr. Jay and Mr. J. Adams. In general, people like the French for they have often seen our fleets and they remember the services we rendered them.

3. Abductions are more common in America than in France. Parents get angry first, and then they are moved by the situation and patch things up after a few months. Everybody is interested in these types of marriage because they seem to conform to the first impulse of nature.

4. The original French term *procédés* can be translated as "methods" or "behaviors."—Trans.

APPENDIX 3

Pierce's 1788 Fourth of July Oration

An Oration Delivered at Christ Church, Savannah, on the
4th of July, 1788, in Commemoration of the Anniversary
of American Independence by Major William Pierce

Friends, Brother Officers, and Countrymen,

To awaken a remembrance of past events, and to call up your attention to that important era for the celebration of which we are now assembled, would be the most pleasing task, that could possibly be assigned me, had I abilities or powers equal to its accomplishment. But, unaccustomed as I am to public speaking, and totally out of the habit of searching after those ornaments that grace and set off style, I cannot but feel a diffidence in entering on the duty which I am called upon this day to perform. It is in obedience to your request, my Brother Officers, that I rise to commemorate the Anniversary of our Independence;—to speak of an event the most important that graces the page of history,—one which contributed to our friendly institution, and which unlocked the secret of political happiness to mankind.

Let it never be forgotten that, on the 4th day of July, 1776, (great and important let me call the period, for on that day we became freem[e]n) the Congress of the United States, amidst difficulties and dangers before and since unknown, "dissolved the political bands which had connected us with Great Britain, and assumed among the nations of the earth that separate and equal station to which the laws of nature and nature's God entitled us." It was on that day, my friends, that the genuine spirit of patriotism was tried. Such as were virtuous remained unshaken, such as doubted abandoned our cause. How glorious was the conduct of those who, not despairing of the commonwealth, ventured to risk both life and fortune for their country's good! To you, my Brother Officers, this compliment is due,—nor to you alone, but to that worthy Band of Citizens who shared the fortunes of a doubtful war, and who continued the steady supporters of a virtuous struggle;—to such an equal praise is due.

Savannah: James Johnston, 1788. I am pleased to acknowledge that a copy of this speech was provided by the Hargrett Library at the University of Georgia, Athens.

When we trace back to its source the cause of our dispute with Britain, and examine well the measures taken by America to counteract her views to enslave us, it is impossible not to admire that spirit of moderation and wisdom which marked every stage of the opposition. When insults and threats were thrown out we heard them with sorrow,—we remonstrated and petitioned against them with tears. When the offers of pardon and protection were sent us, we listened with respectful attention to the terms they conveyed,—but the condition of freedom was wanting. When the sword was drawn, and the plains of Lexington smoked [soaked?] with American and English blood, the passions of men were kept down, and reason with philosophic composure contemplated the mischiefs that were to follow. We had not learned to triumph over those whom we had been accustomed to address by the tender appellation of friends;—we wept over their ashes, and lamented them gone as our departed brethren. And now it was that the wisdom of America was to exert all its powers in the cause of freedom: Instead of this event inflaming the public mind, and pushing forward the people to an intemperate rage, they were wisely fashioned to know the value of that object for which they were all ere long to hazard their lives and fortunes. We had a powerful nation to contend with, and veteran troops to encounter;—great management and resource of course were required. We found them both in that Body of Patriots who were assembled at Philadelphia to manage the affairs of the Union. Delay and an opportunity to make a solemn appeal to the people, were essential to enter seriously on the great business of the war. To effect both these objects, (for I am not willing to attribute it to any other cause) Congress sent forward their last petition to the English Throne, expressed in terms more submissive than the high mounted pride of an injured people would have submitted to, had it not have been to obtain that principle of force from its rejection which was afterwards employed to produce a series of action[s] that effected our Independence and Freedom.

Fortunately for mankind the American Revolution happened at a period when the principles of society, and the nature of government, were better understood than at any former existence of the world. Men were taught how to define the rights of nature,—how to search into, to distinguish, and to comprehend, the principles of physical, moral, religious, and civil liberty. The spirit of free investigation had gone forth and stirred the genius of the civilized world; and men no longer fettered by false habits suffered philosophy, guided by truth, to pursue its way through the dark regions of ignorance and superstition without the dread of persecution. Our Revolution heightened its exertions. It has since gone into the Chambers of the Inquisition, and shaken the pillars on which that awful and bloody tribunal rested;—nay, it has ventured farther,—it has dared to approach the palaces of despots, and pointed out the boundaries of regal prerogative to Kings. But to proceed in detail where should I end? Great events have a principle of force annexed to their births that drives on their consequences through a succession of ages, and as they pass along they unfold their benefits or injuries to the different societies of the world. It is for posterity to enjoy the blessings of the American Revolution. Enough for us, my friends, that we have been the actors in a great scene intended for the good of mankind. God almighty grant that it may compleat the end of our hopes.

Many of the events on which have rested the fate of nations have been founded on accidents and trifles that ridicule belief. A circumstance as light as air has been the cause of a people's ruin, or a country's glory. A love adventure proved the destruction of the Trojan people;—the cackling of geese saved the Capitol of Rome from the ravages of the Gauls;—and the much famed Revolution of Switzerland turned, as it is storied, on the flight of an arrow shot from the bow of a private citizen of Uri.

Among more polished nations controverted points (incomprehensible in themselves) have occasioned rivers of blood to flow. We read of a King of France, a Prince of Orange, and a Duke of Guise, who were assassinated, and a King of England who was led to the block, to gratify the vengeance of ignorance and fanaticism. From the well known times of Charles V. to the celebrated people of Westphalia theological disputes, and ridiculous opinions, made Germany a scene of blood too terrible to behold. And indeed all Europe became a theatre for the most unruly and ungovernable passions to revel in.

How different, my friends, are the times we live in! With what contempt does an American look back and trace over such scenes of past folly!

Our late successful war with Britain stands upon grounds very different indeed! No circumstance of whim or passion moved us,—no fanatic zeal enraged us,—no cause of a popular demagogue inflamed us,—no dethroned monarch to replace,—no sympathetic fury caught from the injury of a favorite citizen urged us to oppose our parent country;—no,—all was the result of reason, and a train of injuries unprovoked, which prompted us to arms. The rights of human nature, and the benefits of civil liberty, we contended for; the cause of all mankind we engaged in. And is it not astonishing, my countrymen, that a people, bred as we were in the toils of agriculture, accustomed only to the reap hook and the plough, should have ventured to brave the hardships of war, and after an eight year struggle with the veteran troops of Britain to deliver up our country independent and free? Let, the volume of records be opened,—let the historic muse come forth, and point to the page where an event of equal magnitude appears.

Our success, if properly improved, will open a vast extent of country, where the oppressed may seek an asylum;—where the industrious may meet a plentiful return for their labor;—and where the virtuous may enjoy safety and peace.

The great scheme of political happiness we have in our power to accomplish: the prospect lies before us;—but as experience alone can teach a people how to direct their way through a wilderness of errors, it is no wonder that we have been so long on our pilgrimage to that happy shore which was unfolded to our view the day we took our station among the nations of the earth. Elated with success,—allured by false schemes of commerce,—and tempted by luxuries which we had for many years before been deprived of, we plunged, without reason or discretion, into habits of expence and idle speculation, that have so entangled and disordered the economy of our affairs as to make us neglectful of every public concern. The different states too, swayed by local

considerations, have been unmindful of the general interest, and have suffered the public faith to languish and sicken with reproach. Our Union, every day weakening, would
before this haven fallen into ruin, had not that wisdom which has guarded us in all
extremes pointed to the propriety of consolidating our interests, and uniting our views
under the direction of a general government. The different states appear by their Depu-
ties at Philadelphia, to undertake the momentous task. At the head of this great Council
presides the immortal Washington, and with him many of those illustrious characters
whose signatures grace the scroll of Independence. After four months deliberation the
great work is produced. It rises to view like a pyramid, whose broad foundation is
the people,—whose summit is their happiness. Let us examine the inscription which
relates the story of its birth:—"In our deliberations" (say the framers) "we kept steadily
in view, that which appeared to us the greatest interest of every true American, the con-
solidation of our Union, in which is involved our prosperity, felicity, safety,—perhaps
our national existence. This important consideration, seriously and deeply impressed
on our minds, led each state in the Convention to be less rigid on points of inferior
magnitude than might have been otherwise expected,—and the Constitution which is
here presented is the result of a spirit of amity, and of that mutual deference and concession which the peculiarity of our political situation rendered indispensable."

This is handed to the people,—-its contents are examined,—and, after the utmost
freedom of discussion, they come forward, and peaceably join in a new compact. Not
led by a blind zeal to favor a system they do not understand, but conducted by reason,
they support a plan that can alone save these states from ruin. Here, my Countrymen,
is the second great epoch of our history. Let us turn our attention to it, and know why
it is that a people smarting under the defects of an old government should maintain
the right of judging, altering, and even renewing the rules by which they choose to be
bound in a new one, without the spirit of innovation hurrying them into those extremes
that have destroyed the liberties of other nations. The reason is with us, and it is fortunate for us too, that the study of government has been attended to by almost every class
of people among us, and that the precise point where the line ought to be run between
obedience and command is better known in America perhaps than in any other country upon earth.

In contemplating our success in this great undertaking, we should congratulate ourselves that no mischievous or ambitious character should have shaken or disturbed the
public mind during the deliberations of the Convention;—and that no popular leader
since should have started up to give us law, and take advantage of our divisions.

When changes in a government take place, it is always to be expected that objections, discontents, and parties, will arise. The various schemes and interests which
men pursue, make it impossible to establish any system, however perfect, that will not
clash with some one or other of their views. Hence arises the feeble opposition made
in some of the states to the new Constitution. '"Confederated" (say the opposers) "as
we have hitherto been, with the addition of a little more power to our Federal Council, will be the only means of preserving our freedom, and supporting the flourishing

consequence of our republic." "But to adopt the new Constitution will be to sacrifice at once all the benefits of civil liberty, and to maintain with our own consent a tyranny that will lash and oppress posterity." Astonishing language! Has not experience sufficiently convinced us that the present government of the United States is inadequate to every national purpose? Has it ever been able to call forth from the different states resources sufficient to pay even the civil list, and keep itself in motion? And as this is the case, and as a blending of our power and interests is essential to our existence as a nation, does it not appear necessary that some such government, as the one proposed, should assume the place of anarchy? The unequal balance of the old Constitution suspends operations, and being placed, as it were, out of the perpendicular, it is like the hanging tower of Pisa, it is kept up and supported only by props, that must one day or another fall. It is impossible for any government, constituted as that is, to exert a national principle, where its parts are compleat only when separate, but discordant when united. In all the state governments the three great branches that maintain each other give each separate part of the Union an efficient power to execute its own laws. But, in the Federal constitution, there is nothing but legislative and recommendatory powers, without even the shadow of authority to support or enforce its decrees. It is impossible to hold together these states by ties so slender,—by powers so feeble and imperfect. To preserve the harmony of a great republic, the strong arm of power should be stretched out against it. Rome never felt her nerves so tightened, nor her people so obedient to the Magistrates, as when Pyrrhus first, and after him Hannibal, shook their swords at the gates of the city. It is the dread of the surrounding nations that has kept together the United States of Holland, and has preserved for better than 400 years the Union of the Swiss Cantons. Whenever that principle of common danger shall cease, farewell to the Belgic and Helvetic Leagues!—they will fall asunder and become petty republics, or unite their interests and become two nations.

We are about, my countrymen, to experience a change, the effects of which cannot yet be told. One false step now may ruin us forever;—should we look back at our former situation and repent, we are undone:—the object lies before us. We must go on, and not halt between disunion and war.

Your country, my Brother Officers, may possibly require your aid. If that holy regard for her interests which once inspired you;—if a sacred love for liberty, (at whose altar libations of American blood have been poured);—are still your first and greatest virtues;—guard over and save the peace of our new empire. Let the true spirit of patriotism induce you to mingle your views with the views of your fellow citizens, and unite with them in every measure that may tend to blend our common interests, and advance our public happiness. There is no pleasure so sublime as that which arises from the reflection of having faithfully served our country. It was to keep awake this reflection, and to cement the friendship we had formed amidst difficulties and dangers, that the Society of Cincinnati was instituted. No base motive (as has been ungenerously suggested) gave birth to our association,—the the purest principles of friendly esteem, and the most sacred regard for our individual rights, urged us to unite. We saw ourselves on the point of dissolution after having given Independence to our country, and could not part without establishing some principle that should occasionally draw us together. It was impossible indeed to separate but upon some such terms. We reflected that in a little time we should be scattered over a vast extent of country, mixed and undistinguished in a large community, the greater part of which in a few years would be composed of adventurers and strangers, who would neither care for nor value our interests;—and to this we added the mortifying consideration that we had spent our youth and our best services in the tented field without reward; but were to go and seek in poverty a resting place in that empire we had but just assisted in giving birth to. Under these several considerations we determined to fix a badge that should mark us out in the most hidden retirement, and make us known to each other, whether in poverty or in affluence,—whether in private or in public station. The emblazoned honors and distinctions of a military order that should mark a separation between our fellow citizens and ourselves we reject. We only desire to be known as a private society of friends who have shared together one common danger; and that posterity may be informed who aided that Revolution which gave freedom to North America.

As the Society of Cincinnati, then, is founded on principles that bind its Members to each other by the strongest ties of affection, it will be impossible for us, my Brother Officers, on the present occasion, to part, without offering a tribute of gratitude to the memory of our deceased friends. Who can forbear, amidst the gaieties of this day, to express their sorrow for the loss of that great and illustrious character Major General Greene? Who is there among us, that could boast his acquaintance, but must lament that those great and amiable qualities with which he was once endowed should now lie buried in eternal silence?—On whom should a grateful country more liberally bestow their praises than on a man who had contributed to her freedom and peace? His character should be remembered by us with gratitude and esteem. Formed for the duties of public life, he discharged the great truths reposed in him with fidelity and honor. Splendid as a soldier, he figured through the Revolution as one of the most distinguished of our Generals. His military achievements form a bright track in the annals of his country, that marks his career fom the blockade of Boston to the battle of the Eutaw. With a mind that teemed with resources, he had always the means of surmounting difficulties;—in every situation of danger he had the address to meet it to advantage;—and, when pressed by necessity or duty into action, he "taught the doubtful battle where to rage," with an equanimity of mind, and a steadiness of soul, that defied its terrors. The southern states hailed him as their deliverer, and received him as the best friend of their oppressed country. He valued the rights of mankind,—he knew them well,—and respected those privileges that secured their civil happiness. A fortunate experience, and a well directed intercourse with the world, had corrected his judgment, and fitted him for all the purposes of society. He was gentle, free and [word crossed out and "chaste" substituted in the margin] in his manners, and was benevolent and friendly in his nature. Objects of magnitude engaged his attention, but he could at all times unbend to social purposes. In private life he was as much esteemed as he was respected in his public station. When that awful stroke was given which numbered him with the dead, all America gave testimony of their regard for his virtues. Cut off, as it were, in the bloom of life, with the most pleasing prospect of domestic felicity before him,—his fall was every where regretted,—his loss every where lamented. Dear departed Greene, over thy relics shall "sorrowing Friendship" mourn!—at thy tomb shall Liberty and Virtue weep!

Nor must we, on the present occasion, forget another late worthy Member of our Society, whose remains were not long since conducted to the grave. If honesty and social worth, if benevolence and an obliging nature, could adorn a character, whether in humble or in exalted station, who will not lament the loss of Hiwill?—Who is there among us that did not esteem him when living,—and now dead, who will refuse him the tribute of a tear?—Over his urn hangs a disconsolate widow, and by her side a little infant inquires the story of his father's fate!—It is your duty, my Brother Officers, to take the infant by the hand, and to wipe the tear from the eye of the afflicted widow.

And now, my Countrymen, to close the duties of this day, let me advise you to look back and take a view of the principles on which our Revolution was founded; seriously observe the objects for which we contended; and examine well the benefits which they promise to society if the great end of them could be accomplished. Weigh with unprejudiced minds the circumstances that have obstructed their completion, and unite in such wholesome measures as may still bring them forward to compleat effect.

To accomplish this, remember that unanimity and a happy understanding among ourselves will be necessary. Permit me, therefore, to recommend seriously to your consideration, the cultivation of harmony and good order in society:—cherish a spirit of industry, as the means of doing it;—abandon all idle extravagance;—introduce economy;—love your country;—and dismiss ill-founded animosities. Let friendship and sociability unite you; destroy all improper distinctions, whether private or political;—and let the spirit of party be exiled forever from among you.

INDEX

ABOUT THE AUTHOR

John R. Vile, a graduate of the College of William and Mary and the University of Virginia, is a professor of political science and dean of the University Honors College at Middle Tennessee State University. He is the author of numerous works about the U.S. Constitution and rhetoric: *The Men Who Made the Constitution*; *The Constitutional Convention of 1787: A Comprehensive Encyclopedia of America's Founding*; *The Writing and Ratification of the U.S. Constitution: Practical Virtue in Action*; *A Companion to the United States Constitution and Its Amendments* (now in its sixth edition); *The Encyclopedia of Constitutional Amendments, Proposed Amendments, and Amending Issues, 1789–2015* (now in its fourth edition); and *Presidential Winners and Losers: Words of Victory and Concession*. He is a contributor to and the co-editor of *The Encyclopedia of the First Amendment*; *The Encyclopedia of the Fourth Amendment*; *James Madison: Philosopher, Founder, and Statesman*; *The Encyclopedia of Civil Liberties in America*; *Great American Lawyers*; and *Great American Judges*. Vile is the recipient of the 2000 Congressional Neal Smith Award for his contributions to legal education and a recipient of MTSU's 2010–2011 Career Achievement Award.